HIDDEN CHILDREN
OF THE HOLOCAUST

HIDDEN CHILDREN
OF THE HOLOCAUST

Belgian Nuns and Their Daring Rescue
of Young Jews from the Nazis

SUZANNE VROMEN

OXFORD
UNIVERSITY PRESS
2008

OXFORD
UNIVERSITY PRESS

Oxford University Press, Inc., publishes works that further
Oxford University's objective of excellence
in research, scholarship, and education.

Oxford   New York
Auckland   Cape Town   Dar es Salaam   Hong Kong   Karachi
Kuala Lumpur   Madrid   Melbourne   Mexico City   Nairobi
New Delhi   Shanghai   Taipei   Toronto

With offices in
Argentina   Austria   Brazil   Chile   Czech Republic   France   Greece
Guatemala   Hungary   Italy   Japan   Poland   Portugal   Singapore
South Korea   Switzerland   Thailand   Turkey   Ukraine   Vietnam

Published by Oxford University Press, Inc.
198 Madison Avenue, New York, New York 10016

www.oup.com

Library of Congress Cataloging-in-Publication Data
Vromen, Suzanne.
Hidden children of the Holocaust : Belgian nuns and their daring rescue
of young Jews from the Nazis / Suzanne Vromen.
p.   cm.
Includes bibliographical references and index.
ISBN 978-0-19-518128-9
1. Jewish children in the Holocaust. 2. World War, 1939–1945—Jews—Rescue.
3. Holocaust survivors—Interviews. I. Title.
D804.48.V76 2008
940.53'183508309493—dc22   2007037557

1 3 5 7 9 8 6 4 2

Printed in the United States of America
on acid-free paper

In memory of my parents,
Ella Weinberg and Joachim (Imek) Donner

For my grandson Adam

"THOU SHALT NOT BE A PERPETRATOR;

THOU SHALT NOT BE A VICTIM;

AND THOU SHALT NEVER,

BUT NEVER, BE A BYSTANDER."

—YEHUDA BAUER

2000 International Forum Conference on the Holocaust,
from *Beyond the "Never Agains,"* edited by Eva Fried
(Government of Sweden, 2005), page 9

CONTENTS

Photo gallery follows page 92

| ACKNOWLEDGMENTS |

That this book has been written is due to three people: Georges Schnek, Deborah Dash Moore, and Mark Lytle.

After I retired from Bard College in 2000, I contacted Georges Schnek, a friend I had known since 1947, when he was the head of the Jewish students' association at the Free University of Brussels. When I wrote to him about my intended research, he replied with enthusiastic encouragement and included in his letter a list of people I should interview. His name opened doors. He had been honored with the title of Baron for his activities on behalf of the Jewish community in Belgium, and he was at the time the head of its Consistory. Throughout my stays in Belgium he remained an unwavering support.

Deborah Dash Moore, a friend with whom I had team-taught the first Holocaust course ever offered at Vassar College, is at present Director of the Jean and Samuel Frankel Center for Judaic Studies and Professor of History at the University of Michigan at Ann Arbor. When early on I showed her some of the results of my research and told her that I intended to do a comparative study of hidden children in Belgium, France, and Poland, she was impressed with the richness of the Belgian material. She convinced me to focus solely on the Belgian case and persuaded me that my work would be a significant contribution to Holocaust studies.

Mark Lytle, Professor of History and one of my former colleagues at Bard College, found great interest in the summary that I forwarded to him. He offered to direct me to Oxford University Press and smoothed the way. He also carefully read and commented on the nearly finished manuscript.

I am deeply thankful to these three persons for their interest, their abiding encouragement, and their confidence in me.

My friends Joanna Gillespie and Andrew Bush read parts of the manuscript at different times, and generously offered me the benefit of their incisive comments. I am also indebted to David Kettler and Judith Gerson, whose questions and challenging remarks led me to think more in depth.

In Brussels, besides the constant and warm hospitality of Georges Schnek and his wife, Sarah Deutsch, I enjoyed the friendship and steady help of Annette and Berti Apelbaum-Szyke, both formerly hidden children, who adopted my work as their mission and made every effort to respond to my endless requests. Jenny and Ralph Stein cared for my well-being with great kindness. Louisette Kahlenberg offered neighborly companionship and a model of how to age gracefully. Early on, my old friend, Rose Leszczynski, drew my attention to her convent experiences. At the Center for Historical Research and Documentation on War and Contemporary Society, Fabrice Maerten was generous with his time and valuable advice, for which I thank him wholeheartedly. I am also grateful for helpful conversations with Anne-Dolorès Mercelis, Jean-Philippe Schreiber, and Hanne Hellemans. The latter provided me with an online copy of a manuscript she was working on. I had a fruitful correspondence with Alice Dermience, who read an early draft of my chapter on the nuns. Professor Luc Dequeker provided useful leads in the early days of my research. I thank Maxime Steinberg, Laurence Schram, Johannes Blum, and Sophie Rechtman for granting me interviews, and my old-time friend Maurice Woitchik for his assistance.

Helene Potezman at the Israeli Embassy in Brussels, Dr. Mordecai Paldiel, and Irena Steinfeldt at Yad Vashem in Jerusalem kindly responded to some of my inquiries about the Righteous Among the Nations (honored non-Jewish rescuers) among the Belgian clergy.

I am very thankful to the U.S. Fulbright Program for two Senior Specialist grants. Though these grants were specifically intended for teaching at the Buber Institute of the Free University of Brussels, they gave me an opportunity to enhance my understanding of the intricate Belgian social context.

The librarians at Bard College were welcoming and efficient. I thank them all, particularly Betsy Cawley, Jane Dougall, and Jane Hryshko.

At Bard College, I was a member of the sociology department and later its chair. In 1979 I also cofounded the women's studies program and later directed it for a number of years. I owe much to the students in the classes I taught throughout my twenty-two years at the college, especially those in Holocaust, women's studies, and social theory classes. It was challenging and stimulating to respond to their keen interest and fresh questions. May they find some answers here. I also remember fondly some of my adult students enrolled in the Continuing Studies program and have been awed by their accomplishments.

Father David Mickiewicz kindly answered my queries. Marlene Yahalom generously offered help. Yaffa Schlesinger, a friend since graduate school, gave me the benefit of her erudition. After having heard my presentation on the book's topic at the Association for Jewish Studies meetings in Washington, D.C., in 2005, Genya Markon from the U.S. Holocaust Memorial Museum offered to request for me access to a transcript of an extensive interview with a Jewish child hidden in Belgium who became a nun. I thank her for her support.

Reed Sparling patiently eliminated some of my French stylistic quirks but was careful to leave me my own voice. May he find here my most sincere appreciation for his skill and also for his kind support whenever my energy flagged.

I am very grateful to Cynthia Read, senior editor at Oxford University Press; Meechal Hoffman, her assistant; and Christine Dahlin, production editor, for their care throughout the publishing process.

Over the years Tammy Valentino has used much energy and devotion to keep my body and soul together. Janice Bernath, Doug Ewing, and Tom Towey, each in their own way, have skillfully helped to run our household and willingly responded to any urgent appeal.

My dear friends Elayne and Hal Seaman and Marcia and Ralph Preiss have provided a stream of unfailing encouragement. By now they have become my extended family and immeasurably enriched my life.

Ben, my husband of more than half a century, has steadfastly stood by me and knows what I owe him. My children and their spouses, Galina and Doron, Jonathan and Sue, have sometimes wondered why I have not really retired. I love them all dearly, but looking to the future, this book is dedicated to my grandson Adam.

Finally, I am indebted to all the formerly hidden children and to the nuns who told me their stories. In translating and transcribing all the interviews myself, I hope to have done justice to their voices. I have chosen not to reveal the children's names or, by request, the name of the nun who left her order many years after the war. My appreciation goes also to Andrée Geulen-Herscovici, one of the escorts in the Resistance, for our lengthy conversations and friendship. Sadly, Paule Renard-Andriesse, the second Resistance escort I met, and Father Julien Richard, the only priest I was able to interview, have both died since we talked.

Belgium and Northern France under German rule, 1940–1944.

HIDDEN CHILDREN
OF THE HOLOCAUST

"Hope is a little wisp of a girl
Yet a girl who spans the worlds
It is she, this little one, who draws all . . .
And who runs the whole world."
—Péguy

This little girl, I would like to give
superabundantly to my dear Suzanne as
she steps towards life. . . . Give it to her and
whatever happens, may she never lose it.
With it, may she step confidently towards her Ideal.

With much affection,

S.M. Tharcisius

E/v[1] Institut Marie José Sept. 45

[1] [customary abbreviation for Elisabethville]

" L'espérance est une petite fille de rien du tout
" C'est cette fille pourtant qui traverse les mondes
" C'est elle, cette petite, qui entraîne tout .....
" Et qui fait marcher tout le monde. —— Péguy

Cette petite fille, je voudrais la donner
surabondamment à ma chère Suzanne qui
va vers la vie ..... La lui donner et que
jamais, quoiqu'il advienne, elle ne la perde.
Qu'avec elle, elle aille confiante vers son Idéal
—— En toute affection,

SOUVENIRS   Sr M. Tharsicius

Sr. Institut Marie José, Sept. 45.

Inscription by Soeur Tharsicius, Institut Marie-José, Elisabethville (now Lubumbashi), Belgian Congo, in *Souvenirs*, by Charles Péguy (1934), a gift to the author on the occasion of her departure for Palestine, September 1945. (*Suzanne Vromen*)

| INTRODUCTION |

In its relentless racist attack lasting from 1939 to 1945, the Nazi Holocaust exterminated 1.5 million innocent Jewish children throughout Europe. The one hundred thousand or so who survived came to be known as the "hidden children."[1] In this book, some of them reflect on their past as youngsters sheltered in Belgian convents. Also included are the rarely heard voices of several of the nuns who protected them. Interviews with members of the Committee for the Defense of Jews, a Resistance network, whose members escorted the children from their parents to the convents, add suspense and complete the picture.

There is an autobiographical reason for the focus of this book. In 1941, after a year under Nazi occupation, I fled from Belgium with my immediate family and was lucky to reach what was then the Belgian Congo. I went to school in a convent run by the Sisters of Charity of Gand (Ghent), the Institut Marie-José in Elisabethville (now Lubumbashi), because all education in this African colony was in the hands of missionaries. I distinctly remember my initial bewilderment at being plunged suddenly into a Catholic milieu. I also recall how I eventually made my peace with the atmosphere of spirituality and the intense socialization that characterize convents. I even became a teacher there. As the colony was cut off from Nazi-occupied Belgium, new missionary teaching nuns could not reach the school. So, in early 1945, after I graduated from high school during a year in South Africa, the nuns asked me to teach Latin, Greek, and English in classes where some of the pupils were older than me. It was a challenging and happy experience. With the salary I earned, I was able to leave for what was then

Palestine when the opportunity presented itself. (What became the state of Israel was called Palestine in 1945.)

Later on, I began asking myself what it was like for children who did not have the comfort of home and were torn from their parents to be plunged suddenly in this strange milieu. My own experience provided me with empathy when I conducted my interviews, as well as an insider's knowledge and ease. In the past I had reflected many times on the war and our escape. Working on this book sharpened my recollections and I was haunted again by the realization that I had been extraordinarily lucky. In a sense, therefore, this work became for me both an acknowledgment and a mission.

On the eve of the Nazi invasion in 1940, Belgium was essentially a Catholic country. It counted nearly thirteen thousand priests and fifty thousand nuns, a gender imbalance partially explained by the more limited career opportunities available to women at the time. The country had many Catholic organizations serving both adults and youth. It was proud of its first-rate Catholic university—the University of Louvain (Leuven)—and of an extended network of Catholic elementary and secondary schools in which the majority of Belgian youth received their education. Orphanages, health, and elder care were mainly the Church's responsibility. Because of its extensive impact on public life, the Nazis did not disrupt Church functions.[2] In fact, it was the only institution to remain untouched by the occupation. Therefore, many Jews sought its protection against the Nazi terror and violence. With a single exception, Belgium's higher clergy—its cardinal and bishops—did not share widely in this humanitarian effort. It was the lower clergy—parish priests and nuns—who spontaneously extended their help.

May 10, 1940, is etched in the memory of every Jewish person then living in Belgium. On that date, Germany overran the country, its tanks sweeping down nearly the same paths used twenty-five years earlier in the invasion marking the onset of World War I. Defeated after only eighteen days, the nation was put under German military rule, which continued until liberation in September 1944. Despite his capitulation, King Léopold III and his family decided to remain in Belgium. However, his ministers fled, first to France and later to London, where they established a government-in-exile.

Then as now, Belgium was a country divided linguistically into French- and Flemish-speaking segments that occupied different geographic regions. Most of the Flemish lived in the north and west of the country, the French-speaking in the south and east. Bilingualism could be found only in Brussels, the capital. (This linguistic division is noted in this book: I use mainly the French names of places, as they were known to me at the time, with the Flemish designations in use today shown once in parentheses.)

In national institutions, parity of Flemish with the more prevalent French was achieved through legal battles and political pressure. Flemish nationalist movements pushed for autonomy for Flanders within the Belgian state. The Flemish National League (Vlaams Nationaal Verbond), founded in 1933, was fascist and anti-Semitic in orientation and collaborated extensively with the Germans during the occupation. These facts are important for two reasons. First, the geographic language division made hiding more complicated and added to the danger of detection. Second, Jews living in Flemish-speaking Antwerp were surrounded by a culture of anti-Semitism.

Estimates of the Jewish population of Belgium ranged between fifty-six thousand and sixty thousand at the beginning of the war; about 94 percent were foreigners. Most had arrived during the 1920s and the 1930s from Eastern European countries and as refugees from Nazi Germany.[3] Jews in Belgium suffered the same step-by-step procedure of annihilation the Nazis instituted in every country they occupied: deprivation of rights, expropriation, stigmatization, isolation, removal, and extermination. After the first, sudden, brutal roundups in the summer of 1942, about half of the Jewish population escaped deportation and death by going into hiding. To ensure the success of this clandestine operation, children often were separated from their parents.

The first rescuers were those parents who made the heartbreaking decision to relinquish their children. They appealed to a wide range of non-Jews—friends, neighbors, acquaintances, parish priests, and convents—and used whatever resources they could muster. Fortunately, in Belgium they were greatly assisted by remarkable Resistance networks whose specific task was to provide shelter for Jewish children of all ages, from seven-day-old babies to adolescents. Parents had to trust their children to total strangers, often with no knowledge of where the youngsters were being taken. Faced with a barbaric onslaught, they responded with unprecedented courage.

In the Resistance networks, rescues were an ecumenical endeavor transcending religious and class differences. Jews and non-Jews worked side by side and at all levels of responsibility in the Committee for the Defense of Jews. Jews and Catholic priests collaborated to place children and respond to their needs. People in all walks of life lent their support, from municipal workers who forged identity papers to the miner who took on more perilous underground assignments to earn extra rations for the child he was hiding. However, these people were a tiny minority. The wider population was largely indifferent during the first two years of the invasion. Its support grew gradually after the call for compulsory labor in Germany was instituted in October 1942, and more steadily as the Nazi defeat became likely.

Within the broader Resistance context, the Committee for the Defense of Jews conducted an efficient and systematic placement of children throughout the country, both within families and institutions. Convents were especially safe havens for Jewish children, and the networks repeatedly enlisted their help. A large number of Belgium's surviving children were hidden in these Catholic institutions.

The research on which this book is based includes lengthy, unstructured interviews with sixteen women and twelve men who were hidden as children; eight nuns and one priest involved in the rescue; the two surviving members of the Resistance who escorted the children from their parents to the convents; the president of the Belgian Association of the Hidden Child, who was herself a hidden child; various persons involved in commemorations; and historians unraveling the history of World War II and its aftermath. People were eager to talk, and a snowball sample of hidden children emerged easily. Most of them were between seven and twelve years old at the start of the war. The nuns and the priest were reached through the ex–hidden children, connections with friends, and lists of honored rescuers kept by the Israeli Embassy in Brussels. The interviews with escorts from the Committee for the Defense of Jews and with nuns from sheltering convents provide examples of the courageous people who made these rescues possible.

This book sheds light on the way nuns safeguarded the Jewish children and integrated them into their convents. Their voices on these subjects have never been heard in such great detail. Surviving nuns point to the major roles their mothers superior played in decisions to accept the children and provide for their care. They recall the women's concerns with secrecy, as well as their management skills, power of decision making, courage, and savoir-faire. They provide well-deserved recognition for women whose actions have been unjustly ignored.

The nuns also relate how, under the guidance of the mothers superior, they coped with unexpected numbers of strange children in their midst. They functioned under the constraints of an occupied country drained of its resources by the needs of the German war machine. They detail their quotidian existence, as well as significant events within the convents, such as the celebration of an anniversary jubilee.

Because the convents and orphanages differed markedly from each other, the hidden children were subjected to a wide spectrum of experiences, which clearly dispels the one-dimensional notion of convents and nuns often held by outsiders. This is in part why the memories of the nuns and children often diverge. However, there are also divergences of memory between ex–hidden children and nuns who lived in the same institutions. These are reflective of the tensions of convent life. For example, few nuns I spoke to allude to discipline problems, while some formerly hidden children recall harsh punishments. By asserting repeatedly that the hidden children were treated like all others, the nuns justify their behavior in their own eyes.

The nuns also tend to evade or deal lightly with issues of baptism and conversion, arguing that the children had to conform to rituals for security reasons but were not pressured into doing anything they did not want to. This is corroborated by some, though not all, of the ex—hidden children I interviewed. That they were treated the same as other boarders is not disputed, but the fact is they were not like the others. They had to change identity rapidly, keep mum about former lives, and repress deep anxieties about their parents. Before reaching the convents, they had been stigmatized and hunted. Convents offered a certain degree of security, but the unpredictable threat of denunciation remained ever present. In their refuge and the collective context in which they were suddenly placed, the children accepted the lack of attention to their differences, but it does not mean they did not suffer from it. Today, the nuns do not refer to suffering. Instead, they remember the children as adaptable, accepting, courageous, and discreet. They do not envisage the possibility that the children may have been masking their real feelings in a situation in which they felt powerless and that they adopted obedience as the sole realistic strategy. Any suffering mentioned by the nuns refers primarily to the Allied bombardments at the end of the war, when some of the convents were heavily damaged and lives were lost.

In playing a critical role in the rescues, the nuns stepped beyond their convent walls and made contact with the wider world in ways they had not expected. When necessary, they dealt with German occupiers with dignity and cleverness. However, in view of church teachings prior to Vatican II, especially the commonly held view of Jews as Christ-killers, their rescue missions had to be reconciled with their beliefs. This was a topic the nuns found difficult to discuss with me, but some of the formerly hidden children cited examples of these beliefs. What is clear from my interviews—and from what happened in Belgium in general—is that the children were rescued predominantly for humanitarian reasons and not purely for conversion purposes, even if after the war there was scattered reluctance to return rescued children to their Jewish heritage.

Formerly hidden children were eager to talk with me about their wartime experiences. They wanted to describe who they had been and who they had become. In particular, they recalled their feelings about their clandestine existence in the religious milieux into which they had been thrust. As psychologist Eva Fogelman and historian Deborah Dwork have noted, there were two types of hidden children: those who stayed out of sight and those who were visible.[4] Children in convents belonged to the latter category. Their visibility forced them to be constantly vigilant about their new identities and resolutely silent about their past. They were protected in the convents at the price of rejecting their religion, sometimes being forced to listen to anti-Semitic remarks. Many, but not all, found the Catholic religion a comfort and solace. Conversion and baptism allowed them to blend into the institutions. These rituals also provided security and the exaltation of belonging.

The interviews with the formerly hidden children show us what life was like for them—the effects of wearing the Star of David; abrupt separation from parents; the swift learning of new names and family histories; a sudden plunge into religious institutions; the conformity to religious rituals and the effects of Catholic teachings; guilty views about their bodies; a fear of detection because of stereotypical Jewish appearance or circumcision; the threat of denunciation; the adaptation to collective life and discipline in a series of different institutions. Beyond silence, their lives in hiding required flexibility and obedience, and the realization that being Jewish was something shameful and dangerous for which one could be killed. It is no wonder that for many, anxiety has been imprinted in them to this day.[5] The end of the war brought further hardships. Those who were orphaned were sent to institutions or to relatives in other countries, often winding up in difficult situations. Others faced parents who were like strangers—camp survivors broken in spirit and body, unable to respond to their needs. For some, suspended between two religions, the return to Judaism was a long process. Others never abandoned the Catholicism they had embraced in the convents.

After the liberation, what the hidden children had endured was not deemed worthy of attention. One ex–hidden child summed up very well the societal roadblocks that prevented her and others from publicly recalling their experiences for decades. "After having once begged for a touch, I was to spend years hungering for an ear. When I tried to break the silence, I was always quickly reminded how lucky I was, far luckier than most," she wrote.[6] Silence did not imply that the children did not remember. When hierarchies of victimization and suffering ceased to matter, when their environment no longer supported a conspiracy of silence, the ex–hidden children finally found the words to express themselves. In the 1990s, they organized collectively. In 1991, Deborah Dwork could write that "within each Jewish child who survived, the past remained intact and undigested . . . an unopened internal package."[7] Today, these "internal packages" have been unwrapped; we are far richer for it.

Talking about the past, connecting the past and the present, finding the support of a collectivity, testifying about their experiences in schools, returning to hiding places—all of these have proven very important to the ex–hidden children. They repeatedly emphasize the importance of the 1991 First International Gathering of Children Hidden during World War II held in New York City, and the subsequent formation of national associations. As Eva Fogelman has pointed out, "healing cannot be done in isolation."[8] By organizing and gaining a voice in Belgium, the children have acquired not only status but also the ability to mobilize resources and make collective claims.

Chapters 1–3, which discuss the hidden children, the nuns, and the escorts from the Committee for the Defense of Jews, relate these lives to the historical and institutional context in which they were lived. The section on the Committee for the Defense of Jews, for example, leads to a general discussion of the different facets of the Belgian resistance. Chapter 4, an extensive discussion on memory and commemoration, then traces the emergence of the concept of hidden children and highlights it as an example of the construction of a collective memory expressed through sharing and collaboration. Chapter 4 also addresses the formal recognition of rescuers by the Israeli government as "Righteous Among the Nations" and offers an interpretation of Yad Vashem—the commemorative institution in Jerusalem that honors the rescuers of Jews—as instrumental in reconnecting and reinforcing bonds between Jews and non-Jews. At the same time, chapter 4 uncovers how gender initially played a major role in the recognition of priests and nuns who were rescuers. The Belgian Catholic Church's former reluctance to commemorate these rescues is also examined. The struggle for the souls of some orphaned Jewish children who were baptized during the war and whose return to the Jewish community was contested is discussed as a particularly painful episode. By raising the question of commemoration, the book contributes to the understanding of how memory is institutionalized and reinforced by mnemonic practices.

In Holocaust literature written in English, relatively little attention has been paid to Belgium, as Dan Michman has remarked.[9] This work attempts to remedy the situation by providing different perspectives on the same series of events, many of which are not widely known. While the book is based on interviews reflecting what is remembered today, these memories are inserted in a wider context. The eminent historian Saul Friedländer, who survived the war as a hidden child, writes at the end of his memoir: "When memory comes, knowledge comes too, little by little."[10] That is what is hoped for here.

1

The Children

THE CHILDREN GO INTO HIDING

A few months after the Nazis invaded Belgium on May 10, 1940, they began to enact increasingly severe measures against Jews. First they required them to register and stripped them of their livelihoods as civil servants, lawyers, teachers, and journalists. By 1942 they forbade them access to schools and other public institutions and ordered the liquidation of all Jewish businesses. On May 27 they decreed the forced wearing of a yellow badge in the shape of the Star of David and implemented the decree a few weeks later.

The yellow star was the stigma par excellence. All Jews six years and older had to wear it in public. The malevolent intent was both psychological and pragmatic. First and foremost, the Nazis aimed to emphasize the Jews' "differences," isolating them from the surrounding population and branding them as members of a faulty, misbegotten species. In that way they activated a systematic dehumanizing process. In effect, the invaders were telling non-Jews: "Beware of these foreign beings. They are unlike you. Dealing with them is dangerous." Pragmatically, the star made surveillance—and eventually roundups—much easier for the Germans.

Children responded to the star in various ways. What mattered to them most was how friends and teachers reacted. One interviewee remembered the shame she felt when other children stared and reproached her, asking, "What have you done to our country?" Their question overwhelmed her with guilt. Another recalled a sense of shock because the star and the word "Jew" stamped in her parents' identity cards humiliated her so deeply.

Henriette remembered what happened to her in minute detail. After sewing the star on her coat, her parents told her, "Hide it inside. Wear your coat with its lining outward." Shortly afterward she went to an entrance exam that would enable her to take special classes to earn a teaching certificate. The daughter of her teacher pointed a finger at her and shouted out loudly enough to be heard by all:

> "Do you know why she hangs her coat with the lining outside? It is because she is Jewish and she wears the STAR." I was stunned. I found these words horrible, especially coming from the daughter of my teacher, who in those times seemed nearly godlike to me.

Not all children had such negative experiences. When Emile arrived at school wearing his star, the other children found it fascinating and wanted to bargain for it, much the way they haggled over marbles. He decided to keep his star and still owns it today. Emile's school seems to have been a special place. He recalled that his principal broke into tears when forced to forbid Jewish children from taking classes.

In the streets, people showed sympathy, although Belgian fascists seized the opportunity to harass the wearers of the stars.[1] None of those interviewed mentioned such harassment, but the escorts (the women who would take the children from their parents to hiding places) fully realized Nazi cruelty when they encountered starred children. Until then, these young women had not been confronted by the invaders' anti-Jewish measures. As we shall see in a later chapter, they found this visible branding so revolting that it triggered their decisions to join the Resistance network dedicated to hiding the children.

For those Jews not alarmed by the decree banning access to school or the forced wearing of the star, the brutal roundups that began in July and August 1942 dealt an insufferable blow. Now it was clear that no Jews, not even women and children, were safe. Finally, as fear overwhelmed all other feelings, there was a scramble to find hiding places. While families would have preferred staying together, parents often recognized this as impossible. Aware that their foreign accents and facial features would make their own hiding more difficult, they first sought shelter for their children. In that quest, they counted on the humanitarian feelings of the Belgian population toward their young ones.

Parents called on all the resources they could muster in their search for hiding places—non-Jewish friends, clients, employees, landlords, renters, street vendors, neighbors, parish priests. According to historian Maxime Steinberg, parents' ability to find safe havens for their children depended on the length of time they had lived in Belgium before the Nazi occupation.[2] Those who had come soon after Hitler's rise to power in 1933 had solid connections with non-Jews through their occupations and businesses. Those who had arrived later in the 1930s tended

to approach the Catholic parish priests, who were considered sympathetic to the Jews' plight.

The children had varied memories of their separation. For most it was sudden. For some it was not complete: Parents periodically visited them in their hiding places, taking great risks to do so. In the interviews, those children didn't dwell much on the moment they left their homes, but their escorts remembered the remarkable maturity the youngsters displayed. As a safety precaution, the escorts could not allow them to shed many tears.

The children themselves rarely recalled how the hiding decision was made, but they remembered where they were taken. When a hiding place was found, it was not necessarily permanent. Temporary refuges prevented immediate danger until safer places could be found, most often through the Resistance network Committee for the Defense of Jews (CDJ). Some children were moved often, for a variety of reasons—fear of denunciation, extreme unhappiness, or the inability or unwillingness of those who sheltered them to provide for their needs. For example, a farmer's wife requested that the Resistance remove a teenage girl because her husband took too great an interest in her. The children had to adapt to the chaos of the war and to the unexpected. In general, they did not recall who had paid for their upkeep. They were young, so it is not surprising that such material concerns did not claim their attention.

Going into hiding necessitated acquiring a new identity. All of my interviewees, without exception, were provided with French or Flemish names—both given names and surnames—that were rapidly drilled into them by the escorts. Even today, an ex–hidden child noted, "I respond to David *and* to Daniel. Why forget Daniel?" Remembering and responding to these names was an essential first step in the process of going underground. This became very clear, as reported:

> A woman came, we took a train, and our escort gave us our new names, which we practiced with mistakes and laughed about it. But when she said to us: "Don't ever tell anybody that you are Jewish or you will be killed" we never again made a mistake about our names.

However, a new name did not remove the danger of denunciation. One boy, given the name Timmermans (a common Belgian surname), entered the crowded dining room of the boys' college where he was hidden and heard himself hailed by a student who knew him from his previous school: "Hey Tabakman, what are you doing here?" Fortunately, the encounter had no dire consequences for him.

When it became clear that Evelyn would no longer be allowed to go to school, her father, the owner of a snack bar, sought the help of one of his customers, a Greek. He was given the name of a woman with two daughters who was willing to hide the girl. Evelyn vividly recalled her feeling of dread when brought to their home. After a while, the host family became afraid of denunciation and requested that she be removed. Her mother went to the local parish priest, who found her a place in the Institut Saint Antoine de Padoue, a convent in Louvain Saint-Pierre. For her younger brother, the priest approached the family of a painter. He accepted the boy and treated him like one of his own children.

Monique recalled a ride on the bicycle of her parents' accountant, who sheltered her for several days after a narrow escape from a Nazi roundup. Her mother then went from neighbor to neighbor, seeking a hiding place for her. The search was fruitless: "I remember her standing one day in front of a neighbor who says, 'I cannot take her. We live door to door! Everybody will see it. It is not possible.'" One of Monique's teachers, who lived in the neighborhood, took her in temporarily until the local parish priest steered her to a convent.

Alice's neighbors were unmoved by the dangers she faced, but a Catholic family further down the road came to the rescue, sheltering her for a few days and obtaining a place for her in an educational institution whose principal they knew. However, her tribulations were not over. She had to flee again after being denounced by the young daughter of the family that had formerly sheltered her. The girl needed pocket money and found the payment for denunciation a handy way to supplement her allowance.

My subjects often mentioned the interventions of priests. Some of the children were hidden in the network of the CDJ. Andrée recalled the night before the CDJ escort was scheduled to come. Her mother spoke to her all night long, dispensing advice that she was unable to remember, being only nine years old at the time. To this day, Andrée is comforted by the fact that she was number 10 on the CDJ list—proof that her parents appealed to the Resistance committee very early.

Paul was hidden through the intervention of Monseigneur Jean-Louis Kerkhofs, the bishop of Liège and Limbourg, the sole bishop in the Belgian church who organized help for Jews at an early stage and also encouraged his priests to do so. A nurse friendly with Paul's mother, who was a doctor, consulted the bishop. He advised that the teenager be placed in a relatively isolated seminary in the south of the country.

Camille had to find a hiding place on her own. Coming home after an outing with a friend, she found her front door sealed. Her parents had been taken away in a roundup. The next-door neighbors were, in Camille's words, "green with fright." After telling her that her sister was at a friend's house, they slammed the door in her face. Just eleven years old, Camille reunited with her sister, who was two years older, and the girls made their way on foot to a hospice. They stayed there for three months. To keep them safe, a sign was hung on the door of their room proclaiming the occupants to be highly contagious. Eventually the CDJ was contacted; it found the girls a place in a rural institution housing poor children and children of prisoners of war in need of a little fresh air.

Bill's father was a tailor who had a lawyer as a client. The lawyer agreed to help hide Bill and phoned the head of the board of trustees of a Protestant orphanage. After several consultations, Bill and his brother were placed there, staying almost until the end of the war. Soon after their arrival, they realized that other Jewish children also were hidden there.

Despite the painfulness of the process, the children showed a remarkable adaptability. Yet to this day, many of them still feel a sense of anxiety and fear when talking about their ordeals. Those who were not moved frequently seemed to benefit from the stability. The others had to keep on readjusting.

RELIGION, BAPTISM, COMMUNION, AND PRAYERS

Abruptly separated from distraught parents and given new names, the children were brought to the convents with a sense of urgency, sometimes under the cover of darkness. They were plunged into this new milieu, different from anything they had ever known, and expected to adapt seamlessly. This meant finding their bearings quickly and learning the rules. Not only did they have to conform, imitating what the other children were doing, they had to blend in. In a spiritual atmosphere, the various prayers that they were expected to learn structured the day and gave it meaning. They were to recite these prayers aloud with conviction, even fervor.

How did the children react to the religion they found in their new environment? At first, they were startled by the amount of time devoted to praying. For example, Camille prayed kneeling on a bench. Initially it hurt, but then, "with the frequency of prayers, huge calluses—like a camel's—covered my knees," she recalled. "I expected them to be there forever." Nicole described her day:

> We got up at 6:3o. We kneeled, we prayed, we dressed, we put on a hat, we went down, we prayed morning prayers, we went to Mass, we ate breakfast, during breakfast prayers, after breakfast prayers, then I think we had a short break. At nine we went to school. Prayer, it was always prayer before and prayer after—after anything whatsoever. And in the evening, and on Sundays, we had beautiful prayers and the salute, also during the month of Mary.

Because of the prominence of prayers in the convents' daily schedule, many of the former children can still recite them by heart without hesitation. When they reflect now on these routines, some describe them as boring, while others recall praying with fervor. In any case, they had to learn the prayers, together with the timing of genuflecting while making the sign of the cross, very rapidly in order to blend into their new surroundings. This was not a choice: it was an immediate and compelling obligation allowing neither time nor concern for a smooth transition. When the culture shock of the sudden encounter with Catholic practices wore off, they lost their foreign quality; such behavior became familiar and predictable. "It was very strange," said Evelyn, recalling the daily morning devotion. "A nun slipped me a prayer book to be able to follow Mass, but I never managed to follow." For Henriette, the prayers, especially the evening ones, "have remained with me. Now, every evening I think of my family and make wishes for them. I don't ask God to fulfill these wishes, but this habit has remained with me." Lucy remembered how "it was difficult to go to Mass every day. It was an unbearable chore every morning, and the vespers—all this religion was boring and unpleasant." Both the rituals and the religiosity were strange and burdensome.

The children were given formal religious instruction. They learned the catechism, plunged into the Catholic narrative of the Virgin Birth, and felt the sufferings of Jesus Christ. Until they were baptized, they could only be auditors during the daily Mass, the ritual reenacting of one of the major beliefs of the Church. After receiving baptism, they could be active participants, able to partake in the sacrament of Holy Communion. (To allow someone unbaptized to receive the host would be seen as a mortal sin.) They were then also expected to go to confession, where they would be cleansed of all sins in preparation for participating in the sacrament.

Baptism and subsequent conversion sometimes created a dilemma for Jewish children. On the one hand, being baptized meant that the rescue strategy was complete: they could shed their stigmatized "Jewishness." By participating in the numerous rites, they became religiously indistinguishable from the rest of the children; the same rules now applied to them as to all of the others. They belonged wholly to the convent community, both sheltered and embraced by it. On the other hand, when there were groups of Jewish children in a convent, those who were baptized and converted saw themselves—and were seen by those who did not convert—as different. This sometimes created among them a sense of separation.

Luc Dequecker has argued in an important essay that baptism did not automatically signify conversion.[3] I do not believe that this difference was significant for the children in convents. Certainly, my interviewees did not distinguish between the two. Their responses demonstrated a great variety of attitudes toward baptism and conversion that could be aligned along a continuum between two poles. At one end was complete and adamant resistance to baptism; at the other was total and zealous acceptance of the tenets and beliefs of the Catholic Church.

Whether the idea of baptism was initiated by the nuns or by the children themselves is difficult to establish. The pressure may have been subtle or sustained, or even blatant in some convents. In others, it may never have existed. The fact remains that not only was the sheltering of the children a humanitarian response to barbaric violence and brutal circumstances, but it also provided a unique historical opportunity to save impressionable young souls in large numbers. Given the relatively low position that Judaism occupied in prewar European culture and the relentless wartime stigmatization, baptism and conversion could be seen in a very positive spiritual light, and also mistakenly justified as a protective measure. The perception of baptism and conversion as protective measures was mistaken, because in view of the Nazi racial ideology they were in fact irrelevant.

As scholars increasingly study the records, their findings indicate that baptism seems to have been more widespread than originally thought.[4] After the war, the practice was vigorously denounced by the CDJ as it pursued a thorough search for children and morphed into the Aide aux Israélites Victimes de Guerre (AIVG; Aid to Jewish War Victims), a Jewish welfare organization. The AIVG argued that children whose parents did not come back from deportation were to return to their prewar identity and brought up by the Jewish community until adulthood—whether they had been baptized or not. For that purpose, the AIVG set up orphanages, and the American Jewish Joint Distribution Committee funded them.[5] (This issue will be detailed further in chapter 4.)

Baptism of the hidden Jewish children served a dual purpose for the nuns. On the one hand, they were saving souls and creating faithful Catholics, thus fulfilling an important part of their life's mission. In addition, baptism was a strategy that allowed them to conceal the children more fully and complete the rescue, making the hidden youngsters undistinguishable from the others. Thus they could credit themselves with achieving both goals simultaneously: the children's souls were saved and their bodies protected from the evil that threatened them.

Communion was a complicated issue. In order to receive the sacrament, one had to be baptized. In a sense, communion is a personal relationship with Jesus symbolized by the host (the wafer) placed by the priest on the tongue of the communicant. To receive the wafer without being baptized was an act of desecration. For the Jewish children to receive communion meant gaining full entrance into the convent community.

The unexpected arrival of the children caused a novel problem within the convents when it came to baptism and communion. Henriette related, "When we went to Mass in the chapel, which we did daily, we were told that we did not have the right to go to communion. I was never told that I had to convert. I wanted to; it is something that stayed with me."

When Renée was asked why she did not go to communion, she was at a loss for an answer. The chaplain advised her to write to her mother, who answered that Renée should be ashamed to want baptism at a time when her family suffered. Monique was baptized very soon after her arrival in the convent; she was later confirmed in a ceremony in which Cardinal Van Roey, the head of the

Belgian Church, officiated. As for Alice, the mother superior had given instruction that she should "pass" as Protestant.

Some resisted the socialization. Nicole, who was hidden in the convent with her older sister, relied on her sister to help her resist conversion:

> Each time they tried to convert me, I said, "Ask my sister. I will do what my sister decides." My sister, who was fifteen years old, knew very well what she wanted. She told the nuns: "Listen, I promised my parents that we would not convert. I will convert when my parents return. During the time my parents are deported, I have promised to stay Jewish, but when they come back I will convert." This way she was left alone.

This reaction illustrates not only steadfast resistance to Catholic socialization but also the mistaken, but common, belief that deportation did not necessarily mean extermination.

In complete contrast, Monique was entirely won over to baptism.

> I was probably naïve. For me, if you did not accept that religion, you would be burning in hell. And this Jesus suited me; he was a good-looking young man, Mary was a beautiful young woman. I didn't ask myself too many questions. And I must say that when I was baptized, all the nuns around me were in tears because, when I had to give my little speech, I spoke with such conviction. I delivered it with much emotion and much fervor and much passion, and the whole convent was really greatly touched and moved.... The nuns wanted to save me. They said to me if one doesn't believe in miracles, one goes to hell, and I accepted this entirely.

Not all convents were equally intent on baptizing the children they sheltered. Some were unwilling to baptize without the parents' consent. Some parents had been deported, others hidden in places whose location neither the convents nor the children knew. Others remained in touch by letters. A minority came at great risk for short and infrequent visits; a few children sometimes visited their parents, also at considerable peril, to alleviate the separation. So parental consent was difficult to obtain, and invoking such consent often postponed baptism for the duration of the war. Alice recalled:

> I had asked the nuns to baptize me, and they refused. "Only if your parents agree," they said. I had been dazzled by the Catholic religion.

I had learned that there was a god who loved me, that he had died for me on the cross, that he had sacrificed himself for me. It was something I had ignored and which pleased me. When my brother and sister joined me in the convent, I was so enthused by that religion. I wanted them to share my happiness. So I told them immediately: "You know there is a god, called Jesus, and he wanted to sacrifice himself for us, and he died on the cross for us." My sister looked at me and, without a moment's hesitation, declared: "If you continue to say such nonsense, Dad will laugh at you." My faith was immediately shattered in a thousand pieces. . . . It broke at my feet. I really heard it breaking like crystal.

Evelyn was slowly won over to Catholicism, and one of the nuns asked whether she would like to be baptized. Having witnessed the baptism of others, which she found very pleasing, she agreed. However, as she was only eleven years old, the nuns demanded that she first receive her parents' permission:

I asked only my father because I knew that he was more open-minded. You know children feel that, and my father said, "Why not?" I never dared tell my mother. I was baptized on Easter in 1943 without my mother's knowledge, and received baptism and communion effectively together.

Her mother was told about it much later and felt greatly hurt.

Camille and her sister decided to be baptized for practical reasons—not out of faith, but for the advantages it offered them. In their convent, there was a Catholic Girl Scout troop whose leader would take the girls out of the convent for walks and other diversions. Camille and her sister decided to be baptized so they could participate in these pleasant activities and especially to have the opportunity to roam beyond the convent walls. Camille was baptized on a Sunday, creating an obligation to go to confession on the following Thursday. "But what was a sin?" she recalled asking herself. "I didn't know exactly what it was. I knelt, I could feel the priest's smoky breath, and I made up what I thought to be sins. For example, I said that I had lied five times, et cetera, et cetera."

Every morning, Camille went to communion, and every week to confession. One day, a high church dignitary came to visit. She followed the others who went up to him, not realizing that she was supposed to kiss his ring. Instead, she stuck out her tongue, as she did while receiving the host during communion. The dignitary shoved his ring on her tongue, and then she realized what she was supposed to have done.

For Charles, there was no explicit Catholic pressure. In his seminary class, there were twenty-two students; seven of them became priests, so there was a very fervent ambience that could influence a young boy:

> And I was influenced. When I left in September 1944 [after the liberation], I told the director that my ideas had evolved, and that I was very interested in Catholicism and wanted to continue in that direction. The director hesitatingly answered that I would be living in a city surrounded by life's turmoil; nevertheless, as I insisted, he agreed to offer me a director of conscience and gave me the address of a priest teaching in a well-known Catholic institution in Brussels. That man was austere; he answered my questions poorly and seemed totally uninterested in giving me a Catholic foundation and explanations.

While some parents refused to grant permission for their children to be baptized, in other cases whole families were baptized as a protective strategy. Paul and his mother went to different convents for instruction. He recalled vividly the very pretty nun who had been his catechism teacher. Mother and son were then baptized together. Afterward, he helped to celebrate Mass in the convent where he had studied. About his faith he remarked, "One day I lost the faith. Perhaps I never really had it, but I felt that I owed a debt of gratitude to the people who protected me. I think that, in fact, it was a gesture of gratitude, but not real faith." Paul sometimes served as a choirboy later on, but during a special Mass at the Collège d'Enghien, the choral director whispered to him repeatedly to stop singing because he was so out of tune.

The last time she saw her mother, Andrée asked for permission to be baptized. "We come from a family where there were rabbis. We are religious, if not Orthodox," her mother replied, with tears rolling down her cheeks. So Andrée did not pursue the matter at the time and did not recall being pressured by the nuns in her convent to be baptized. Then toward the end of the war, the town in which the convent was located was repeatedly bombarded as American planes passed overhead on their way to Germany. Gripped by the fear of death in the midst of one bombardment, Andrée asked an older girl to baptize her. The girl pronounced the words, but then Andrée said: "What if I don't die?" The girl replied: "I baptize you under condition"—that she die. She survived and was baptized again, after the war ended a few days later. She went to communion wearing the white dress she had yearned for so badly. This second baptism seemed possible because the first one was "under condition."

For Isaac:

> Those who wanted to convert converted. I never forgot that I was a Jew. I remember my mother's parting words: "Never forget that you are Jewish. Don't forget that you have a sister and parents. And never

look the Germans in the face because brown eyes may betray a Jewish origin." I never forgot these words though I acted like a Catholic, and went to Mass, and still can recite all the prayers.

Roger was baptized early in 1942. He emphasized the sense of emotional security he acquired by becoming part of the majority: "Yes, I was Jewish, but what did it mean at the age of nine? On the other hand, everyday life was Catholic. It represented an acceptance by a totality, an insertion into a majority. It meant not being a black sheep left on the margin." Catholicism left a profound impression on him. It provided a secure emotional anchor. He was placed in a seminary by Father Joseph André, who had created his own Resistance network and whom Roger greatly admired. The institution's director and principal, as well as the nuns in the infirmary, knew that Roger was Jewish because he never left for vacations or holidays. The impact of Catholicism on him was so profound that even after the war's end he continued religious studies for some time, and even helped to celebrate Mass in the presence of his sister and her friends.

As for Simone, she requested to be baptized and celebrated her first communion without her mother's knowledge.

Once baptized, the children were expected to go to confession. Some children did not quite understand its meaning. As Camille remarked, "I invented sins." The unbaptized could not go to confession. Nicole mentioned:

> Once a week, the priest came to hear confessions and we did not go. I think the other children didn't react to that. These were children of divorce, and young delinquents placed there by a judge, who did not go out and had very few visits. As for the nuns, I know that the mother superior once was frightened as she said that one or two nuns there were pro-German.

Charles also recounted the fear of discovery and denunciation as a result of non-conformity: "As I did not go to communion and confession, I was left alone, immobile, in the middle of the church. This aroused gossip. There weren't any consequences; the witnesses kept mum. They were good people."

Henri remembered sitting in church and being told to go to the confessional. "When I entered, the priest asked me, 'What did you come for?' I answered that I was sent, so he thought that I was making fun of him. Then I realized that those who had told me to enter had played a joke on me."

Monique, who had been deeply devout, pointed to a photograph and said:

> Here is the corridor, and when I did my communion, here is where we passed to go to confession. And I know that when I went to confession

I was terribly afraid to forget something. I wanted to cleanse myself from every sin because I understood the concept of a sinner, and when I came back after communion, and I had said the prayers, I jumped with joy in these corridors because I was forgiven. I remember this joy so well.

Nuns are not allowed to celebrate Mass, nor can they hear confession, so chaplains served the convents, and their influence is addressed in many accounts. Often, chaplains assumed the teaching of catechism; in some cases, they supervised it. For some children, both girls and boys, they became father substitutes. Girls sometimes loved them as male figures. "The chaplain came for the children," Renée recalled. "They loved him very much and jumped around his neck."

Renée had a special relationship with the chaplain in her convent. She cherished their frequent discussions and conversations. She never forgot his telling her that if she ever received her mother's permission to convert (which she didn't), "in any case you will not be converted to Catholicism, at best only to Protestantism." This was his response to their many arguments about her unwillingness to accept Catholic dogma. She remembered him as much more open-minded than the nuns in her convent. To this day, she keeps a photograph of him, cut out from his obituary in the newspapers.

Henriette described how "the chaplain came to ask questions and to see how well we knew our religion course." Alice's chaplain was also her religion teacher:

When I arrived the very first day, there was a religion lesson given by the chaplain. And he asked me: "How many cardinal sins are there?" I didn't know what sin was, and I didn't know what cardinal meant, but as he had asked how many, I hazarded a guess and answered fourteen. So he said to me, "Ah, you have double vision!" And then I told myself, "So there are seven." And very rapidly, I applied myself to learning everything by heart.

In Andrée's convent, there were two priests, one called Père Blanc (White Father), the other a cigar-chewing Capuchin. Andrée was the best student in her religion class. She asked lots of questions, and through the priests' responses she discovered that the religion contained many "mysteries":

The priests were important because they represented the religion. It is to them that we addressed our questions. And I, as I had always been very curious, very open, I questioned them. In fact, I was not really shocked because Jesus was Jewish; he never renounced being Jewish.

However, when at the end of the war the children of Wezembeek (who had been raised as Jews) took refuge for a short time in our convent, and we argued with them, we had become nearly anti-Jewish.[6] After all, we had been taught that the Jews had killed Jesus. That was the mentality at the time.

Henri also had a priest for a religion teacher. When that priest taught the class the story of Adam and Eve, Henri argued with him and insisted on correcting him. The priest was angered, and Henri realized that he had behaved stupidly. After all, the priest knew that he was Jewish, and that he was only a student.

In her interview, Monique raised a more troubling aspect about the chaplain she had known: "I ask myself whether he was not a bit perverse. I think that when he came to the infirmary, he had the habit of caressing. I have the memory of a man with caresses."

Representing a male presence in female institutions such as convents, the chaplains were endowed with an aura of superiority and authority. It was they who celebrated Mass and received confessions. For the nuns and the children, they were often the sole accessible male presence. It is no wonder that the ex—hidden children referred to them frequently. In seminaries and boys' schools, chaplains were just another type of priest among many others. In my interviews, Monique's remark about caresses was the only suggestion of possible sexual abuse by clergy.

Responding to Catholic teachings, the children embraced the rituals and were sensuously captivated by the rich intensity of the feasts. At Easter, Renée picked violets and placed them at the feet of the statue of Christ in the tabernacle. "These little violets smelled so good," she recalled. Irene loved the religious feasts, the decorated chapel, "the priestly adornments—mauve for Easter, white for Christmas, red for the end of the year." Emile knew by heart the Latin Mass and was especially enthralled by midnight Mass. The singing pleased him deeply, as did the walk in the snow and all of the Christmastime decorum and ceremonies. Charles found the Gregorian chants sublime. For Bill, singing Handel's "Halle-lujah" chorus at the age of twelve remained unforgettable.

Religious instruction also introduced the children to the concept of sac-rifice. In personalizing this notion, they bargained with God: perhaps in exchange for their sacrifice, God would spare their parents from harm. Renée decided to stop eating so that "Dad would come back." Monique walked intentionally on thorns to replicate the suffering of Jesus, and sewed a dozen holy medals in the lining of her father's suit to protect him while he waited at the church's entrance, risking great danger while she prayed inside. Henriette forced herself to eat more of the dried cod, which she disliked intensely. She hoped that, in divine recog-nition of her sacrifice, her parents would be safe. In a sense, the children brought their parents spiritually into the convents, as silent witnesses. This was even more palpable when siblings were hidden together, influencing their resistance to baptism.

The children did not refer to belief in miracles, except in one case. The convent in which Alice was hidden ran out of coal, and it was very cold. The coal merchant had no more coal to sell.

> As the weather became colder and colder, one day the nuns put their statue of Saint Joseph with its nose against the wall. There still was no coal. So the nuns placed the statue under a gutter. On March nineteenth, the day of the feast of Saint Joseph, as the statue was soaked, coal arrived. That was the miracle: Saint Joseph did not want to be soaked. This made such an impression on the nuns! I found it all so stupid that I never forgot it.

Alice was once asked by the mother superior: "You are Jewish, but you do believe in Jesus Christ, don't you, now that you are thirteen years old?" Alice understood that it was impossible, inconceivable even, for the nun to love a girl who was an unbeliever. She recalled another time, when talking about Jews and Judas, that a different nun said, "I recognize Jews right away. They are dark, they have yellow skin [yellow is the color of treason], and a large hooked nose . . ." She said this in a convent where she did not suspect many Jewish children were hidden. This anecdote illustrates the efficiency with which secrecy was maintained in this convent, but also how, even in their refuge, Jewish children could be exposed to stereotyping anti-Semitism.

There were ways the children dealt with the Judaism in which they had been brought up. Emile sang in the choir, and he loved the hymn that began "Laudam Jerusalem" (let me praise Jerusalem). He explained:

> This Jerusalem—I integrated it into my early religious upbringing. I integrated Jesus, the Apostles—these were Jews—and the Virgin. I integrated them all into my religion, and I accepted them rather fast. I recited the Rosary with sincerity and I said "Our Father" and "Hail Mary" with conviction. I was addressing myself to those who were mine, who belonged to my people. I did not ask myself many questions, but I included all these persons in my faith. It was as if I were saying a Jewish prayer.

He then added: "After the war, I evacuated them very rapidly, without drama. As rapidly as I had integrated them, I let them go, just as fast."

The use of the word "evacuated" is significant. By using it, Emile implied how swiftly and thoroughly he abandoned all that he had considered holy, at once recapturing his past identity and obliterating the spirituality he had embraced.

This easy flipping of identities was far from common; it represents one extreme of a continuum at whose opposite end are those who responded so totally to this intense resocialization that they remain practicing Catholics to this day.

Henri followed a different trajectory, still expressing some indignation:

> I was still praying in Ashkenazi Hebrew and said "Shma Israel" before we went to sleep. All this I knew by heart from my grandfather. When I went to sleep, I could cover myself with the blanket, and I prayed until slowly, you know, toward the end of the war I realized we had become Christians. I was in the choir there in the church, and when I came back from it I was an outstanding pupil. Why? I loved neatness very much; my bed was made beautifully. I received a dedication on a sort of card of the Virgin Mary, and on the other side they wrote a dedication to me for being an outstanding pupil. With that, I returned to Brussels, and first of all I hung up the card in my aunt's home. She said to me, "What are you doing. We are Jews here. That's the Virgin Mary!" I felt terribly offended, and then she understood that I had been influenced. I was really insulted. She hurt me. . . . It is a pity that this card is lost; it would have been a memento.

When Renée came home after the war, she tried to sneak out to Mass on Sundays. One day her widowed mother followed her, caught up to her, ripped her prayer book to shreds, and hauled her home. Renée then wrote to the nuns who had hidden her, saying that she wanted to convert and become one of them. She received no reply, and thus the relationship ended. Other parents were more prudent and understanding, and the resocialization process lasted longer.

It is possible to theorize that the adoption of a new identity served as a form of "passing." However, one would have to refine the concept before applying it. The children did not choose to pass: there was an imposition on them, not a free selection of one identity over another. At the onset, this "passing" was not expected to be permanent. Some saw it as a survival strategy, a mask to be discarded after it ceased to be useful. Others were more deeply affected by it.

The interviews attest to the strength of religious socialization in Catholic institutions. As we saw, according to their own accounts, some children wanted to be baptized. They found their new religion comforting, warm, hopeful, an oasis of spirituality in a world gone mad and rendered incomprehensible. They cherished crosses, rosaries, prayer books, and holy images. They looked for and sought their mother when they contemplated and prayed to the Virgin Mary. They prayed to her with devotion for the safe return of their families. In one account, when a daughter came to meet her mother just returned from Auschwitz, her first words to her mother were, "Now you come to the chapel to thank the Virgin Mary for saving you." And for the first and last time in her life, this mother went to the chapel. The children embraced the rituals with little difficulty and found solace in them. They were responsive to the powerful emotional appeal of Catholicism. They also wanted to be like all the others around them: belonging, accepted, embraced.

The presence of siblings seems to have encouraged resistance to Catholic socialization. In the presence of a witness to one's past, it was easier to maintain one's convictions and feel protected by a sense of familial solidarity. The institutions provided very different milieux. While some defined parents as the final arbiters of their children's religious identities, others entirely ignored parental wishes. There was no policy common to all convents. Some children remained pragmatic and considered baptism for the practical advantages it brought. Some girls were enticed by the white communion dress. In retrospect, the most complex responses linked faith to a sense of security or to an expression of gratitude for the clergy's rescue actions.

Though the children found solace and comfort in the religious rites, they did not assuage their anxieties about their parents. Undoubtedly, some were torn in their loyalties, but their use of malleability and intelligence for survival remains undeniable.

Children Who Chose to Remain Catholic after the War

I was able to interview former hidden children who decided to remain Catholic after the war. One still fervently practices her faith; the others belong to a group that tries to bridge the Judeo-Christian divide. Its participants explore their Jewish roots and the commonalities between the two religions. Sponsored by the Sisters of Zion, the group collectively celebrates Jewish and Christian holidays.

Hugo, the only man among these interviewees, was protected during the war by Father André, the priest who created a Resistance network to hide Jewish children. When neither of Hugo's parents returned from deportation, Father André became his surrogate parent and his anchor in life. Baptized during the war in a convent in which he was hidden, he saw no reason to give up the Catholicism that had provided solace and bonded him to Father André. After the war, he lived for a time with the priest, who helped him find work. He eventually became an electrical engineer. What seemed to matter most to him during our interview were the varying attitudes of surviving relatives, none of whom had offered to help him during the difficult postwar years. Decades later, an uncle berated him for his conversion, yet some of his cousins invited him to Israel and organized a festive get-together. There he met a young relative in whom he "found the face of my mother." Hugo and his wife, Pauline, who was also baptized while in hiding, raised their son Catholic, although he knows that both his parents are Jewish.

Pauline was baptized in the convent to which she was brought by Fernande Henrard, who later became notorious for her fanatical postwar efforts to ensure that Jewish children who had been baptized during the war remain Catholic. Pauline's father was deported and never returned, leaving her mother destitute with two children to raise. Henrard took in the family, who were forced to follow strict Catholic rituals. Henrard even had Pauline's brother baptized without his mother's knowledge.

After Father André married Pauline and Hugo, the couple built a house and added an apartment for Pauline's mother and her aunt, who had emigrated from Russia and joined the household. Thus the two elderly women finally left Henrard. At the age of sixteen, Pauline's brother also escaped the woman's grasp. He moved to Israel, where he returned to a traditional Judaism. He has maintained ties to his sister.

During our interview, Pauline complained mainly about being seen as a renegade by her Jewish relatives, who did nothing to help her mother after the war. In fact, they humiliated the family, considering them strangers because of the stigma of their conversion. A fragile reconciliation eventually took place following the visit of Pauline's nephew—her brother's son—from Israel. While religion is important in her life, and she and Hugo attend Mass on important holidays (but not daily), she insisted "I am not a bigot." She noted that she even fetched a rabbi to her mother's deathbed.

Evelyn, who belongs to the Judeo-Christian group, was baptized in her convent with her father's permission, but without her mother's knowledge. After the war, her mother tried unsuccessfully to entice her to date Jewish boys. Her family remained in touch with the family that had sheltered her brother; one of its sons became a priest, who took Evelyn under his wing. After the war, she was "baptized and disoriented," attracted to Catholicism through the priest and to Judaism through her mother. She did volunteer work for the priest's parsonage, joined the Judeo-Christian group he fostered, married a non-Jew, and concealed her children's baptism from their grandmother. Evelyn appreciated the group's support, as well as the opportunity to deepen her knowledge of the two religions. She also stated firmly that she wanted her granddaughters to know her roots and her war history. When her husband was kind enough to take me home after our lengthy interview, he remarked how, during their courtship, Evelyn did not disclose to him for a long time that she was born Jewish. She was afraid that this fact, stigmatizing to her eyes, would deter him from proposing.

Simone spent a large part of her childhood in various boarding schools because her parents separated when she was young. She was baptized in the convent she was hidden in during the war, and remained there for a year following liberation, while her mother remarried. Deeply affected by her father's deportation, she had a difficult relationship with her mother during adolescence and was shunned by family members because she insisted on remaining Catholic. Their attitude wounded her deeply. Still a practicing Catholic, she feels her Jewish origins are stigmatizing. In fact, she has never been able to tell her children and grandchildren about them. She thinks it would be dangerous for her grandchildren to know about their Jewish roots.

Through the Holocaust Museum in Washington, D.C., I was offered a transcript of a lengthy interview with Rina, a Jewish girl who chose to become a nun. Hidden by a Catholic mother and daughter during the war, she was so moved by their dedication to protecting her family and by their deep spirituality that she decided to convert. After the war, she took her vows as a nun, and was sent to teaching missions in various African countries before ending up in the United States. A large part of the transcript details her family's reaction to her conversion. For her father, she ceased to exist, although the two reconciled shortly before his death. One brother who lives in Belgium continues to ignore her, refusing even to mention her existence to his children. Yet she was welcomed in the home of her other brother, who lives in Israel. Rina feels she has been able to bridge the two religions and perceives herself as belonging to both.

The common thread between the experiences of the hidden children who remained Catholic is their rejection by Jewish relatives after the war. In a sense, they acquired a pariah status. As adults, they considered themselves entitled to choose their religious trajectory. However, their relatives were not willing to grant them this freedom. My interviewees were deeply wounded by this intransigence. For Simone in particular, her Jewish roots were both a stigma and the cause of a deep fear, seemingly unrelieved by her fervent Catholicism. Three of the converts found relatives in Israel who were more accepting of them than those living in Belgium and elsewhere. Perhaps more at ease in Israel with their Jewish identity, these people could give preeminence to blood ties and disregard or dismiss issues of religion as an inevitable consequence of the war.

The Body

On entering convents, the children confronted a vastly foreign conception of the human body. In convents the body had to remain covered and inconspicuous. It was not to be pampered by heat or softness, nor scented or adorned. It was also not to be touched or washed frequently. While some convents had central heating and hot and cold running water, others had antiquated stoves, only cold tap water, and toilets that had to be flushed with pails. Even when water did not have to be specially heated for bathing, the weekly bath or shower was an entrenched custom. More frequent bathing was seen as a wasteful, and even sinful, indulgence.

Understandably, when water had to be heated in cauldrons, bathing was a major event that required a considerable expenditure of physical energy and money. As a solution, many children were often required to take turns sharing the same tub of bathwater. Of course, to be among the first in line was highly desirable. Fights sometimes broke out to attain such a position.

Lack of hot water was not the only problem. The children received detailed instructions about *how* to wash. As nudity was considered immodest—as well as unacceptable and sinful—surveillance was undertaken to ensure that no flesh would show. As Camille recalled:

> At night, to wash themselves children put a nightgown over their clothes, and then undressed underneath the nightgown. We went to the sink, opened the top buttons, slipped the washcloth through the top opening of the nightgown, and tried to wash without exposing any flesh. The first time I didn't know what to do. I looked at a girl to see how she was using her washcloth. She insulted me by screeching accusingly, "You dirty girl!"

The surveillance also helped to prevent any sexual temptations. Charles, a teenage boy at the time, remembered that

> we had ten minutes to get dressed and wash our faces, and once a week we were entitled to a shower that often did not work. We had to stay in it the least time possible, for who knows what temptations we would encounter when alone in the shower. There was not much warm water. There were sudden bursts of hot, or of cold, or—nothing at all. Sometimes the supervisor called out agitatedly, "What are you doing?" I would answer, "I am soaping myself, sir, I am soaping myself" and in my hurry I often forgot and left the soap in the shower.

The fear of the male body—and of genitals in particular—is perhaps best illustrated by Alice. She was hidden with her younger brother, who was four or five years old at the time. When the nun who had been in charge of the boy for about two years became ill and was absent, Alice was told,

> "You will take care of your little brother." And in the evening, I undressed him to wash him, and he was white from his head to his navel, black from his navel to his knees, and white from his knees to his toes. His underwear had never been taken off. Would the nun have even known that he had been circumcised?

In winter water froze in the individual washbasins, so washing was avoided. And, Nicole relates, once a week

> we washed in a hall where we received warm water, but we were forbidden to take off our underwear. When my sister saw this the first time, she took the warm water, undressed me completely and proceeded to wash my naked body. The nuns screamed that this was a scandal, but the next time they provided a screen behind which we could wash properly.

Nicole's sister seems to have been a resourceful adolescent. She complained to the nuns about the glacial water and succeeded in leaving some warm water in her sister's basin before she left in the morning to go to another school. As Nicole gratefully remarked, "I was privileged and always protected by my sister."

Lice were a frequent problem, casually mentioned by some, remembered more emotionally by others. When Camille and her older sister arrived at the convent in which they would stay for some time, they found all of the children lined up to have their hair washed and cut. The nun in charge, Sister Louise, was "a bitch on wheels," Camille recalled. All of the children had their hair washed in the same water. Camille's sister was at the front of the line, while Camille was at the end. When it was her sister's turn to have her hair washed, Sister Louise found it full of lice and screamed at her, "Dirty girl!" Witnessing this, Camille left the line, went to the toilet, and furiously combed her hair, watching the lice fall out by the hundreds. Back in line and eventually in the hands of Sister Louise, she was found to have very few lice. This caused the nun to berate Camille's sister all over again. All hair was cut very short, except for one girl who was allowed to keep her long, curly tresses, which her mother brushed when she visited. Needless to say, all of the girls were jealous of her.

The youngsters in Bill's orphanage also were infested with lice:

> The small children especially had lice and lice eggs. The heads were washed with kerosene, and there were these special combs, like scrapers. We had white towels to dry our heads so that we could see if the lice had been vanquished. . . . Most of us had shaved heads, not really good-looking. People said that these bald heads were the distinguishing mark of orphans.

The convent in which Jenny was sheltered, Notre Dame des Sept Douleurs, was very dirty. Hair was washed every Wednesday with vinegar, and heads were examined for lice:

My poor friend Ariane sobbed all the time because of the lice, and through her tears complained, "Why lice?" The nun came and asked her: "Why do you cry?" Ariane answered: "I do not want lice." The nun replied: "If Jesus made lice, you must not cry." But then Ariane came to me and asked: "If Jesus has made lice why does she kill them off if they are so good?"

Her logic really was impeccable.

Scabies was also prevalent. It was treated with a cream containing sulfur, which had an unforgettable smell. The scabs were scrubbed mercilessly.

What is forbidden often becomes attractive. Adolescent girls often discussed the bodies of the nuns, which were hidden beneath large robes that concealed their shapes. The question that preoccupied them was: Did nuns have breasts? "We tried to look at them from the side, to try to guess. We laughed and made fun of them," said Camille. For her, the question was answered when her sister, who worked in the convent laundry, reported that the nuns strapped large, wide bands around their chests to prevent their breasts from protruding. (Her sister, in turn, was required to wear such a band as her breasts developed.) Another remembered taking walks to the nearby lake, where the nuns "seemed as if liberated" when they lifted their robes to step into the water. When skirts were sewn for the girls, they had to kneel, to determine the garments' appropriate length. But one remarked that since the girls were not nuns, their skirts could be shorter.

When a nun died, the children had to honor her by viewing the body. "It was horrible to see her inert on a bed . . . it took me years to recover from the terror," said Nicole. So, while the body had to be covered habitually, it was honored in death, and was deemed important for others to view it.

EVERYDAY LIFE, DISCIPLINE, SCHOOLING, LANGUAGES, AND FOOD

The Catholic institutions in Belgium that sheltered Jewish children were not necessarily similar to each other. Some were regular boarding schools, others orphanages, and still others facilities where judges sent young delinquents not yet deemed to be hardened criminals. Children of war prisoners and other deprived youngsters were sent to places where they could "breathe fresh air" and recover from crowded urban conditions and family stress. There were also homes for so-called feeble-minded children, and seminaries and schools called *collèges* for boys.

For simplicity's sake, I will use the word "convents" to refer to this spectrum of institutions, most of which were run by nuns. (Priests headed the seminaries and the boys' schools.) The main threads linking them were Catholic ideology and practices. The institutions varied in their wealth, ability to accommodate unexpected children at a moment's notice, educational standards, and styles of management and discipline. French or Flemish was spoken on a daily basis, depending on geographical location. Almost none of these places were bilingual. Some institutions were coeducational; the boys in them tended to be young. The exact number of these many institutions that sheltered Jewish children is unknown and will probably never be possible to determine. A reasonable estimate is two hundred.

Relationships with Nuns

Severed from their parents and plunged into the convents, the rescued Jewish children had to form relationships with nuns—the parental surrogates and new authority figures who now ruled over their lives. Who were these beings dressed in wide, shapeless, austere robes, their hair completely covered by the stiff headgear called a cornette? All had to be addressed as "Mother" or "Sister." The youngsters' feelings for the nuns ranged between two poles—from love and admiration to virulent hatred. Often in the same convent, children adored some nuns while attaching to others slang insults such as *chameau* (camel), the English equivalent of "bitch," and *rosse*, meaning "vicious beast." Whether a nun was recalled as an "angel" or a "bitch on wheels," the children remembered her name decades later without a moment's hesitation.

Many of the children were searching for the parental affection they had recently lost. With those nuns who lavished maternal feelings on their needy new charges, the youngsters sometimes expressed the same emotions they had for their mothers and fathers. Some children wholeheartedly adopted the values the nuns advocated. Some were implicitly aware of the power of the Church's pedagogical methods and the many techniques the nuns used to motivate them. On the other hand, the children hated overly strict disciplinarians, heatedly recalled anti-Semitic incidents, and struggled with experiences of intense cruelty that would be forever etched in their memories.

Henri was lucky:

> There was Madeleine. She was also a nun. "Sister" she was called. She was a nurse, and I will not forget her. She loved the children very much. I remember one day I had to undress because I had boils, and I was very much ashamed. I was afraid that she should see that I am

Jewish. So she told me: "You can undress, and you have nothing to fear from me." I adored her. Not only I, all the children. They all wanted to be examined by her, they loved her so.

Sister Madeleine helped Henry overcome an anxiety felt by most Jewish boys in hiding. At the time, only Jews were circumcised, so their true identity could easily be revealed if they were forced to remove their clothes. As a nurse, Sister Madeleine also calmed physical pain and dressed wounds. But Henri most fondly recalled her gentle reassurance and caring attitude, which went beyond her professional duties. The infirmary was a place where each child was seen as an individual, a luxury in a life lived in a collective context, so the opportunity for a visit was eagerly seized.

Anna experienced both good and bad treatment in her convent: "There was a nun who received me very warmly the first evening. It was Sister Angélique. She was sensational. Seeing me crying, she came to hug me, and she made the sign of the cross on my forehead to reassure me a little bit." Anna understood that Sister Angélique was trying to comfort her in the best way she knew. Even if the sign of the cross seemed strange to her at the time, Anna realized that it was a protective gesture. She believed in its effectiveness and felt consoled.

Yet she also remembered instances of cruelty:

> I did not like catechism and was punished for it. I had to lift my arms and keep them up for a very long time. That was Sister Anna. She was wicked. And there was another one, Sister Paula. I remember her very well. One day a girl had forgotten a pair of pants. Pants were not worn often at that time. Sister Paula asked: "To whom belong these pants?" As nobody answered, she shouted: "These surely belong to a Jewess." As for Sister Anna, each girl in turn had to wipe the blackboard at recess with a dry wiper. I was lazy. Instead of leaving the classroom and shaking out the wiper in the playground, I shook it out under the blackboard; after all, it was only chalk. Sister Anna called me and said, "Did you see what you did there?" I remained silent. And she slapped me. I have never forgotten it. These women were probably forced to receive us—it was in all likelihood an order from the mother superior— but I ask myself whether these women were afraid. I think that it is fear that made them act like this.

Anna needed to find a rationale for such vicious behavior, especially when contrasted with the sympathetic attitude of Sister Angélique. The arrival of unexpected children—and Jewish ones at that—certainly caused tension and might bring to the surface latent feelings of anti-Semitism, which before Vatican II were not rare within the Church. Anna recalled other instances when Sister Anna made anti-Semitic remarks, especially when she mocked the "useless hands" of the Jewish children who did not know how to clean school benches and classrooms at the end of the school year. Some of the nuns may simply have been bitter people.

Anna's experience was not unique. Camille recalled:

> Sister Louise and Sister Ida were very mean, but Sister Clotilde was very nice. I spoke very little Yiddish, but Sister Clotilde asked me to translate the sentence "Shloof git mein kind" (Sleep well, my child). Once a month, when Gentile children had visitors who brought them "goodies," Sister Clotilde would lean close to my ear when we were all in bed. She would whisper, "Shloof git mein kind," and would slip a piece of candy into my mouth. I suppose that she did that to the other Jewish kids, and apparently knew who they were. While I enjoyed the candy melting in my mouth, my heart enjoyed her tender loving care. The next day, however, Sister Clotilde treated us as she did the other children.

Sister Clotilde's concern was surely maternal, perhaps even more multilayered. She endeavored to alleviate the marginality of the Jewish children and grant them the same privileges enjoyed by all of the others. She knew how to comfort by using familiar and familial language. Certainly the pleasure the candy provided was important, but it was the sweet way it was offered that remained so memorable. The sister's timing was also perfect: night was when the children were most vulnerable to homesickness.

A former child who was hidden in another convent recalled:

> Our teacher was Sister Helene. She was an angel. I loved her because she was so special. She tried so hard to educate us, to teach us, because she was not prepared for us. She did extraordinary things. One day, she came to wake me up very early in the morning to watch the sunrise. Perhaps she wanted to tell me that I was a human being. She wanted to show me something beautiful. I have never forgotten. . . . Everybody loved her very much.

This instance of being treated as a worthy human being instead of an object to be hunted, stigmatized, and dehumanized has remained with this woman to this day. Sister Helene showed her how to find beauty, but she made the experience special, forever bonding the two.

Admiration and enthrallment were sometimes linked in the former children's memories:

I transferred my desire for family to one of the nuns, who was very beautiful, very blond, and very intelligent. She fascinated me. I waited to see her, and the moment she appeared, I was ecstatic. She was not maternal; she was dignified, shining, and prestigious, probably from a very good family. There were others who were cute and nice and jolly in their relationships. There were nasty ones . . . primitive, very vulgar, vicious, but I personally do not remember big tears or fear.

The mention of the sister's blond complexion refers to the Aryan ideal of blue-eyed blondness that was eagerly sought by Jewish children during the war. To be blond was safer, less "Semitic," and nonstigmatizing. These recollections—by someone who was obviously acutely aware of class distinctions—illustrate the diversity of the nuns in this particular convent community.

Isaac remembered the heartache after his mother's sole visit:

My mother came to see us once, bringing a cake. Sister Marguerite said: "This is for Sunday." We never received that cake. I don't know where it disappeared, but we never ate it. I remember this very clearly. It is a feeling of frustration that has remained with me.

With serious wartime food shortages, a cake was an extraordinary luxury. It required much effort to provide it, and the mother risked her safety in bringing it to the convent. No wonder that in a time of hunger, Isaac rejoiced in anticipation of eating the cake. More important, it represented what his mother meant to him: it was her gift of love to him and his brothers. He remembered the frustration so strongly because he had been doubly betrayed—denied the rare pleasure of delicious food and deprived of the precious token of his mother's love. The nuns' greedy act, seemingly inconsequential, inflicted a wound still remembered after more than a half a century.

Zalman recalls most vividly the corporal punishments:

Sister Marie Camille was a witch. She taught catechism. We had to learn it by heart, and when we didn't know it, we had a day of dry bread. One day, somebody talked to me while eating. She pulled my hair and beat me until I was bloodied. . . . During Holy Week, the nuns would listen to the story of how Jews spit at Jesus and hit him, and they would look at us as if we had committed all of these deeds. . . . They would hit us. They would slap our faces any time we talked to each other, and children do talk. . . . We felt an anti-Semitic hostility. When I left, I was twelve years old. I relearned that I was Jewish and I felt ashamed. We had killed Jesus, we had spit in his face.

Not only was Zalman physically hurt, he was morally damaged as well. Burdened with feelings of guilt, he was ashamed of who he was. The orphanage that sheltered him also housed young delinquents. The regime was relentlessly severe, at times sadistic. The Jewish children were not delinquents, but they bore the stigma of their Jewishness, so they were deficient in a different way and made very much aware of it. Children attempted to flee from this institution. During Zalman's stay, one Jewish boy managed the exceptional feat of escaping.

Some of the children, such as Irene, thrived on the values instilled by the nuns:

> I adored the nuns; I found that they gave me values. I tell you frankly, to this day when I do something I always say to myself, "Ah, God sees that you have not cleaned well." This is what they made me understand. When I finished cleaning, a sister would come to ask me: "Are you sure that all is clean? Do you think that God does not see that you haven't cleaned well?" They gave me values, and I think that I am tolerant of others because they were tolerant. I think they were complementary to my parents. I have never regretted having been in the convent, in spite of the circumstances. But, of course, I was lucky to find my parents.... Everything was well organized; it smelled of cleanliness. We were taught not to be lazy, and to be useful to others. I think it has become my nature.

Wrapping routine activities in a spiritual guise granted them a sacred character and was an effective pedagogical tool for shaping young minds. Irene's extremely positive view also stems from the sense of order and security this particular convent conveyed. Secure from the chaos and brutality outside the convent walls, some children responded with great relief to the order and predictability of the well-run institutions. And by fulfilling tasks within the convents, the children gained a sense of purpose and belonging to the community.

Charles developed a special relationship with his college principal, who had arranged his placement after he was expelled from another boys' school. The man became a father figure to him:

> I attached myself to Carlier not only because of all he had done for me, but because he was a man of character. When I asked him one day whether he had protected me as well as others on his own initiative or whether it was due to instructions from the Church, he told me that it was his own initiative.
>
> When others could leave for home visits I had to remain in the school. He would call me into his office and we would chat. We had

much affection for each other. I think he would have liked to have me as his son just I would have liked to have him as a father.

On the other hand, the former children made numerous remarks about narrow-mindedness, the inability and unwillingness to understand nonbelievers, censorship, and the hatred for everything male. For example, Renée was still indignant when she recalled how a hated nun opened all letters, both incoming and outgoing, with "a shameful disregard for privacy." Nicole remarked, "We were told to hate men and anything masculine. We were warned that we would go out in a depraved and terrible world. The nuns were looking for recruits and wanted to transmit to us the fear of the outside world." These nuns also abhorred homosexuality and repeatedly admonished Nicole and the other girls "not to walk by twos, because if you do so, the devil will be in the middle."

Everyday Activities, Food, and Hunger

Routine structured days in the convents. At dawn, the children removed blankets and sheets from beds and aired them in front of open windows. Later, they remade beds, wrinkle-free and with tight corners. The nuns verified that ears had been washed well. Girls were taught to knit gray stockings for prisoners of war and priests. Saturday afternoons were devoted to a thorough cleaning of the convent; corridors and toilets—everything—had to shine. At the end of every month in one convent, the mother superior rewarded the good workers with a bar of soap, a rare wartime commodity. Irene enjoyed giving the soap she earned to her mother when she made periodic visits. And Andrée, who had never lifted a finger at home, proudly pointed out to her mother how the convent's entrance hall shone because she had scrubbed it so well. The laundries had large mangle rollers. After they were washed, sheets were spread on the lawns to dry. Later, the children helped fold them. Tables had to be cleared every day and the large kitchen sink cleaned with chicory.

Potato peeling was an activity the children recalled iconically. The children dropped peelings into German army helmets salvaged from World War I; they then collected peeled potatoes in buckets that they emptied into large vats of water. Potato peeling was a daily activity, but "we did not eat many potatoes; these were eaten by the nuns," said one of the former hidden children. "We had peeled two or three buckets and we received nothing, so it meant that the nuns ate well."

Food and hunger were distinctive memories. The children frequently charged that the best food during this time of great shortage went to the nuns and not to them. These accusations did not apply simply to potatoes: "When we received soup, there were filaments floating in it. I had the impression that there had been meat in it, but that it had been removed."

The children described in detail various ways they coped with hunger. Unsavory experiences and comments on the poor quality of what was given also abounded:

> We had a small slice of bread in the morning. We cut it in four, and we ate slowly to make the pleasure last. It was a small slice. . . . I remember a pea soup that made me vomit. I could not swallow it. The others ate it and did not die from it. . . . Meat was tough. I chewed it until it became sticky and gooey, and I took it out of my mouth and threw it high up so that it stuck to the ceiling.

In the winter of 1942–1943, the sea yielded a miraculous abundance of herring. North Sea fishermen caught some 40,000 tons,[7] and when the fish reached the convents, one former hidden child recalled that

> we were very hungry. One time, there were many dried herrings, and we were allowed to eat as many as we wanted. We hid them in the pockets of our aprons to eat them later. When we went back to class, the stink accompanied us. We had to leave the room and go out into the fresh air.

For Jewish children brought up to follow the rules of *kashrut*, eating required special adaptation. For some, this was not a problem: "We ate pork. It did not disturb me. We were happy with what we had to eat." Others constructed a more complex rationale to assuage qualms:

> I come from a very Orthodox family, and here I was brought to the large dining hall. I said to myself: "I have to eat. If it does not please God, He has to open the sky and take me suddenly." I was sure something terrible was going to happen, and I ate, and nothing happened. Since then I do not eat kosher any more, because I said to myself: "It worked once, it will work for the rest of my life."

While hunger seems to have been widespread, not all children suffered. "We ate bread that stuck to teeth, but we were not hungry," recalled one. Rutabagas (Swedish turnips) were plentiful, though eating them became monotonous. Some convents had vegetable gardens and orchards, and children picked apples and plums. Still, the amount of food available varied greatly among the convents, as illustrated by Nicole:

We were hungry all of the time. My sister went to another convent every day where she ate well. So, morning or evening, she would leave me food on a plank under the table. She left me a slice of bread or her dessert, so I ate a bit better.

Some commented on the special efforts of nuns and priests to feed their communities, sometimes by calling on surrounding farmers and begging for food:

> The mother superior ruined her health going from farm to farm, begging for food. She would come back with two heavy baskets. She went by herself. Maybe she paid something.

> We had a headmaster who dedicated himself body and soul to us. He died soon after the war, for he went beyond the limits of his strength to provide us with decent food.

Food became a source of inequality because some boarders received packages from home, while others did not. This food was handled in a variety of ways. There was some sharing among the children. Alice poignantly remembered:

> Occasionally children received food packages. In our convent were two little girls, three and five years old. One day, while we were on a walk, I heard one say to the other: "These children receive packages and we never do. Do you think mother has forgotten us?" It hurt me so, I reported what I had heard to the mother superior, who then arranged a package for them.

The food shortages caused by the war also created a new structure of privilege that was indignantly recalled. In one boys' school,

> these farmers' sons had a table to themselves; they ate white bread, fresh eggs, butter. They enjoyed a privileged regime. It represented really a chasm between the haves and the have-nots, those who were excluded and those who were invited to the banquet. Some of the farmers' sons had friends among the others, and so they gave a little bit.

For the children, food was an integral part of the radical changes they had to endure. Their former likes, dislikes, and finicky appetites were ignored. They ate what was available. To assuage their hunger was what mattered. As Monique recalled, "My father, who had come to visit, watched me with unbelieving eyes as I tore ferociously into black bread with pear syrup. I was no longer the child he had known." Undoubtedly, food was a source of concern and tension not only for the children but also for the adults. Organizing a sufficient supply was a task constantly fraught with difficulties. Forged rationing cards had to be obtained for the hidden children. The black market presented an ethical dilemma and an economic challenge. Seeking the help of farmers required negotiating skills and diplomatic appeals to compassion. Truly, life in the convents revolved around food.

The Problem of Bed-Wetting

The consequences of bed-wetting have remained one of the former hidden children's worst memories. Many mentioned that bed-wetters were compelled to carry their sheets on their heads during the day so all could see and shame them. Ivan remembered urinating during Mass when he was five years old. Bed-wetting was common, he claimed, but what he had done was rather exceptional.

Camille had an elaborate arrangement with her older sister, who slept in the same dormitory. When she wet her bed, the sister removed the sheet, folded it, and spread it underneath the mattress to dry. Then she helped Camille make up her bed. All of this was accomplished before anyone else stirred, thus sparing Camille from punishment. Interviews with nuns indicated that attempts to cover up bed-wetting did not always work.

In Zalman's institution, bed-wetters were treated with exceptional cruelty. At the exit of the chapel, the nuns stood in two rows and whipped the offending children without mercy. From our contemporary perspective, such punishments have come to symbolize in an iconic way the shortsightedness and lack of understanding by the rescuers for the emotional suffering endured by the hidden children.

Language and Identity

Arriving in the convent demanded a change not only of identity but also, in some cases, of language. Some children had to repress and try to forget the Yiddish they spoke at home. And depending on the location of the convent where they were hidden, many now had to speak French instead of Flemish, or vice versa. They learned quickly, sometimes to their teachers' astonishment. For many of the children, it became a point of pride. Some linked the language to their acquisition of a new name and identity:

> In April 1943, I considered myself a Flemish Jew. In one hour, I became a Walloon Catholic. I was given the name Michel, and my brother's name changed from Abraham to André. Then, after the war, my father came to bring me back into a Yiddish-speaking family. So while it had

been traumatic to pass from being a Flemish Jew to a Catholic Walloon, there was also a reverse trauma. I was used to being a Catholic Walloon, and suddenly I had to metamorphose into a Brussels Jew.

And for one who was older when hidden:

> When we had to clear the tables, I met another boy, also a Flemish-speaking one in an environment that was entirely French-speaking. We quickly realized we were both Jewish. One day, while clearing the tables, we screamed at each other in Yiddish, trying to find as many swear words, insults, and curses as we could. All the while we were giggling. It was a way for us to exteriorize our Jewishness.

Many Flemish students were placed in a French-speaking convent to learn the new language. These children continued to use Flemish among themselves. Henriette managed to conceal the fact that she spoke Flemish—so she could be privy to what the others were talking about—until the day she received the top grade on an exam in Flemish class. Zalman, who was placed in a French-speaking institution, was at first held back in his classes, but then learned the language so rapidly—and against all expectations—that by the end of the war he was at the head of his class.

Because they were young, children easily became bilingual, despite their difficult circumstances. This was in marked contrast to adults, whose accents—which were difficult to overcome—made them an object of suspicion.

Children became expert at concealing their identities. While going to the toilet, one boy made sure that his friend would not see that he had been circumcised. After the war, the two discovered that they were both Jews. So friendship went only so far and left much unrevealed. Identity remained concealed, and children learned early to keep silent. Alice related that in her convent the Jewish children had been instructed to ignore each other. Toward the end of the war, the mother superior assembled all of the Jewish children to warn them of an impending search. The youngsters were amazed to see who else was Jewish. The mother superior was astounded at how well the children had respected her instructions and carefully kept their secret from each other. In other convents, Jewish children formed cliques, so secrecy within convents was not uniformly enforced. It depended on the circumstances and the rules each convent considered necessary for its own safety.

Contact with Parents

Contact with parents took place in person or by letter. On the whole, it was infrequent. One child received letters in German, so this revealed to the other

Jewish children that he was Jewish, though he never admitted it. When one mother stopped visiting and her son became anxious about it, the other boys played a cruel joke on him. They told him that his mother had arrived, and then witnessed his despair when she wasn't there. She never again appeared. Some parents visited throughout the war in spite of the danger of roundups. Others did not know where their children were hidden. The CDJ did not allow parents to know the hiding places for safety reasons. The children who received visits from their parents were a small, privileged group.

Jenny's father remained hidden indoors for three years, but her mother would come to visit from time to time. Jenny had a lovely voice. She and Sister Angélique were planning to sing together one Sunday when her mother was expected to visit. When the woman did not come, Jenny lost her voice suddenly and completely. The mother showed up a few days later; she had been unable to inform Jenny about her change in plans. Yet the girl never entirely regained her beautiful voice.

Letters from parents in hiding were often transmitted through the priests who had helped to place the children and were in touch with the outside world. It must have been very hard for those who did not receive letters—or when the letters stopped coming. What was happening to their parents? The anxiety the children felt throughout the war was fed by this silence. Some were luckier:

> I received a letter every week, and in it there were small paper rect-angles. At first, I didn't understand. Then I realized that my father was sending me back my spelling mistakes! We wrote to our parents through our landlord, who transmitted the letters. When my father found spelling mistakes, he cut them out and sent them to me. My father loved me very much. I saw his efforts to improve my spelling as an expression of his love and never as criticism.

In the middle of chaos and brutal persecutions, hidden in an attic, cold and hungry, this father maintained his ties to his daughter by checking her spelling! This was his way to pursue another reality and to assert his humanity. He expected his daughter to understand, and she did.

Visits were dangerous. In one convent near Louvain where many Jewish children were hidden, mothers would come for short visits, traveling by tram. The Nazis did not come to the convent to search and confront, nor were the nuns aware of any formal denunciations. However, on one occasion, while making their way home, the visiting mothers were denounced. Policemen boarded the tram to check identity cards and to make arrests. Young and alert, Irene's mother calmly said "Excuse me" to a policeman while he was busy checking somebody else's papers. He let her pass, and she succeeded in getting off the tram. She hurried back to the convent to alert the remaining visitors to the dangers that awaited them.

Learning

What the children learned in the convents depended on their gender. Former hidden boys described being engaged in serious studies, while the women reported taking classes in catechism, knitting, embroidery, and vocations they did not particularly want to pursue. Henriette was put in a class to learn to become a professional seamstress and cutter. She really wanted to become a language teacher. To this day, she has not forgiven this and is both unwilling and unable to handle a sewing needle. Jenny learned sewing and ironing but needed a tutor after the war to catch up in her studies. None of the women interviewed recalled a regular education; all were academically disoriented and had to make up for years lost.

It was different for the men. For Charles, classes at the institution where he was hidden were a great improvement over his prewar school. "We learned in two years more than in the preceding ten," he recalled. Ivan also praised his institution, arguing that it provided a quality education that allowed him and other children to readapt easily to regular classes after the war.

That the gender differences were so significant is of course due to the Church's different educational expectations for priests and nuns.

Age Divisions and Responsibility

In many convents, children were grouped by age. Older children took responsibility for younger ones. Roger recalled:

> I was eleven years old. In our group, we each were responsible for a two- or three-year-old. The boy I was responsible for had scabies, and I had to take care of him with a kind of smelly cream that, I realized later, smelled of sulfur. In case of air raids, I was in charge of him. He knew how to walk. He was called Simon. He was blond. That is all I remember. I was the big one, and all the big ones were responsible for the small ones in case of bombardments. That was the discipline.

So the "big" Roger remembered his twofold responsibility: caring for the wounds of a little one and shepherding him during emergencies.

Camille detailed the emergency measures in her convent, which was located in Louvain. Dormitories for the youngest and the middle ones were adjoining; this was important during bombardments, which virtually flattened the city. When the Americans wanted to warn of an impending bombing, they released yellow flares, then green ones, then red ones—and then the bombs. Camille remembered the distinctive sounds they made. As soon as yellow flares lighted up the sky, the order came: "Pick up your little one." She never failed to snatch the child who had been assigned to her. Together, they ran to the basement. There the frightened children sat at a long table, their heads bowed. Camille did not see this as an occasion to pray.

Some older children also had other functions. They served as guardian angels and godmothers (*marraines*) for the little ones. When a girl was baptized, the guardian angel would stand behind her throughout the ceremony (see fig. 9 of the photo gallery). They served as precocious role models, helping to ensure the rapid socialization of the hidden children. Guardian angels were only mentioned by the women interviewed, though boys were in principle also protected by them.

In one convent where she stayed, Renée passed as older than she actually was, so she was named a monitor. She found the task tiring, especially washing the children's hair with kerosene to kill lice. But the responsibility allowed her to seek permission once or twice to leave the convent for short periods.

Dormitories and Privacy

At first, the collective arrangements for sleeping struck the children as strange. Their descriptions of the dormitories—with or without partitions—sometimes small, Spartan cubicles separated by curtains, as in hospitals—primarily stressed the lack of privacy (see fig. 14 of the photo gallery). There were exceptions. For instance, during Easter, when all of the other children went home, Charles was allowed to stay in a room normally belonging to a priest. In her convent dormitory, where there was no privacy at all, Renée felt privileged to have her bed in a corner, surrounded by a curtain. In addition, she was allowed into a room with a piano, on which she could practice. In general, the children's desire for private spaces was rarely met. This lack of privacy required of them a major adjustment, and they alluded to it frequently.

Other Issues

In addition to scabies and boils caused by malnutrition, interviewees often mentioned other illnesses. One remarked that children fainted frequently at morning Mass because of the incense. Jenny fainted easily. Whenever she did, a doctor hidden in the convent took care of her. She recalled:

Sister Helene always came to tell me: "Do not faint. The war will soon be finished. We will all be well, and everything will be all right." I was sure she received direct news from God until I heard that there was a radio in the basement. She really had the news, and it was great that she gave it to us.

Scouting, countryside walks, even visits to a swimming pool were some pleasurable activities recalled. In Irene's convent, a blind nun played the piano, and the children sang. In good weather, they went to a lake where there were canoes. Irene remembered that the nuns seemed more relaxed and inclined to banter when outside the convent walls. The interviewees said little about toys and games, with one exception. Monique said, "I had a shoebox. In a cheap copying notebook I had cut out a cardboard doll and a whole wardrobe of dresses. This was my treasure, this shoebox with the paper dresses that were not very sturdy."

Vacation time made the hidden children particularly conspicuous and highlighted their marginality. While the boarders went home, the Jewish children stayed on. Roger was the only youth who remained at his convent during these holidays. He realized after the war that the nuns, the principal, and the prefect all must have known that he was a hidden child. In effect, those children with nowhere to go were singled out. They had to trust that others would keep their existence a secret. Kathryn could not stay in her convent during vacations and was sent to orphanages that she hated. She found the need to adjust and readjust extremely difficult. On the other hand, Charles cherished vacations; they provided him with occasions for long conversations with his director, Father Carlier.

Liberation and Aftermath

The days of liberation from the occupation remain vivid for many former hidden children. Jenny recalled the smell of cigarette smoke:

> I knew that they [the Americans] were there. We knew one song, "Tipperary." We sang it the whole night. My throat was sore and I could not speak for a few days. I also saw Germans with dirty boots, and then we knew that it was the end.

On the day of liberation, Camille and other children in her convent lined up along a main road. She saw a little black dot that grew bigger and bigger: "They looked like gods—big, smiling, black. (I had never seen a black person.) We yelled, 'Chewing gum, chewing gum.' I was thinking, 'Now my parents will be back for my birthday.' This was not to be."

When Emile heard that the Americans had arrived, he also thought about chewing gum. With a group of children, he went out to see the soldiers. He found a group of them praying in an orchard. Among them was a chaplain wearing a Jewish prayer shawl:

> I approached them . . . and at one point, under the envious gaze of the other children, the chaplain asked me in an Americanized, heavily accented Yiddish: "Are you a Jew?" I chatted with him, I don't remember exactly about what, and I felt very happy. The children around me were astonished that I, one of them, had a common language with an American soldier!

Many sobering moments soon followed the exhilaration of Liberation. Catholic upbringing provides rewards in the guise of holy medals and cards, while rosaries facilitate concentration when praying. The children had become attached to these holy objects and felt protected by them. With the end of the war, parents or relatives came to retrieve the children and expected them to relinquish immediately all of their wartime religious practices. As we have seen, this transition was far from simple. Some confrontations were abrupt and painful, for Catholic socialization had been very effective. It was difficult to flip identities again so rapidly and give up instantly what one had been taught to consider significant and comforting.

More important, many children slowly began to realize that, contrary to Nazi lies, "deportation" had been a synonym for extermination. Many youngsters had to face the fact that their parents were never going to return. The prewar life with their families that they imagined so nostalgically throughout the war had disappeared forever. The AIVG established group homes for some of these orphans; others were taken in by relatives. Many parents who did return from the camps were broken in body and spirit. Girls who had been hidden had to make up much of their schooling. Those who were orphaned and lived in the AIVG homes were steered toward occupations in which they could quickly earn a living, such as nursing, elementary school teaching, or secretarial work. In contrast to boys, they were not offered scholarships for higher education. My interviewees are still resentful of paths not taken and opportunities not offered. The women, by now of retirement age, do not consider their lives failures, at least within the limits of the interviews, yet viewing their past from the perspective of the present, they judge harshly the stereotypical gender blinders that were worn by those who had the power to steer them to adulthood.

CONCLUSION

The variety and intensity of the human experiences described here show the impact of Catholic institutions. The sample is of course too limited to account for many contingencies of everyday life, but the reach of this study is predicated on what it suggests, not on any definitive statements.

That the former hidden children were willing to talk so readily about their convent experiences is significant both for them and for us. In effect, they were talking about their survival, and highlighting the conditions in which they survived and adapted. Being in a convent saved their lives. Their survival, with all its ramifications and impact, is the main issue. To place one's child in a convent was not an easy decision, and it was not the children's to make. But the desire to understand and to narrate what happened at the time is theirs. As a group they had a variety of reactions to the strong Catholic socialization, and they used diverse coping strategies. What strikes us today is how essential their adaptability was to their survival.

It is plausible that some hidden children benefited from the orderly life the institutions provided. While unpredictability and sporadic chaos reigned outside the convents' walls, the structure and regulation of Catholic life within them offered a measure of stability. While these structures did not give rise to a uniformity of responses, they offered space and encouragement for adaptability. Some children appreciated what was offered, whether at the time or in retrospection. After all, nuns have been honored as Righteous Among the Nations thanks to the energetic efforts of former hidden children.

Adaptability also led to variations in return to former identities. These range from those who have returned to Judaism to converts who see themselves as bridging traditions. In effect, the latter have created a new category of religious people—Judeo-Christians—as they seek to fulfill their religious needs through this bridging of the two religions.[8]

In spite of their innocence, the children suffered incalculable losses and unjust pain. Though they were robbed of normal childhoods, they became competent adults. They recalled willingly the lives they spent in the convents that sheltered them. In reconnecting their past with their present, they nurtured their individuality, while providing us with valuable insights into the institutions into which they were plunged.

2

The Nuns

The voices of the nuns are an essential part of this story. These voices tell us under what conditions the nuns rescued the children, what motivated them, and how they proceeded. Just as the former hidden children's memories are selective in what they remember about their lives during the war's upheaval, so are those of the nuns and the only priest I interviewed. Though they were of advanced age, they were clear-minded. Occasionally a few received a visit from some of the children who were hidden in their convents. One of them, Soeur Marthe Sibille, even receives to this day weekly Sunday visits from a woman she protected and cherished as a child. Others relied entirely on their memories of the past. These memories have been refreshed in cases where the nuns have been honored as Righteous Among the Nations or have accepted the medal and diploma on behalf of nuns being honored posthumously.

This chapter draws on voices from various places, two of which are highlighted. From the Couvent de la Miséricorde (Convent of Mercy) of Héverlé (Heverlee) near Louvain, there are detailed memories that are sometimes juxtaposed with those of former hidden children who stayed there. So this one site is illuminated by various points of view. In contrast, an extended interview with a former nun from an orphanage near Charleroi, south of Brussels, where about fifty Jewish children were hidden, reveals her wealth of experiences and feelings during the war—a single point of view from a single site.

Clearly, the Jewish children were very different from the boarders who were living in the convents of the teaching orders and in orphanages. The hidden children were utterly unprepared to fit into the existing institutional structures.

They had suffered an unexpected and sudden separation from their parents, and they were stepping into a strange milieu lacking any familiar markers. Loss of home, name, identity, *kashrut*, and sometimes even language—the children were ushered into the convents carrying all these losses. To boot, they were under orders not to acknowledge them. Their lives were safe momentarily, but they realized it was a fragile safety. They did not know their parents' fates; that, too, was a constant worry. The nuns had to understand these children's anxieties, yet on the other hand they were often instructed not to treat the Jewish children differently from the others; the situation could present them with dilemmas. Simultaneously, they expected to teach their own rituals to these nonbelievers, so very different from the children they usually educated.

The convents stretched all their resources to accommodate the new arrivals, yet many who called on them took these efforts for granted. Space in dormitories and classrooms had to be rapidly expanded, a feat not so easily accomplished and likely to bring discomfort. The nuns had to be especially careful to avoid German scrutiny, enforce secrecy, and ensure that false identities were not discovered. With more mouths to feed, additional food had to be provided in a war situation in which hunger predominated. Without any doubt, rescuing Jewish children demanded from the convents special qualities and competence.

This chapter explores first who were those responsible for the acceptance of the Jewish children into the convents. It then addresses the problems presented by Catholic rituals and baptism. It also illustrates how the war forced the convents to deal with the Nazi occupiers and food shortages. In the nuns' relationships with the children, Sister X's special contribution played an extraordinary role—her reminiscences about these relationships bring an additional perspective. The chapter concludes with thoughts about the agency of these convents and their mothers superior.

RESPONSIBILITY FOR ACCEPTANCE OF JEWISH CHILDREN

The narratives show clearly that the mother superior of the convent independently made the decision to admit a Jewish child, without formal prior consultation with the members of her convent community. In some cases, she possibly sought advice from the Church hierarchy, but there is no clear evidence for that assumption. Neither do we know which convents were solicited but refused to accept children. As already mentioned, in the provinces of Liège and Limbourg, Bishop Kerkhofs had instructed his clergy to extend all help possible to Jews, so in those provinces it is unlikely that the convents felt the need to seek advice. In the rest of the country, vagueness shrouded the issue, leaving the decisions whether to shelter Jewish children with each mother superior individually. Some of these decisions, though not necessarily all, had to be made rapidly, often on the spur of the moment, despite their long-range consequences. As Sister Hélène Baggen related, speaking of her mother superior:

> The next day she comes with two children just like that, and says to me: "Listen, Sister, we have to make room. I leave you to find room; you know how to manage that better than I can." I don't know how I managed to add all the beds for these children, twenty-two beds in my dormitory. I asked myself later how I managed, because each child had all that was needed.

The nuns I interviewed were unanimous in designating their mothers superior as bearing the entire responsibility for making the decision to accept and hide the Jewish children. Without a moment's hesitation, Sister Hilde Casaer from the Paridaens Institute, a Catholic boarding school in Louvain, declared that it was the head of the sisters, Sister Marie Bernadette, who decided to hide a Jewish girl. "She was courageous, a great woman, really a great lady. . . . She said that we would be told as little as possible." And Sister Marie Beirens was just as categorical in her claim that her mother superior, Mother Cécile, took all the responsibility for hiding a large number of Jewish children in the Couvent de la Miséricorde. Father Julien Richard, teaching in a renowned boarding school for boys, the Collège Saint Pierre in Brussels, was told by the priest who was the director: "I am putting a Jewish child in your class; you will not speak about that, dead or alive." Two other Jewish boys were hidden in the school, but Father Richard was entirely unaware about them until after the war.

Without a doubt, the heads of convents and other institutions enjoyed much leeway and exercised an unchallenged authority in their convents. Therefore, it is not surprising that the surviving nuns highlighted the initiatives of their superiors; it would have been more surprising if they had not. My interviewees were young nuns at the time of the war, and they could not be expected to know whether their mothers superior had sought advice from the bishop or the head of their order. For them, their mothers superior were powerful, all-knowing figures.

After being contacted by the Resistance, by priests or by parents, and agreeing to shelter and rescue, the mothers superior generally restricted any knowledge of that activity to a small intimate circle around them. The other nuns in the convent community were kept in the dark as much as possible, or acquired their knowledge indirectly through gossip, or were gradually briefed as needed by those in the know. In any case, once the nuns knew, they were not supposed to talk about the rescue activities, nor were they to treat the Jewish children differently from the others. Aware of how self-absorbed children can be, they assumed rightly that the non-Jewish children would not pay too much attention to the rescue mission and to the new boarders. When denunciations occurred, the informer was generally an outsider who had once been employed by the convent and had a grudge against it, or somebody who expected to profit by being paid for the denunciation.

Here is an example of how one mother superior proceeded, in an orphanage near Charleroi. Jewish children and adults were brought there from Brussels through an intermediary. My interviewee reported that the mother superior assembled the nuns and told them: "We cannot leave the children in danger of being taken away. I ask from you the greatest discretion, above all don't talk to the boarders about it, and don't even talk about it among yourselves." So the nuns followed instructions and kept silent about the presence of fifty Jewish children and three Jewish mothers who were hidden in their midst at different times during the course of the war. The regular boarders did not seem to perceive the new children as strange, and the three adults helped in the convent kitchen. In general, when convents sheltered Jewish adults, members of the Belgian resistance, and labor draft evaders, they employed them as domestics, gardeners, cooks, and general help—both to lighten the daily burden and especially to avoid detection.

The convent of one of my interviewees hid a Jewish couple with two small children in addition to numerous Jewish girls. On a nice Sunday, the weather was so beautiful that the family wanted to go out for a walk. The mother superior suggested they go out into the garden instead, warning that stepping outside might be dangerous. They did not heed her advice but went out and were never seen again:

> We notified the Resistance, who had placed them with us. My heart was broken. The kids were so cute, lovely. And the mother, too. She was tall, I see her before my eyes, a tall, beautiful person. It was dangerous to allow them to go out. We had a garden that was quite large. Maybe they wanted to go out for the children, maybe to buy them some small thing. Never came back. We didn't dare to try to find out anything. We think they did not have our address on them because nobody came to check on us.

This case illustrates that some nuns were well aware of the dangers of the German occupation. On the other hand, in some of my other interviews, I was told that there was ignorance about what was happening in the outside world. For example, Sister Beirens said: "We did not know what was happening outside. Now, I have goose flesh when I think of it." Roundups and deportations were not necessarily seen as leading to subsequent extermination, at least in the early months of the deportations. The Germans were intent on keeping the pretense that they were deporting Jews for forced labor, and succeeded for a while. But little girls could hardly be considered useful labor!

CATHOLIC RITUALS AND JEWISH CHILDREN

As discussed in chapter 1, all the important Catholic rituals—baptism, communion, and confession—played an essential part in the children's adaptation to convent life. By baptizing children, the nuns were saving souls and creating faithful Catholics, as well as completing the strategy of concealment: simultaneously saving souls and protecting bodies from threatening evil.

In view of the low prewar status of Judaism and its constant stigmatization during the war, there was undoubtedly a strong desire to save the souls of Jewish children, and to convert them. In contemporary interviews, however, these members of the clergy fully articulated the difference between past and present, played down the conversion aspect, and emphasized the humanitarian goal:

> Sister Marie Bernadette told the little girl called Rosalie from the beginning to behave like everybody else, and at communion time Rosalie walked forward. . . . I would say that the presence of Jesus in the consecrated wafer was nearly seen materially. At that moment Sister Marie Bernadette said: "my God she is going to communion. I have forgotten to tell her," and she took the girl's arm quietly and led her away. Rosalie was then baptized in secret so that she could take communion. This really had little to do with faith, but it was a way to save her, to save a human life. At night, she would say her Jewish prayer in her bed . . . the poor little thing.

The nun downplayed the religious aspect, the saving of a soul. From her contemporary perspective, it was the humanitarian initiative, the rescue of a child's life, that mattered. However, then and now, baptism is an expression of faith, a ritual not to be performed lightly for purely instrumental reasons. In the interview situation, the nun adopted the retrospective view that prevailed among Jews at the time of the war—baptism was seen as purely a strategic device to deflect persecution. It is probable, however, that the nuns at the time were also greatly concerned with the spiritual aspect of baptism, even if admitting it today is difficult. In mentioning the Jewish prayer, the nun wanted to show her belief in tolerance. The girl of whom she spoke was the only Jewish child hidden in this convent as an intern. There were some Jewish children who were day pupils, but their teachers found that out about them only after the war.

The irony is that baptism per se did not preserve Jewish lives. For the Nazis, the rationale for exterminating the Jews was fueled by a racial ideology; religion, and therefore conversion, were beside the point. As targets of this savage onslaught, Jews considered any strategy for survival better than none—baptism, signifying conversion, was considered a resource for claiming and seeking the protection of Catholic clergy and institutions. In a certain sense, it created for them the illusion of an entitlement. For the nuns, hiding nonbaptized Jewish children presented a double predicament. Allowing the children to take the consecrated host without baptism would be blasphemy, but if these children did not participate in important Catholic rituals, their hidden identity could be compromised. So baptism could be justified for tactical reasons—to complete the cover-up.

All the other interviewees denied that there had been any pressure to baptize the hiding children. Today these nuns do not consider this whole aspect important, though it was certainly different in wartime. After the war, some convents were reluctant to relinquish Jewish children whom they had baptized during the war and whose parents did not return from deportation. Humanitarian concerns ceased to be relevant, and the saving of souls mattered to them greatly. The painful debate that developed around the baptized, orphaned Jewish children in the aftermath of the war will be addressed in chapter 4. Because this debate was so contentious and painful for all concerned, it is easy to understand that people would squash and prefer to ignore the subject today.

Father Richard, who has died since I interviewed him, reported the following dialogue with the Jewish boy in his class, as they went on a walk together:

HIDDEN BOY: You will baptize me, it will be a proof.

FATHER RICHARD: I only baptize believers.

HIDDEN BOY: I am a believer because I am Jewish.

FATHER RICHARD: Stay what you are. We shall see after the war.

The boy attended Mass. There were other children in his class who were not baptized, so there was no problem of standing out.

Sister Beirens took care of very young boys and said that the issue of baptism never came up for her. As for the rest of the convent—"the other side," as she put it (where the girls lived)—she was unaware of what happened there. However, two women interviewees who were hidden in her convent reported that they were baptized because they themselves insisted on it.

Recent archival research seems to indicate that baptism was more widespread than has commonly been believed, and more than the nuns I interviewed reported.[1] In these recent interviews, baptism played a relatively small role. In a period when tolerance and multiculturalism are deemed politically correct, in theory if not in practice, it is no wonder that the nuns did not highlight the practice. The issue only became controversial after the war, as members of the Catholic clergy argued that baptized orphans should remain Catholic if they wished, while the Jewish community wanted to retrieve the orphans and raise them until adulthood as Jews, as they and their parents had been.

When asked what motivated Mother Urbain to accept the children, Sister Marie Reine, after having emphasized that the children were never pressured toward baptism, responded with a most appropriate sentence: "Mother Urbain did it for charity. We are called Sisters of Charity. Above all we must honor the name we carry." She had found a very elegant way to communicate her humanitarian goal.

Interviews with formerly hidden children indicate that in some convents, the solemn communion after baptism was considered a significant and festive occasion. Women in particular emphasized the white dress they were given on the occasion of their First Communion, at a time when clothing was in short supply and clothing choice an illusion. These formal events were captured in numerous photographs, attesting to their significance for both the convents and the girls. For the nuns, the ceremony was the consecrating high point of their mission.

While baptism and communion, though frequent, were not imposed in all convents, with few exceptions, going to Mass was the rule. Mass structured the days in the convents; it was imperative that Jewish children be integrated into these structures and that they conform to all their rules. That was vital for security, and it was also essential for ensuring the daily routine.

Sister Baggen was amazed at how easily the hidden children followed the Mass: "They behaved as if they had done so all their lives. They never said: *This I don't know, this I can't follow.*" Interviews with the formerly hidden children, however, did not necessarily reflect such untroubled adaptation. Perhaps children did not want to convey to Sister Baggen their doubts and hesitations. And perhaps they learned so quickly because they felt their lives depended on it.

Because the Catholic religion does not allow women to celebrate the Mass or to hear confessions, chaplains fulfilled these functions in each convent. Some of them also oversaw catechism instruction. Again, diversity predominated, ranging from chaplains who were remembered as personalities to those some nuns perceived as insignificant. For example, Jesuit priests were lavishly praised and considered "very fine, and also excellent for the children." But in the convent in Auderghem, a suburb of Brussels, all that was said about the chaplain was "he was a good man, very pleasant, but nothing special." In another convent (Héverlé), language divided the chaplain and the nuns. The chaplain was Walloon and French-speaking, while the nun interviewed was Flemish, and so, "on the whole we hardly knew him." Another arrangement included a Dominican priest who came to the nuns for confessions, retreats, and conferences, and a vicar and a parish priest who visited at fixed intervals to hear the children's confessions. On the whole, the chaplains did not seem to be remembered as greatly significant—either for the nuns' religious consciences or for the running of the convents. In the accounts of the formerly hidden children, however, this consistent masculine presence was frequently invoked, and sometimes seen as vital.

RELATIONSHIPS WITH GERMANS

The Role of German Nuns

The Sisters of Charity ran the boarding school Notre Dame du Bon Conseil (Our Lady of Good Counsel) in Auderghem, a suburb of Brussels. Sister Marie Reine recalled in great detail the German army's partial occupation of the institution over four long years. The institution as a whole included a day school, a boarding school that attracted mostly Flemish-speaking children who were sent there in order to learn French, and a convent that housed the nuns. The Germans requisitioned the day school building for general staff headquarters. Subsequently, when the Germans wanted to occupy an additional building, the mother superior promptly delegated Sister Rodriguez to protest. Sister Rodriguez, whose secular name was Franziska Catharina Weber, was German. She was a tall, strong, and distinguished woman, with a reputation for valuable negotiating skills. She went straight to the commander-in-chief, protested the planned takeover, and succeeded in preventing further inroads into the institution. At least twelve Jewish girls, as well as three families, were hidden right under the noses of the Germans (see fig. 22 of the photo gallery). The soldiers were noisy and often drunk. Toward the end of the war, the nuns noticed fewer and fewer soldiers. One day they heard nothing, but they did not go and investigate until after the Liberation. The soldiers had quietly disappeared, leaving the building in total shambles.

Sister Rodriguez protected Sister Bridget (Bridget Fitzgerald), who was Irish and therefore, in the occupiers' eyes, an enemy alien. In my interview with Sister Bridget, she told me that she had to show herself at the German Kommandantur every six months, as evidence that she had not fled the country clandestinely. Sister Rodriguez always accompanied her and smoothed the tense encounter. In addition, Sister Rodriguez was often called on to serve as an intermediary for people outside the convent when they had matters to settle with the occupiers, and apparently she also helped in issues connected to the nuns' medical clinic. Sister Rodriguez was not the sole example of what German nuns could achieve. German nuns in other convents were remembered. They would persuade the Germans searching for Jewish children in the convent that there were none, and these nuns were convincing liars! They were also praised as being very good cooks—"They baked carrot cakes that were so good!" Having in a convent German nuns who could communicate in the occupiers' own language gave others a feeling of security, a much-appreciated recollection.

The different national backgrounds of their members gave some convents a view on the world outside their walls, and provided an advantage in dealing with the unpredictability and the chaos brought about by the war. From the occupiers the German nuns elicited a certain respect, along with a reminder of their common and familiar homeland. All this worked to the advantage of rescue activities.

Reactions to German Incursions into Convents

Sister Beirens did not remember a German incursion into her convent. Two women interviewees who had been hidden there, however, recalled that they were taken unexpectedly out for a walk into the woods and kept there until the all-clear was signaled. This was the preferred method for dealing with these incursions. Children were whisked away, especially those who looked "Semitic": having dark and frizzy hair, dark eyes, a prominent nose. These types could, and did, with luck, pass as Italian or Spanish in rare cases.[2] During the whole war period, exterior physiognomies acquired extraordinary importance. The more "Aryan" the look, the smaller the risk of being arrested in the street, for example—on condition that one had identity papers whose authenticity could not be easily challenged. The notorious Jacques the Jewish traitor roamed the streets of Brussels specifically to detect Jews he could denounce.[3]

Sister Baggen would leave the convent with the children when it was searched. She remembered the Germans questioning the mother superior, without dire consequences. Late in the war, when the town where the convent was situated was heavily bombed and badly damaged, she found refuge with the children in a large house near a wood. As she went to reconnoiter the neighborhood and to investigate patches of white she had glimpsed in the woods, she nearly stumbled on a German encampment and retreated in haste. Not only were the Jewish children with her but also her own sister, who was hiding from conscription for forced labor. Priests from the order of Dom Bosco came to the rescue. They housed her and her charges in their monastery, and fed them all until the end of the war. They told her that they would treat the children as if they would be baptized at some later date. To this day, Sister Baggen marveled at their generosity, at the abundance and quality of the food they provided for free, and at the easy way they related to the children. She told her mother superior that these priests were an answer to her prayers.

The Germans came to Sister Casaer's convent (Paridaens) in search not of Jewish children, but for a young woman who had come to the convent posing as a postulant, in reality in order to evade forced labor conscription. She had been denounced. She was not in the convent, having gone to the dentist, and the Germans caught her there.

In another convent, the first child hidden was a two-and-a-half-year-old boy who was brought through an intermediary. The nuns never knew his real name. When the Germans arrived one night, Sister X recalled being given instructions to hide him, but as he was sleeping so soundly in his crib, she did not wake him. He was not discovered.

On the whole, when there was time, the plan was to escape by back doors and to stay away in whatever way possible until the danger had passed. Because the occupiers did not want confrontations with the religious orders, when they didn't find any Jewish children or resisters or labor draft evaders on the spot, they retreated.

Suffering from a growing labor shortage, the Germans conscripted young people for forced labor in Germany on a large scale in the fall of 1942. By the spring of 1943, thousands of workers went underground to escape being sent to Germany. Some convents and colleges hid not only Jewish children but also Jewish adults, rescued pilots who had parachuted from Allied planes, people in the Resistance who had been denounced, and those who had been called up for work in Germany but refused to go. A formerly hidden boy recalled that when he was assigned a new room in his Catholic institution, he was soon ordered to take off his heavy shoes, bearing protective metal plates, when he entered his room. He was not given an explanation, only an order. After the war, he found out that his room was above a cellar in which three parachutists were hidden. His heavy footsteps had frightened them, as they thought they were Gestapo boots.

In the memories of the nuns I interviewed, the fears evoked by the Allied bombardments and the German responses toward the end of the war were much more vivid than the sense of danger that the children might be discovered hiding in the convents. In the Belgian situation in general, reprisals against nuns who had engaged only in the rescue of Jewish children would not have been extremely harsh. The nuns, on the other hand, would have been deeply distressed by the fate of the children, who, if discovered, would be deported and exterminated, and thus by the failure of their mission. The German response was not always predictable, however. In one secular institution where Jewish children were discovered, the principal and her husband were deported and assassinated.[4] If the rescuers could be accused of having obtained false identity and rationing cards, prison sentences were likely. When resisters, Allied pilots, and people avoiding labor conscription were discovered, those who were sheltering them were deported to concentration camps, and rarely survived. This was also true in the case of people who organized rescue networks. When I interviewed historian Maxime Steinberg and queried him about risks, he explained that these varied according to region. In Antwerp and Liège, those hiding Jewish children would be arrested, while in general this was less likely in Brussels. As for the nuns, Steinberg explained, they perceived their rescue actions as risky and envisaged the possibility of dangerous consequences and reprisals.[5]

Ensuring a Sufficient Supply of Food

Convents by definition are enterprises functioning to fulfill the various needs of their members. What was usually an important but routine function in peacetime— assuring an adequate food supply—turned into a daily challenge during the war. Staples, obtained with rationing stamps, were meager.[6] Some of the food was supplied from the convents' own resources, such as vegetable gardens and orchards. As mentioned in chapter 1, much depended also on good relationships with local butchers and farmers. The widespread black market posed both an ethical and an economic dilemma. Information on how the institutions where Jewish children were hidden used the black market is not readily available.[7] The number of mouths to feed was not stable, as children were brought in and taken out; this also posed a challenge. And the appetites of growing children presented constant dilemmas. In short, in such trying circumstances, learning to make do with what was available and creating substitutes for what was unavailable were prized skills. The Secours d'Hiver (Winter Aid) extended some help, especially in cases where the children had been categorized as sickly or weak.[8] The soup it provided was characterized by some interviewed children as diluted, perhaps even in the convents' kitchens.

As in the population at large, there was hunger:

> We were cold, we were hungry. Every day we ate the same food, carrots, turnips, rutabagas. A nun was in charge of setting up the weekly menu, and we were convulsed with laughter as she would write: Monday, carrots, turnips, rutabagas, Tuesday, rutabagas, carrots, turnips—every day the same—but once a week we had meatballs.

People in the neighborhood were generous to this orphanage. The butcher would sometimes give them meat he had not sold. The sister who was the main house-keeper came from Brussels. Because she had formerly lived in the city in contrast to other nuns who came from a simpler rural background, the congregation expected her to be both shrewd and worldly. Charged by the mother superior with the task of obtaining food, she went to the local German Kommandantur (administrative offices) where she tearfully pled for help on behalf of the 150 orphans who were dying of hunger because they were deprived of potatoes. Her performance was successful. The next day, the Germans brought in a truckload of potatoes. How many times the stratagem succeeded is not clear. Some children also received packages from the Secours d'Hiver. These children were not sick, but in connivance with doctors, those who were a bit pale were declared feeble and thus were entitled to receive supplements.

As a rule, in all institutions, the nuns did not eat with the children. Commensality is not commonly practiced in highly stratified institutions. The nun from an orphanage remarked simply:

> We had to eat in silence, while listening to a reading. Sometimes the mother superior would allow us to speak, the reading was stopped, and we were allowed to converse. We never ate with the children. We ate somewhat differently. It wasn't luxurious, but it was a bit different, for we were less numerous. The children at one moment numbered 140, even 150, while we were about twenty nuns.

What exactly did Sister X mean by these figures? Probably that some food would be available for a small number of mouths, but could not be offered in large quantity—eggs, for instance. It was an open admission that when it came to food, the nuns occupied a better position than the children. Of course, none of the nuns interviewed admitted openly that they had eaten better than the children. Those who were hidden as children at various institutions, however, repeatedly accused the nuns of shortchanging them and keeping the best food for themselves (as reported in chapter 1).

Another angle is shown by Soeur Marie Reine's assertion that the Resistance, in this case the White Army, brought some food.[9] That particular convent was also hiding adults. She recalled, perhaps with some exaggeration, that "her convent always had enough for the children."

As for Father Richard, he claimed there had been no hunger in his institution. During vacations, however, he took his hidden Jewish boy to stay with distant relatives, a couple of farmers, with whom he ate white bread, and learned at what angle to set his knife in order to spread the largest possible quantity of butter and jam on his slice of bread.

There was also a sharing of resources between convents, not necessarily belonging to the same orders. For instance, the Fathers of Dom Bosco at first provided food for Sister Baggen and her children when their convent was badly damaged in bombardments. When the nuns' temporary residence proved to be uncomfortably near a German encampment, as noted, the priests opened their monastery to them and housed them for the last months of the war, supplying food and advice generously. According to Sister Marie Reine, the more prosperous convents would help the poorer ones; she considered this a unique feature of her order, the Sisters of Charity. In fact, Sister Baggen's story suggests that it may not have been a unique occurrence. Whether institutions run by men command better resources than those run by women is a question still to be answered.

Convents owned orchards and vegetable gardens, even potato fields. Secours d'Hiver provided dried beans to make soups, according to Sister Beirens. And the nuns were allowed to milk the cows the Germans had requisitioned from farmers, before the cows were slaughtered. Sometimes convents had a bakery, and one had a pigsty, in which Sister Beirens remembered she had to caulk the windows, despite her fear of pigs. And one day, in that convent, Sister Cunégonde arrived carrying in her apron a load of newborn piglets.

It was evident that the war and the food shortages, created by the occupiers' requisitions and the inability to import goods via prewar channels, fostered the emergence of a new aristocracy of farmers. These new aristocrats commanded plenty of resources and at times could afford to show generosity, if they wished.

Some convents resorted to begging and were reasonably successful. One nun asserted that begging required the permission of the bishop in the diocese on which the convent depended, but this did not present any difficulty. On the contrary, the activity benefited from a long tradition and was blessed. So when the need was pressing, the nuns went begging: "I went with a wheelbarrow to the big farms asking for potatoes. I remember that I asked for potatoes, and I received beans! I thanked them anyway. The cart came from Héverlé to pick up what we had collected." Begging was a method used to obtain not only food but also money. Sister Beirens remembered doing so with a German nun, for the Vatican had ordered nuns never to go out alone.[10] Not only convents but also many social services appealed to charity.

Convents were not necessarily similar to each other. A kaleidoscope of orders was involved in the rescue. Some orders were quite wealthy—the Sisters of Charity of Ghent for example; others, like the Sisters of St. Vincent de Paul, were very poor, and some orphanages were destitute. Securing sufficient food was a constant preoccupation—requiring resources and first-rate management skills. It did not prevent the development of malnutrition.[11]

In many cases, parents or the Resistance paid monthly sums for the upkeep of the hidden children. The Resistance obtained money through donations, and illegally from the Belgian government in London, through the connivance of local banks. When parents were deported and the payments stopped, the Resistance often took over the payment of the necessary pension. But as with baptism and conversion, an explanation of the convents' activities in instrumental terms would be simplistic and tendentious. The many cases in which either no income accrued from hiding Jewish children or they represented an economic drain on scarce resources make it clear that financial self-interest—like missionary zeal—did not represent the single most significant motivation.

RELATIONSHIPS WITH CHILDREN

It is pertinent to reiterate here the advanced age of the nuns at the time of the interviews and the especially impressionable age of the children when in hiding. The interviews with the children yielded a broad range of insights into the complex relationships of the children with the nuns. How did the nuns refer to the children? On the whole, the nuns addressed specific events. Still, they recalled not only events but feelings as well. The nuns' memories, however, were much more limited in their scope than those of the children.

The boarding school Paridaens was run by nuns who belonged to the order of the Daughters of Mary. Those sisters who supervised the dormitories had been instructed to wake up Rosalie when she dreamt in German. They did so without asking any questions. "The fewer people knew 'it,' the better it was for all of us." The reason, of course, was to prevent arousing the suspicions of the other children, who had said to the Jewish girl, "What do you speak? Why do you dream so strangely?" The nuns who supervised the dormitories suspected who she was, but they were not officially informed. During vacations she had to leave the convent and was placed in orphanages, about which she complained bitterly. When she would come back, she would declare that returning to Paridaens was like returning to paradise—a play on words of which Sister Casaer was very proud.

Sister Casaer wrote an account of this girl's time in hiding, and it was published in 1988 in the newsletter sent to the alumnae of the institution, which recently celebrated its bicentennial jubilee. Mentioning in her article that at night Rosalie secretly recited the traditional Jewish prayer Sh'ma, Sister Casaer addressed the alumnae directly: "Who among you, dear former students, would have expected that in your 'Holy Virgin' dormitory a small girl was living such a drama?"[12]

In our interview, Sister Casaer commented on the nuns who had taken care of Rosalie. Sister Loyola was like a mother to the child; Sister Dominique especially befriended her and spent much time with her; the director of the boarding school, Sister Michaela, an excellent musician, gave her constant attention. Rosalie seemed to have been cherished. She was the object of great concern, perhaps because she was the only hidden child. The nuns may have felt that she offered them the opportunity to do a good deed. She needed maternal care; they responded and provided it. In our interview Sister Casaer thought that hidden children in general felt that the Virgin Mary represented their mothers.

Sister Casaer also believed that discovery would have had dire consequences for the whole convent. She did not realize that the German authorities tended to avoid violent confrontations with Catholic institutions. "For a mother superior, it was a very difficult choice ... the Germans, when they massacred, they didn't stop at one person." This perception of danger and of the fickle unpredictability of the occupiers' behavior is in line with the remarks of historian Maxime Steinberg reported at the beginning of this chapter.

In subsequent correspondence, Sister Casaer referred me to a recent brochure published in honor of the school's bicentennial. In this brochure's discussion of the institution's history, a page is devoted to the story of the hidden Jewish girl.[13] Some of the events in this account differ from what Sister Casaer recalled vividly in our interview. The author specifically mentions that the Jewish girl was not baptized and that she later remembered one of the nuns telling her: "Do not give up your Jewish beliefs, just go along with us for a while." According to this author, a couple of other Jewish girls were also hidden in the school during the war, one of them as a postulant. The discrepancy in recollections about the baptism illustrates how the subject is fraught with tension, even so many decades after the war.

Soeur Marie-Reine, from the order of the Sisters of Charity, stressed that

> we had to be good to these children. They needed to feel secure. We had to reason with them when they cried. One child could not get used to staying with us, so an uncle came to fetch her. The children were not compelled to go to Mass; we left them free. None were baptized.

The convent could be flexible up to a point, but the children needed to put up with its structure and its fundamental rules. The constraints under which they lived bear to be repeated. They had to accept the disruption of their families, the absence of their parents, and the uncertainty of their parents' return. They had to participate in a collective way of life in which their former habits and routines were dismantled, new religious practices were followed, and their own names ceased to exist. Sometimes even their own languages had to be discarded. No wonder, then, that some children could not adapt. On the contrary, it is remarkable that the majority of children adjusted to such difficult circumstances and showed much maturity. On the whole, the nuns seemed to have taken in stride the arrival of "strangers" in their midst.

Sister Baggen admired the way the Jewish children understood that they had to be careful, without being told explicitly. Perhaps this was because they had already learned how to live silent lives before they arrived. They never said who they were, nor did the other children refer to them as being Jewish. She was astonished that they acted as if they had gone to Mass all their lives. Those who had been baptized before being hidden went to communion; the others were left alone. "We left it up to them." When Sister Baggen and the children found refuge with the Fathers of Dom Bosco, the children talked a lot with the fathers and asked for explanations. Sister Baggen repeatedly exclaimed with much emotion that in her convent, "they never cried during all that time. I don't know where they found that courage. They never cried, they never asked where their parents were, I don't know how they did it." When the Germans came into the convent, she remembered that she left with all the children, but didn't recall where they went. When they returned to the convent, the children went to question the mother superior, but Sister Baggen did not know what they were told. The Jewish children joined in all the games; they played together with the other children. They never asked, nor were they asked, "Who are you?" When they arrived in the convent, they spoke French, but very rapidly learned Flemish. The nuns did not know their real names. After the war, the children departed with their war names, and so the nuns could not find them again. Four hidden children eventually found each other. They reconnected with the convent, and in time they succeeded in having Sister Baggen recognized as a Righteous Among the Nations.

In the Convent of Mercy in Héverlé

According to Sister Beirens, in her convent, the nuns who cared for the Jewish children knew who they were. However, most of them did not exactly realize all the dreadful events that were happening outside the convent's walls. In recalling these events, Sister Beirens still shuddered: "These children were like all the other children. We cared for them as for the other children. We made no distinctions. We accepted them. . . . We were completely ignorant of the danger that these children faced."

When we talked about the children and I asked Sister Beirens whether she had been frightened, she misunderstood my question. I had meant afraid of the Germans, but she responded by telling me in great detail about the bombings. What she recalled most vividly were the bombardments after the Allied landing on the Continent and the push of the Allied forces toward Germany. In Tertres, in a convent that belonged to the same order, a bomb fell on a shelter, and a nun was killed together with the two small children she had sitting on her lap. Sister Beirens's convent was located in Héverlé, a suburb of Louvain, which was in the path of the Allied armies and was heavily bombed. Sister Beirens detailed her preparations:

> At the time I slept in the dormitories of the youngest boys. The children put on their bed at night their coat, their slippers, and a

washcloth, in case they had to go down in the cellar. . . . Sometimes we watched through the windows as the bombers passed us on their way to Germany, they passed us. . . . I believed really that guardian angels were everywhere. In these kinds of moments, one dares to hope and believe that God's goodness will save these children.

That the fear of bombs was dominant in the minds of my interviewees is understandable. For the convents, bombardments were the major dramatic events just before the end of the war; they were new, intense, and deadly. The anxiety about Germans looking for hidden children had already prevailed for two long years, but in a sense my interviewees, young nuns at the time, were to some extent shielded from it by their mothers superior who had taken the major responsibility for the rescue actions. Sister Beirens expanded on her feelings during bombardments:

When we went down in the cellar with the small children, a Benedictine father often came with us. We prayed together. It calmed us. We believe in God. It is in such moments that one must have the hope of living, especially the children who love life, who have barely begun to live. I did not believe that God would allow harm to happen to these small beings. And that gave me confidence.

The presence of the Benedictine priest helped Sister Beirens to handle her feelings, to overcome her fear, to find solace in prayer; her remark illustrates the role some priests played for the nuns. Her confidence, unfortunately, was not historically justified. Immense harm happened to small beings during the war. By the time of the interview, she knew that a great many children had been killed, but neither she nor I went on to comment that her prayers had not been answered in the world at large.

In the Héverlé convent, there were boys and girls of all ages, some as young as three years old, including orphans, children of prisoners of war, children of divorce—all kinds of children. There were also sick children, subsidized by the Oeuvre Nationale de l'Enfance (ONE; the National Children's Bureau), who came to recover and stayed in three-month shifts.[14]

In 1943, this Benedictine convent celebrated its fiftieth anniversary jubilee. It was a grand affair for which no effort was spared. The children had to be suitably dressed. As material was scarce, the nuns engaged in a labor of love. They ripped apart suits they had received and saved the material; they bought some special tobralco cloth that did not wrinkle in Louvain and sewed identical sailor suits for each little boy. The result was immortalized in splendid photographs. Sister Beirens recalled this collective effort with much enthusiasm.

She gave many details about the running of the convent. The older girls helped in the kitchen, as there was very little outside help. This ensured security and secrecy and was also economical. The municipality distributed bags of dried vegetables, which provided a substantial soup. The convent also ran its own bakery. Because order and cleanliness ruled, there were no lice. When new children arrived, they were checked and combed and deloused. Scabies had to be healed. The convent had a very good infirmary, whose cornerstone had been laid in 1928 by the primate of Belgium, Cardinal Van Roey. The doctors came from the neighboring town of Louvain, renowned for its university and excellent medical school.

Sister Augusta, who was a novice in the same convent, helped with the youngest children. In our interview, she remembered little of the war, mostly the bombardments. When asked whether she knew that the children were Jewish, she did not hesitate to say that she had been aware of it but that one did not talk about that issue. What she remembered most about the very young children was that they didn't like to drink milk, and so she patiently fed them with a spoon whatever milk was available.

The convent was bilingual. Classes were given in Flemish in one part of the convent, in another part in French. It was an unusual and convenient situation; it did not require a rapid adaptation to a new language, in contrast to what was so often demanded from children hidden in other places.

When asked about baptism, Sister Beirens brushed the question aside, saying that she was taking care of boys too young to be concerned with the ritual. When asked who had been privy to the rescue, she estimated at most a dozen sisters. She then added that it was the mother superior, Mother Cécile, and her helper who regularly went to the municipality to obtain rationing stamps. This was not a simple matter, because the rationing cards had the false names that had been given to the hidden children, and the cards' authenticity might be challenged. Significantly, it was the mother superior herself who went to the municipality. She counted on her standing and prestige to prevent any undue inquiries. Sister Beirens carefully and repeatedly insisted that Mother Cécile should be given the most recognition for all that she did. Sister Beirens also praised Mother Cécile's leadership qualities and her ability to resolve conflicts the day they happened, not allowing them to fester. When Mother Cécile felt she had been wrong in some way, she would apologize in the evening after prayers.

During holidays, there were excursions into the woods. The food was packed in two special carts, and both nuns and children enjoyed a nice picnic. Sometimes there were outings to ponds in the vicinity of Héverlé, fondly called Les Eaux Douces (Sweet Waters), and a trucker would help to bring the children there.

Mother Cécile had vowed that if no one in her charge died during the war, she would go every Sunday with all the children to the Grotto of Our Lady, located on the grounds of the Capuchin Fathers. It was a ten-minute walk. So after the war, all the children, praying and singing, crossed the road, formed a long procession, and walked there to thank the Virgin Mary for having spared the Héverlé convent from any deaths during the war (see fig. 4 of the photo gallery).

In a letter written in 1998 to one of my interviewees who was hidden in that convent and who worked energetically for the recognition of Mother Cécile as a Righteous Among the Nations, Sister Beirens provided the following details about daily life that she later omitted in our interviews.

Mother Cécile was French and had arrived at the convent in Héverlé in Belgium when French Catholic orders had been expelled from France before World War I. She did not hesitate to hide a large number of Jewish children during World War II. Sister Beirens wrote the number "66" with a question mark. She described daily life that was informed minimally by radio and one newspaper. She continued:

> There was much discretion about the children's origin, and thanks to that discipline, there were no denunciations. It is only after the war that I learned of the sad fate of the numerous deported. Among them were many family members of our hidden children. Incomprehensible, terrible! The children lived their lives, ignorant of and unconcerned about what the future would bring. The head of the Oeuvre Nationale de l'Enfance, Yvonne Nèvejean, controlled the situation. A pediatrician came to examine the very young children every month.

Sister Beirens praised the Héverlé municipality for generously issuing rationing stamps in the newcomers' names (false cards were provided for false names). Secours d'Hiver provided not only dried beans for soup but also flour, which was quickly transformed into bread in the convent's bakery. People far and wide were forthcoming with gifts in goods and money: potatoes, vegetables, beets, milk, eggs, blankets, clothing, and shoes. From Flanders came bales of cloth for sheets and clothing that rapidly passed through the talented hands of those nuns who were seamstresses. The group photographs of nuns and children all dressed uniformly attest to their skills (see the Heverlé photos in the photo gallery). From America, she wrote, came smoked fish, honey, oatmeal, and cod liver oil.

Each year the Alexian Brothers, who were neighbors, gave the convent much fruit, from which the nuns made jellies, jams, and stewed fruit. They also picked their own fruit. The meals were frugal but carefully prepared. Sister Beirens believed that the children were not hungry, though those I interviewed did not corroborate this.

While Sister Beirens's letter provides some details she did not mention in our interviews—about food and clothing and neighborly help, as well as supervision by the ONE—on the whole the letter describes the same efficient management, mobilization of resources, and capacity for making do with what was available that she depicted in the interviews. And her letter communicates the same sense of agency.

In this convent, appropriately called Convent of Mercy, at least sixty Jewish children were hidden for shorter or longer periods between 1942 and September 1944; nobody knows the exact number. Mother Cécile and Sister Marie Beirens were honored as Righteous Among the Nations in 1999—posthumously for Mother Cécile.

Sister X: The Orphanage in Marchienne La Docherie

My interview with Sister X, a nun during the war who left her convent in 1960, yielded many insights into discipline and relationships with the children, indeed more than any of the other interviews. She asked to remain anonymous because in her long life outside the convent, nearly half a century, friends and acquaintances had not been made privy to her past. At the time of World War II, Sister X was a nun in an orphanage in Marchienne La Docherie near Charleroi, an industrial area with many coal mines. Besides orphans, there were many children sent by the courts, and some children from problem families placed there through the intervention of welfare committees. The order to which this convent belonged was the Daughters of the Cross. According to Sister X, a 1998 exhibition at the Free University of Brussels on hidden children made reference to the mother superior, Mother Marie de Saint Joseph.

Sister X, trained as a nurse, was a person of many skills. She knew how to take care of children and was put in charge of older boys during part of the war. She was also an able seamstress, responsible at times for the entire convent's clothing needs. In her own words: "I did many things. I worked a lot I must say, a very hard life—one didn't have a choice. It was a little in my nature."

Asked about her mother superior, Sister X described a situation she thought was irregular. She assumed that mothers superior were generally elected for three years with one possibility of a second term. In her convent, however, when she entered in 1939, the same mother superior had reigned already for more then ten years and continued to do so for the entire time Sister X lived there, another twenty-one years. The mother superior would periodically wage a quasi electoral campaign, with surreptitious food inducements—an egg or a bit of butter—suddenly appearing in the nuns' refectory drawers. Her longevity in leadership was the source of her strong authority.

The daily routine was strict: everybody awoke at 5:15 in the morning, for hours of endless praying throughout the day until lights out at 9 p.m. The convent included both girls and boys and included around 150 children during the war. During the evening prayer, Sister X would direct her charges to examine their consciences and to reflect for a few minutes on what they might have done wrong during the day.

The Jewish children arrived in 1942, through the intervention of a woman living with the Ladies of the Assumption who was neither a nun nor, presumably, Jewish. It was she who urged the mother superior to take in the children. So the mother superior said one day, "We absolutely must do something, it is serious. We must shelter them, and we must conceal them." After she had gathered her nuns, she urged discretion and secrecy.

The first child who arrived was a boy two and a half years old. His name had been changed, so nobody knew his real one. Because he was so young, he was not housed in the boys' dormitories. In general, the children accepted into the convent were at least three or four years old. Sister X was told that he was a little Jewish boy; he was placed among the girls. She was warned to be careful when he was washed so as not to reveal to the other children that he was circumcised. The girls were greatly excited about having a little boy in their midst.

Later in the war, many more Jewish children were accepted, and three Jewish mothers also moved into the convent with their children. The Jewish children never said anything to reveal their identity, and Sister X remarked that their silence was quite extraordinary. The small ones adapted without too much difficulty, except for missing their parents, of course. All had to go to Mass—there were no exceptions. Some fainted from time to time at Mass, although this was not considered serious. The convent did not insist on communion or on confession.

The few Jewish families housed at the convent had been suddenly rendered fatherless due to deportations. In great distress and at a loss what to do, they arrived at the convent in search of shelter and solace. The children slept in the dormitories, the mothers in a small room on the top of the building where there were a dozen beds. Sister X remembered three mothers. One mother who came to the convent with her three children was put to work in the kitchen, where, Sister X recalled, she was very clumsy and committed blunder after blunder. Her daughter was with her, and her sons were in the boys' orphanage section. She saw them each week, and she lived in the belief that her husband would come back from deportation.

Sister X particularly remembered a very pretty girl who arrived in 1942. Her new first name, whose initial was identical to that of her real name, was Solange. She was an only child and very spoiled. Her mother had asked the convent to hide her. The father had died before their eyes—a mined bridge had exploded when he stepped onto it in front of them. Solange, a mature twelve years old when she arrived, at first was unhappy to have to go to Mass every day, but then she adapted. To remain pretty was important to her. The girls washed their hair every two weeks with black soap and soda; shampoos did not exist. Solange always came to ask whether she could have some hydrogen peroxide because her mother rinsed her hair with it so that her hair should stay blond. She knew Sister X was a nurse and had access to all medications, and she begged her for the peroxide. Sister X gave her a little bit each time, warning her not to tell the others, because all the girls might have begged for it.

Sister X remembered Solange so well because she stayed long after the end of the war. She did not want to leave but rather to convert. Her mother didn't allow it, so they fought for more than a year. Finally she converted without her mother's permission and chose to keep the name Solange. She eventually left the convent and married a non-Jew. One day, the women met again in a chance encounter; Solange recognized Sister X in a store, by her voice at first. By then Solange was the mother of a little boy. They visited each other for a while and then lost touch. Recently, as more nuns were recognized as Righteous Among the Nations, Sister X tried to reconnect with Solange so that Solange could testify on her behalf. She did not succeed, however, because Solange had moved away and her phone had been disconnected. Sister X thus lost touch with an important witness to her wartime activities in the convent on behalf of hidden children. In a sense, the formerly hidden children's pursuit of Yad Vashem recognition triggered for Sister X an emerging sense of entitlement. There was now an open stage on which the knowledge of her wartime caring could be communicated beyond the intimacy of the convent walls. Public importance, recognition in the outside world, legitimate prestige—all could be hers if only she could find witnesses willing to testify.

The convent housed many children who were eight or nine years old, and some who were older. At one point there were two boys, Pierre and Jean Legrand, aged fourteen and sixteen. They looked nearly like grown men, and they stayed until the end of the war. They had been given new names from one day to the next; so in the beginning, they did not realize when they were being called or addressed. They would fail to answer, and they seemed a bit lost. Nevertheless, the non-Jewish children did not look suspiciously at the Jewish ones; they seemed unaware of anything unusual. The convents could not have imagined the Nazi horror. The convent's rationale was that Jews needed to be hidden so that they would not be taken and deported. Deportation was feared as cruel and dangerous; systematic extermination was not imagined until that horrific information leaked out toward the end of the war. The Jewish children went to school with all the others. Across the street were the kindergarten and the lower elementary classes. The others went to school in the village, Marchienne La Docherie, a working-class mining community. The village school was Catholic, and the principal was one of the nuns. There were no denunciations. And Sister X was astonished again and again that the children did not betray themselves. That they had learned so well and so young to conceal their identity she considered an extraordinary feat.

The convent heated its large buildings centrally with coal, but there was not enough fuel. Yes, it was cold and there was hunger. Yet, in spite of the hunger, Sister X recalled incidents that seemed to indicate that the children had a rather playful attitude to food.

The boys who, with the connivance of doctors, had been categorized as sickly in order to be entitled to additional foods sat separately in the refectory. They used to joke around and to question why they were sitting apart. Every day they were allowed to have a dried herring, and some dared to squander these—fling them around, pocket them, even throw them in the garbage. During two war years, Sister X was in charge of the older boys, as noted, and she had to supervise them. She was very young and did not welcome the responsibility. Some of the boys were taller than she was, almost like grown men. One day she threatened one of her charges because he was always messing around with his herring. She told him:

> "If you do not eat your herring and mess around with it, I'll hang it on your neck. Some boys plead to receive a herring, but you mess around and waste it." One day he didn't eat his herring; I didn't know what to do, and so I attached the herring to the collar of his jacket in the back with a safety pin. He went out to play a quarter of an hour in the playground. When all the boys had to go out to the toilets, they left the refectory in a file with their hands behind their backs to ensure order, and I watched them as they passed me by. All of a sudden, I said to myself: "it is not possible, I dream"; the boy behind the one wearing the herring on his back had eaten the herring—only the bones and the head were left.

Sister X realized that she should have scolded the boys, but she had an uncontrollable fit of laughter, and they all laughed with her. "Look what remains," she exclaimed as she exhibited the herring skeleton. The story, naturally, spread throughout the convent community.

Sister X was aware, of course, that when she was challenged, her threats had to be carried out. But she could not entirely predict teenage behavior or imagination. Meals were one area that offered the children space for transgressive behavior, and they made the most of it. The following anecdotes also illustrate how the children reveled in behaving improperly and challenging authority.

One day at Christmas time, there was a Christmas tree at one end of the refectory. The children were eating pasta from prewar supplies, and that day spaghetti was on the menu. One of the big boys was playing with his food—not eating. Suddenly Sister X looked at the Christmas tree and saw spaghetti on its branches. Glancing at the boy's plate, she ascertained that the plate seemed less full. She never actually saw him eating, nor did she catch spaghetti flying in the air.

> I said to myself I have to catch him, and each time he thought I had my back turned he would throw the strands with his fork. He was rather far from the Christmas tree, I don't know how he succeeded, and he was really very skillful and aimed it right. So the Christmas tree was adorned, and when the others saw it they all broke out laughing, and I, too. I was so young, twenty or twenty-one, I should have scolded them but I didn't know how to scold them much.

The children enjoyed making a young nun laugh. They must have realized that her sense of fun would triumph over her demands for proper behavior, and they were right. Though Sister X asserted repeatedly that her youth was a handicap in handling the older boys, and that she did not welcome that responsibility, it was the funny episodes with them that she chose to remember and to relate.

Another episode, in the same vein, emphasizes her youth even more. One day a boy she had scolded and punished over the way he handled his meal became angry. In the middle of the refectory he proceeded to undress: he pulled off his pullover, then his shirt, he stripped off everything. "He stood naked as a worm." Sister X didn't want to appear embarrassed, yet she blushed, and the other boys laughed. "He was the first naked man I ever saw," she revealed.

As Sister X recalled these incidents, she was reliving both her youth and her relationship with the boys. Both seemed united in her mind, and in turn connected with an expression of titillating sexuality that was usually repressed in the context of convent life. She repeatedly asserted that she did not like to be with the older boys. It was not an appropriate place for her, she said; she felt "too young to be with this band of big kids" and found it difficult to assert her authority. On the other hand, the boys welcomed having a youngish nun; they found her most amusing. In fact, as she recalled, they never really bothered her—they laughed, they made her laugh, she could not resist because they were really funny. Her feelings were ambivalent: she actually enjoyed their transgressive behavior but, as an authority figure, could neither admit nor condone it. In addition, as noted, because these were older boys, the relationships were undoubtedly fraught with a sexual tension that could not be acknowledged. These anecdotes were among her best memories from her convent years.

Madame Nèvejean of the ONE distributed subsidies because the convent housed many children for whom nobody paid. She inspected the convent to make sure the subsidies were being appropriately used—whether the towels were too near each other, how many washing facilities there were for the number of children. There were no daily baths, but the children did wash daily. There were no sinks but only basins set on benches, for the nuns as well. Madame Nèvejean changed some procedures and improved some others. Her intervention was seen as justified. A warning went out when she came to inspect. She spoke with the children, who apparently never uttered any complaints.

Sister X battled lice, not only on her head but also on her body, and the children had scabies. During the war, the nuns treated the lice with DDT. An elderly doctor came without charging for his visits. He was very kind and devoted, and he liked Sister X very much. As a nurse, she accompanied him very often on his rounds.

The inspection of washing facilities and Sister X's recollection of deficiencies in this regard point to the common fate the nuns shared with the children. When Sister X was not supervising the older boys, for instance, she lived in a nun's cell. These cells had been created with mahogany paneling salvaged from compartments of beautiful old railroad cars. These railroad compartments had been placed in an attic, and each became a nun's cell. Since there was no heating, it was icy up there. Sister X and the other nuns would go up in the evening with warm water, and wash "like cats," as she described it. In the morning, the water left in their basins was frozen. Similarly, the children washed after four o'clock in the afternoon, during study hall. They were called by groups, and also washed "like cats" in small enamel basins without undressing. Thus Sister X described how nuns and children shared a common fate and common shivers.

She recalled another incident in the routine washing that served, on the contrary, to highlight a decided lack of sympathy. The incident involved a nun who was responsible for supervising the children's ablutions. She inspected ears and everything else. One day, she scolded a girl who had not washed her neck. So the next day the girl told her, "You can look," and the nun did. The girl had washed herself well, but the nun's only reaction was to say, "There is nothing superfluous"—not "You did well." Sister X's recollection expressed an implicit pedagogical critique. Why had her sister nun not commended the girl who had washed her neck well? Why express only a concern for order, rather than praise the child who wanted to please? Sister X did not elaborate on the anecdote, but her position was clear: praise should be given when deserved.

The limited facilities were further demonstrated when she recalled the weekly bath. Once a week, the children had a bath, sometimes with two bathing in the same water. The tubs had no running water; they were filled with water heated on a coal stove. The nuns heated large basins of water and then scooped water out with a pot or a pail, and so could not fill the tubs very high. They always tried to take the youngest children first. Sister X talked of two children bathing in the same water. The children, however, generally remembered much larger numbers, ten or more, sharing the same bathwater. Given the exertions even one bath required, the larger numbers are more likely.

As Sister X had made an implicit pedagogical critique of one of the nuns, I in turn inquired about a practice many of the children I interviewed had reported. Was it true that bed-wetting children were made to walk with wet sheets on their head? "It happened, so as to teach them not to do it," was Sister X's reply. Thinking back, she admitted that she might have been perhaps too harsh. She never put a wet sheet on a child's head, but she saw other nuns do it. When the children woke up in the morning, they had to get out of their beds, kneel next to them, and say the morning prayer. Sister X slept in the dormitory and watched over it from her own curtained-off space. Her first activity in the morning was to open the beds wide to air them. While the children dressed, combed their hair, and said their prayers, the beds had time to air. Those who had wetted their beds were usually up before the wake-up signal and had already made their beds. The nuns were not duped by the stratagem, and they knew that wet beds should not be covered over. Everything would rot, since the mattresses were made of horsehair. This was a point Sister X argued heatedly. When latex became available after the war, the mother superior immediately bought latex mattresses. But at the time, everything could rot and stink. The bed-wetters had to stay with their sheets in their hands near their beds so that everybody could see that they had wetted. There were pails in the dormitories that were to be used during the night. Before going to bed Sister X made sure that the girls who were known bed-wetters used the pails; this strategy, however, did not help. Sister X discussed this problem at length. She even cited bed-wetting experiences of relatives and their children. An English school one of her relatives attended had a special dormitory for bedwetters, a convenience for the other boarders who were thus spared unpleasant experiences. And she praised a relative who showed great understanding for one of his children, protecting him from censure by other family members.

In our interview, Sister X defended the harsh practices of her convent while simultaneously denying that she adopted them completely. The bed-wetters in her dorm did not have to wear the sheets on their heads; her more benign practice let them hold it in their hands! She accepted and employed the usual practice of publicizing the behavior as a deterrent. At the same time, she was fully aware that the punishment would be ineffective. Clearly, she realized in retrospect that the practices were cruel, yet she did not condemn them. She emphasized, rather, pragmatic reasons for the strong discipline, and her own practical but unsuccessful effort to help the children avoid the problem. Then she deflected criticism of the convent by turning the conversation to ways her relatives had handled the same problem in more recent times and more modern surroundings, clearly expressing her approval for a less punitive approach. In her reactions, she did not connect the bed-wetting issue during wartime to the emotional problems the children were encountering. At no time was there a realization that the hidden children perhaps needed more attention to their emotional needs. They were treated just like all the others. The problem was a general one in her eyes, and the authoritarian reactions to it were universally accepted, not only in convents but also in the outside world. Her sharpest distinction was chronological—between then and now. She acknowledged that past practices, though common, had been difficult for the children, and demonstrated that in the present she understood that the problem needed to be addressed with kindness and understanding. How difficult had it really been for the hidden children? When I listened to them talk about the war years, they searingly remembered the humiliating punishment suffered for bed-wetting. It represented for them almost iconically the harsh discipline of some convents.

As mentioned previously, Sister X was a skilled seamstress:

> I dressed everybody. I worked a lot because during the war we received bags of used clothing from the United States, among them many nylon items. Some bags contained bras. The children had never seen bras. "They are so nice, oh please Sister, will you give me a bra?" Every Saturday I prepared their little package. The whole week they wore the same underwear except in case of a mishap. On Saturday we prepared for the baths, and I had about 150 packages to prepare. It was not personalized; they did not have their own personal clothes. I had to search the sizes, see what was appropriate for the one or the other, and number what was to be distributed. There were women's clothes in these donations, also suits, too large—but the materials were beautiful, and we ripped and retailored. I sewed a lot.

Here was a detailed description of an aspect of collective life. Clothing ceased to be a response to personal needs; institutional norms and constraints predominated, so individual tastes and preferences of any sort did not matter.

Because of other work and hours of prayers, the nuns did not have enough time during the day for all the sewing that had to be done, so in the evening Sister X requested permission to continue working. Together with three or four other nuns, she stayed up sewing till two o'clock in the morning. And at 4:45 or 5:00, she had to be up for another day. Sewing at night had one great compensation, however: listening to Radio London. The mother superior owned an old-fashioned radio, and the night seamstresses borrowed it. They wrapped the radio in blankets in order to be sure that nobody else heard it, and so they could listen to the Free French broadcasts from London and the patriotic and inspiring speeches of General de Gaulle—"the French speak to the French"; "here is Free France"—while refashioning new clothes from old ones and mending what was torn.

A few times a year, the nuns produced plays. They taught the children to act and also acted themselves. One nun was a talented musician who taught the children dances. Every year in summer, the convent organized a fancy fair to bring in a little bit of money from the community.

To increase its resources, the convent began to send nuns to collect alms from door to door, even as far as Brussels. Those nuns who were from Brussels and knew the city were sent there, so Sister X had the great honor of collecting in Brussels twice. In principle, they begged for money, but people also gave them clothes. As they couldn't carry the clothes they had received, they would pick them up later or at the end of the week. They always went by twos and would sleep over in Brussels or in Liège.

During the war, the convents had no outside domestic help. Everything was done by the nuns themselves, aided by the few hiding Jewish women and the older girls, orphans and welfare cases, who were fifteen or sixteen years old. Some came very young and stayed for many years. They had stopped going to school, having received all the schooling available, and were paid a small sum for their help. They would eventually be placed as domestics in places a judge would find for them. Meanwhile, the nuns told them, "Make some money and when you leave to become a domestic, you will have a sum to spend on clothes." The nuns liked these older girls. They were taught to clean, to work in the kitchen, and to garden a little, and some proved very capable. There was not enough space in the sewing room to teach them to sew, however. After they were placed as domestics, they would come back to see the nuns. Some married and came to visit, showing off their husbands and children. Sister X spoke with much affection about these girls. Her attachment to the children kept her in the convent for a long time, and she missed them above all when she finally left.

The nuns did much hard physical work, some of it added under war conditions. After the Allied forces debarked on the Continent and pushed their armies forward, there were frequent bombardments. As soon as a bombardment began, which happened sometimes in the middle of the night, the children were hastily evacuated in their nightshirts to the cellar, where they slept on the ground. The next day, the nuns would move about a hundred beds down to the cellar. When the bombardments stopped for two days, the beds would be brought up. Moving beds up and down two floors was a constant chore that required strong backs. Sister X developed just such a very strong back and became a skilled mover. She was not the only one.

She was moved to recall a little Moroccan girl, Fatima. Her father was in prison, and her mother had died. She was twelve. During a bombardment, she became very ill. She had been taken down to the cellar with all the other children, and as she was ill and bedridden, she was not brought up after the danger passed. The nuns did not want her to be moved up and down repeatedly. She stayed in the cellar, with a constant vigil at her bedside, and daily visits by the doctor. And there she died. Unable to reach her parents, the nuns buried her in their own cemetery. Sister X believed that her father came to find out what had become of her years later.

In September 1944, the Americans liberated the area. In a single week, Sister X sewed American and English flags, put them everywhere, and distributed small ones to the children. The American soldiers frequently visited the convent, giving chewing gum and chocolates to the children. They were touching, Sister X recalled; they were young and showed photographs of their own children. They didn't know a word of French, and the nuns not a word of English, so they communicated by gestures. They had arrived in September, and they promised that for Christmas they would organize a big celebration, with a Christmas tree for all the children. It was not to be. They left to be killed in the battle of the Ardennes, just before Christmas. That particular Christmas was a very sad one: none of the Americans who had visited and befriended the nuns came back. This tragedy touched the nuns deeply. They had made extensive preparations for a feast. They wanted to provide as much as they could for soldiers so far away from their families. The soldiers in turn had sought to show their generosity in a grand celebration. Before going back into battle, the soldiers, wanting to give something to everybody, had distributed gifts. They had even given the nuns cigarettes, though they were not allowed to smoke. Some soldiers had given away their watches, as well as candies and chocolates. Sister X didn't know what to ask for. One soldier gave her a string of cartridge shells; the soldiers wore these in fringes on their belts when they were shooting. She was not supposed to keep anything for herself, but she was so happy to have received this gift that she kept the cartridge shells in her night table until about a year before she left the convent. Nobody knew she had them. Eventually, she became afraid they would explode. She told herself, "One never knows, perhaps it could happen on a hot day." How could she dispose of them? She felt that there was no way she could tell the mother superior that for more than ten years she had been the secret owner of American cartridges! What could she do? She did not want to simply throw the cartridges away because she was afraid they would explode. She really did not know much about cartridges, nor could she be expected to—learning to shoot had not been part of her nun's education. The convent garden adjoined the cemetery. One day Sister X bravely threw the cartridges over the wall into the cemetery, flinging them as far as she could. Then she listened carefully; no explosion greeted her, only silence. The cemetery guardian probably wondered what they were.

This convent hid about fifty Jewish children during the course of the war. The three mothers hidden in the convent did not leave immediately after the war. Having lost their husbands in the camps, they were glad to have a place to live, and they stayed a year or two, along with their children. As for the other Jewish children, parents came to retrieve them. That order of nuns eventually merged with the Sisters of Christ religious order.

Though the convent housed orphans and welfare cases, its discipline, as Sister X describes it, does not seem to have been as harsh as the one a former hidden child recalled in a similar type of orphanage. For Sister X, the interview was an opportunity to talk about a part of her life she had left behind. She talked freely about the war—and about her reasons for leaving the convent, which had to do with what she perceived as the autocracy of her mother superior.

REFLECTING ON NUNS AND MOTHERS SUPERIOR

More generally, the interviews with the surviving nuns were essential to reveal the way the rescue of Jewish children was carried out, and how life was lived within the convents' walls during the war. The interviews were also valuable for providing ample evidence of the nuns' general agency. In church historiography until the 1960s, as Wynants has shown, nuns in the past have often been represented as "docile auxiliaries of the clergy or as simple cogs in the ecclesiastical apparatus." To highlight the low esteem in which the nuns were held, Wynants says that they were seen as "good girls whose devotion is uncontested, but of limited intelligence and an incredible narrowness of mind."[15] The roles the convents played in rescue and resistance, as these interviews demonstrate, appropriately disprove such mindless generalizations. During World War II, neither of these accusations—lack of intelligence and narrowness of mind—could be upheld, considering how successfully convents cooperated with the Resistance and sheltered Jewish children and adults, labor draft evaders, and Allied parachutists.

In attempting to set the record straight, one needs to note the novel ways some religious houses inserted themselves into the society at large. With a war raging around them, these noncloistered congregations allowed themselves to be drawn into an outside world where former rules had broken down—a world filled with new threats. Collaborators and denouncers had to be avoided or forestalled, brutal occupiers eluded or appeased, living with strangers willingly accepted, lying and cheating and using false papers routinely practiced to save lives. Not all the congregations chose to enter this world, but those who did found that their intelligent participation was essential for effective resistance, and they accepted its consequences. They put their communal structures at the service of outside organizations they considered worthy of their help—organizations engaged in activities the congregations perceived as moral and in accord with their major values.

My research has shown that during World War II the nuns exercised initiative, and in the process they revealed the complexity of their universe; they expanded the meaning of the lives to which they were dedicated. They were in control of their destinies, and they revealed the creative side of convent life to outsiders. While religious women in Catholic organizations had generally been underestimated in the past, they proved profoundly indispensable during the war.

Historically, religious congregations provided abundant and competent personnel to schools, hospitals, hospices, and orphanages—all the institutions that cared for people from birth to death. In the nineteenth century, they were active in education, social welfare, and health, in parallel to emerging state structures. They alleviated the distress of the have-nots. However, in the past they have been viewed as communities of simple-minded Catholic women, their lives judged unworthy of investigation. Their activities during the war should have remedied their omission in the historiography, but this did not occur. In pursuing his survey, Wynants criticizes some feminist scholarship from the mid-eighties for its attempts to search for "strong women" while presenting a "total history" of active women's congregations including daily lives and beliefs. Recent scholarship, however, he considers more valid, because of its focus on the meanings the nuns give to their existence and their apostleship, their experiences, their practices, and the diversity of situations and perceptions.[16] My interviews have been a partial and modest attempt to draw attention to the nuns' wartime lives and remedy their omission. As Wynants has argued, oral histories are precious because they highlight the way protagonists have understood and felt different situations.[17] They are also important because they overturn the apparent rigidity of convent structures. Clearly, as Wynants underscores, many dimensions of convent life during the past century remain to be examined. The field is vast: in 1956 Belgium counted 371 women's congregations plus 117 independent monasteries belonging to 12 different orders.[18]

My interviews also attest to the authority that mothers superior wielded. Historically, they exercised their power in social relationships and through the transmission of values. They were often charged with heavy responsibilities, even when relatively young. Within the four walls of the convent, the mother superior was sovereign, on top of a feminine hierarchical society in which she enjoyed both permanence and power in the service of the Church. The monarchic character of her function could be abusive, Sister X felt. It could also be tempered by elements of democracy when the mother superior consulted her institutional council on important matters.

Her authority had a dual aspect: she exercised it in relationships with individual nuns as well as when organizing the community's collective life. Her functions were multiple and diverse, formal and informal: "she is at the same time the keeper of the law, mother, spiritual counselor, organizer, inspirer."[19] A nun who specialized in psychiatric care affirmed that "the all-powerful mother represented an archaic phallic person for, as keeper of the law and exercising authority, she assumed the role of the father."[20] Be that as it may, a mother superior was a vocation endowed with power.

A mother superior was in everyday life not unlike a CEO. She had to harness all the resources of an organization and ensure its development. Beyond spiritual qualities, the talents demanded from her were those expected from an entrepreneur: initiative, hard work, knowledge of people and the field of activity, rigorous management, ability to form and to inspire a team of leaders to whom one can delegate responsibilities.[21] She had collaborators, such as an assistant, a general secretary, a housekeeper, a mistress of the novices.[22] On some matters she was required to consult with the male ecclesiastical hierarchy or seek its permission.

Spiritually, the mother superior led her daughters "on the road to perfection." She counseled those who wavered and strengthened the anxious, though by the second half of the nineteenth century the Church limited her initiatives further, so as not to interfere with confessors' prerogatives. She was in charge of the community's property and was expected to pursue a policy of patient and systematic acquisitions, while resisting the urge to exteriorize her power with feverish building ambitions.

The power of mothers superior obviously varied, depending on persons, circumstances of time and place, and institutions. Mothers superior could have charismatic personalities, with spiritual talents, social status, and education that gave them a large influence over others. Their extensive knowledge was often acquired by first filling the role of head of novices, and then an assistant—the accepted steppingstones to power. Experience accumulated during a lengthy tenure gave them an additional advantage, but this could also be a source of abuse. A stable and homogeneous team, forged through a life in common, ensured permanence of power and coherence of decisions.[23] This could give rise in certain persons, however, to a routinization of power and to its habitual abuse.

Mothers superiors' relationships with their nuns were often characterized as very affective mother–daughter relationships. They sometimes allowed a superior to have great personal influence on a young nun. If the mother superior was considered to be a voice of God, her power could seem nearly unlimited. Some superiors ruled on all goods and property. Sometimes specific instructions were identified with or claimed as divine will. Many superiors wanted to regulate every detail of behavior by precise norms, including looks and posture. Directives were to be followed without argument. Certain superiors tended to transform their power into autocracy. However, such power was limited by constitutions, by director-priests delegated by bishops, by chaplains and confessors not chosen but imposed, and in general by submission to the masculine hierarchy of the Church.

The nuns interviewed for this book all accepted the authority of their mothers superior without reservation and without criticism, except for Sister X. On the contrary, her mother superior was the model for agency—a leader on the "road to perfection," a road that had changed markedly during the war.

The biggest astonishment in my research for this study has been that the roles the mothers superior played in this story of rescue have been taken for granted and seen as auxiliary, not autonomous. Up to now, these women have not been considered worthy of extensive consideration or focused commemoration. They were the ones, when contacted by the CDJ or directly by parish priests or heads of other Resistance networks or parents, who made the decision to accept and protect the children. They were saddled with the material arrangements, the search for space, and the logistics of everyday living in a time of war, amid shortages of food and heating fuel, and Allied and German bombardments. They were the ones responsible for secrecy, which they enforced by keeping only a small circle privy to their rescuing activities. It is they who agreed to employ Jewish adults in various domestic tasks so as to provide them with shelter within the convents. Undoubtedly, they were major players in the complicated rescue mission. Their invisibility derives from the place of women in the Church. As convents are gendered institutions, and women occupy a lowly position in the Catholic Church hierarchy, there had been little incentive to underscore the important role that mothers superior and their institutions played.

On the other hand, in the immediate postwar period, there was a reluctance by some scattered convents to return baptized orphans to relatives who came to claim them. There were also cases when orphans were returned to relatives only against payment of considerable sums of money. For example, the notorious Mademoiselle Henrard, who fanatically prevented baptized children from returning to their Jewish roots, prevailed on various convents to hide for about ten years a boy who was claimed by his uncle. In these cases, the admirable wartime agency, not sufficiently recognized, changed in peacetime into more narrow-minded behavior in which the saving of souls became the predominant value. This issue will be addressed more broadly in chapter 4.

3

The Escorts and the Resistance

PAULE RENARD

At the time I undertook my research seven years ago, two women from the Committee for the Defense of Jews (CDJ) who had escorted hidden children were still alive, and I had the privilege of interviewing both of them. Andrée Geulen (now known as Andrée Geulen-Herscovici), who was living in Brussels, has been widely honored. She fulfilled important tasks in the CDJ; after the war, she kept in touch with the children she had saved. A recent movie has documented her activities.

The second escort lived in Antwerp. For a long time, she kept quiet about her wartime work and only recently realized that it deserved to be remembered. Paule Renard (now known as Paule Andriesse-Renard), was eighty-four years old at the time of our interview, and much less is known about her.[1]

When the war broke out, Renard was studying at a Catholic school of social work in Brussels, preparing for her final exams to become a fully certified social worker. During the first days of the war, she was part of a group that cared for refugees fleeing advancing Occupation troops. Some of these refugees were at a loss about where to go; they ended up in a shelter Paule and her friends set up. They fed the refugees, using money that came from private funds. They also fed Turkish students who had been studying at the Free University of Brussels. Their country was not at war, but since the university was closed, they ate what was provided. Members of the White Russian colony also came to eat at the shelter, until the Germans ordered it closed.[2]

At that point, Paule was expected by the German occupiers to leave for work in Germany, which she did not want to do. She went to her school for advice. Officials there suggested that she register for another class to avoid being forcibly conscripted to work. A few days later, she was informed that someone had contacted the school with a request for a social worker. This person turned out to be "Jeanne," whose real name was Ida Sterno, head of the section of the CDJ that was responsible for rescuing Jewish children. Paule was interviewed and hired; later she was told that the CDJ members had doubted that she would fit in. The other escorts had been recruited from the municipal, secular school for social work, while Paule had acquired her professional education in a Catholic school. People in the CDJ, all secular and left-leaning, apparently fretted: "What kind of person are we hiring?" Their fear turned out to be unfounded; Paule got along fine with everybody. Ida Sterno explained the rescue activities and asked Paule if she would undertake the work and assume its risks. Paule was willing. She never provided her real name, and was known in the organization only as "Solange." She lived with her mother, who thought she was working for an official organization, the Oeuvre Nationale de l'Enfance (ONE; the National Children's Bureau). Paule never told her mother what she really doing. What motivated her to undertake this risky work? "To thwart the Germans and to save," she said. "It was not normal that people would be arrested because they were Jews." Paule was one of three social workers: Claire Murdoch, who was called "Catherine" within the CDJ; Andrée Geulen, who retained her name; and Solange. Catherine was hired in the fall of 1942, when the CDJ was in its infancy. Andrée and Paule joined the organization within a month of each other, in the early spring of 1943, at a time when the activities of the CDJ were expanding, thanks to subsidies provided by the ONE.

Paule detailed the history of the CDJ. The organization was created by Yvonne Jospa and her husband, Ghert, at the time of the first roundups. It had three important tasks: (1) the search for safe places for children, which was carried out by Yvonne Jospa and Brigitte Moons, with the help of Yvonne Nèvejean; (2) the actual placement of the children, accomplished by Ida Sterno and the three social workers; and (3) the securing of rationing stamps and clothing, which was handled by the office.

The placement of children involved two different groups: the escorts and the payers of the children's pensions. Paule defined herself specifically as a "social worker escort"; it was not her task to pay for the children's upkeep. The payers were women employed by the ONE, which was headed by Yvonne Nèvejean, who provided addresses. These payers went to the hiding places to bring rationing stamps, pay the pensions, and check if clothes were needed. The clothing was stored at a secret address.

Paule repeatedly lauded Yvonne Jospa's wisdom. Early in the Occupation, when the Germans gave the order for all Jews to register, Jospa wisely tried to dissuade as many people as she could from doing so, advising them instead to go into hiding. Later, armed with addresses obtained through Nèvejean, Jospa searched for homes and institutions willing to take the youngsters. "The mothers superior agreed to receive children," Paule added.

The escorts received their assignments through Ida Sterno, who phoned and fixed appointments. She also decided where each child would be placed. On the whole, tasks were well defined, though Sterno often sent Paule to pick up addresses or to follow up when someone called with information about a child who needed to be hidden.

Andrée and Paule's main task was to contact parents and convince them to hand over their children so they could be removed to safe hiding places. Understandably, this job carried a very high emotional cost. How could parents send their children off with people they had never met before? How could they send them into the unknown? To make matters worse, Paule was not Jewish and did not speak Yiddish—the language of many of the families in Antwerp whose children she had to remove. In spite of language differences, it was essential to inspire trust, and Paule did. It was easy for her, she said, to relate to people.

She vividly recalled her first assignment—convincing a mother in Antwerp to give up her children. She traveled there with Andrée to pick up the youngsters, two small boys and a girl. She remembered this assignment so clearly because it took so much out of her. The mother, a woman of very modest means, had been instructed to prepare a small package, so she wrapped the children's few belongings in a blanket. As the escorts and the children arrived at the railroad station, the package unraveled, all of its contents spilling out. The party missed their train and had to wait for the next one. This was dangerous: it was crucial not to draw the attention of bystanders. When the little group finally arrived in Brussels, Paule and Andrée separated. Paule and the children went by streetcar to Héverlé, near Louvain. As soon as they were settled in the streetcar, the children demanded to go to the bathroom. That was impossible. To distract them, Paule gave them candies, told them stories, and sang to them until they arrived at their destination. Nearly half a century later, while attending the First International Gathering of Children Hidden during World War II in New York City in 1991, Andrée reported that she met two formerly hidden children, now grown men, who told her that they remembered traveling to their hiding place by streetcar with a lady who told stories.

Paule recalled another difficult assignment: picking up a baby girl who was just seven days old. "I think I would have never given away my own seven-day-old child," she said. But the baby's crying was a nuisance to others hiding in the same location. Worse, it posed a threat: it could reveal their whereabouts. Finally, they insisted that the mother give up her baby to ensure the safety of all. The child had no father; he had been executed in France as a member of the Resistance.

Paule, having won the mother's trust, accepted the baby, which she then placed with a woman running a nursery for very young children.

After the war, Paule searched for years for that baby. She finally found her not long ago. This was an achievement, for it was difficult to locate the children after the war. Both she and they had used false names. Sometimes she had the real addresses, but she and the others had been told: "*Remember* and *tear up.*" For this search, she enlisted the help of Andrée, who had saved the lists of false and real names. One day Andrée figured out the baby's real name, but this was only the first step of the process. After many more efforts to trace the child, Paule was finally advised to put an ad in a Jewish periodical, with special columns for people searching for persons they had known during the war. Two weeks later, she was contacted by an uncle of the baby, who invited her to his home in Brussels. There he showed her a home movie. Paule instantly recognized the baby girl. She wrote to the now grown woman, who was living in Tel Aviv, apologizing in her letter for suddenly emerging in her life. "I was, after all, a stranger who suddenly appeared," she recalled thinking. No apology proved necessary. The person who had been the object of so much concern came to Belgium to participate in the ceremony honoring Paule as a Righteous Among the Nations, and the two have remained in close contact ever since.

Reflecting further on her assignments, Paule differentiated them by the age of the children. Those who were nine or ten years old understood what was happening and were aware of the danger. But the little ones were more difficult: "I had many very little ones, those I kissed and the tears would stop. I cajoled them, and the tears would stop." The children not only became attached to their escorts, they clung to them. Soon, however, they had to be separated from this last link between their families and the new place. They were losing everything, including their names.

For Paule, false names were immensely important, and she referred frequently to them during our interview. In retrospect, they symbolized for her the cruel reality of the war. With her own false name she had to create an entirely new persona. She *became* Solange, and nobody in the Resistance knew her real identity. In addition, one of her main tasks was to give new names to the children she was delivering to their hiding places. In a very short time, she had to convince them to remember these names and to respond to them without hesitation when they were addressed.

When she and her charges arrived at the hiding places, she gave the caretakers only the new names. In recalling the importance of names, Paule could not resist recounting an episode that had happened to Andrée. A six-year-old girl had been told when she was picked up: "Your name is not Sarah, your name is now Simone. Remember, you are Simone." Soon after, as the child and the escort took a train en route to the hiding place, a lady sitting opposite them gushed: "Oh, what a lovely little girl you are! What is your name?" The child turned to Andrée and asked: "What do I tell her, my real name or my new one?"

Paule found the children painfully aware that it was dangerous to give their real names, even when they realized that there were other Jewish children in their hiding places. In some cases, principals and directors were not even told that the children were Jewish. Sometimes even medical records were falsified. For example, when youngsters were to be hidden in an institution for sick children, a spot was added to the X-rays of their healthy lungs in order to secure a legitimate place in the facility.

Paule herself realized that a false name could lead to difficulties. One day she was sent to an appointment and happened to be wearing a dress adorned with a scarf. The scarf was special—it was decorated with a monogram, a large P for her real name. The man she was meeting immediately remarked: "When one is called Solange, one does not wear the letter P." Quick-wittedly, she answered on the spot that the dress was a present she had received—a plausible explanation. In wartime, clothing was scarce, and one did not have the option to be choosy.

Did some parents refuse to give up their children? Not to Paule's knowledge. On the other hand, she noted that the escorts and the employees of the CDJ knew very little about each other's doings and rarely met.

In relating the different aspects of her work, Paule recalled that she was often sent to investigate reports that a child was not happy. She once was assigned to check on the well-being of a boy on a farm who was reportedly not well treated, but this was hard to determine. She was never left alone with the boy, since the farmer's wife insisted on being present throughout her visit. He did not seem to have been beaten, nor did he look malnourished; these were Paule's two main concerns. Happy he was not, but given the circumstances—and the fact that the farmers might be inclined to denounce the boy if he was removed—Paule felt it wiser to leave him there. Her decision was a rational compromise but not an easy one for her to accept emotionally.

Paule referred repeatedly to Father Joseph André, who had a parish in Namur, in the southern part of the country. Father André was an important figure in the Resistance and was responsible for the rescue of many Jewish children and adults. Paule often brought children to him for placement.

Namur was a vital Resistance center, but it was not easy to travel to that part of the country, especially when escorting Jewish children. Paule recalled that once, while she was trying to determine how best to reach Namur, a friend put her in touch with a man who regularly traveled south without restrictions. He could do so because he was in charge of the region's gasoline supply for automobiles and might be willing to give her a ride. One day, she had to bring two children to Namur:

I was very imprudent, but when one is young, one does not think that way. I approached this person, and said: "You are going south. Could you take me and two children?" He agreed. We left with the two children in the back seat of the car. On the road we were stopped by the Germans, and we said that the children were ours. The Germans did not investigate any further (they didn't suspect anything), and we continued on our way. If we had been caught, the children would surely have been deported. I was really not cautious enough.

She did not mention what would have happened to *her*, recalling only her pluck and her luck. The two children were placed in families or institutions through Father André's Resistance networks.

This trip was also memorable for Paule because it marked the beginning of a relationship with a person on whom she would rely frequently in her rescue work. The relationship eventually evolved into a romance; at the end of their rides, he often invited her to dinner, and after the war, they married.

She described two other episodes with this man. The first occurred after she had picked up a baby boy in another city and was coming back to Brussels by train. She intended to bring the child to an outlying suburb, but she had barely stepped out of the railroad station when a bombing alert was sounded, and all transportation came to a standstill:

The moment I stepped out of the Gare du Midi [South railroad station]—alert! What should I do with my wisp of a child? I stepped into Côte d'Or [a well-known chocolate store], and everybody there admired "my" baby. I told myself that the streetcars would be very crowded after the alert. They have been stopped for a long time. I can't face this with the child. I have to reach Boitsfort [an outlying suburb of Brussels at the time].

So she called her gentleman friend and told him, "I am here with a baby that I have to bring to Boitsfort." She did not tell him it was a Jewish baby, but asked: "Could you pick me up?" He did, and they brought the child where he needed to go.

Just after the Liberation, she again had to meet Father André in Namur. And again, her gentleman friend agreed to give her a ride. She told him, "We have to hurry. The Americans close the bridge [over the Meuse, which flows through Namur] at lunchtime from noon till two o'clock. We will lose two hours if we come late." They did arrive too late and found the bridge closed. She had a letter from the CDJ describing her assignment (related to retrieving children), which she showed to the American soldier guarding the bridge: "This American, a tall one, took me in his arms, threw me in the air, and hugged me. He was Jewish. He was so happy that he opened the bridge for us."

Who paid the children's pensions? Paule did not know at the time, but after the war she inquired of Andrée. The money came from Belgium's government-in-exile in London, which asked its country's banks to supply it to the CDJ with future guarantees of reimbursement. The American Jewish Joint Distribution Committee provided additional large sums. Occasionally, if parents had placed their children somewhere by themselves, they paid the pensions. When the parents were deported later and the payments stopped, some people did not want to keep the children; then the CDJ took over, providing both money and ration stamps. A well-connected CDJ employee obtained authentic stamps with the help of sympathetic municipal workers who had access to them. Paule also remarked that the Catholic Church helped: "They considered it a duty. It came from the bottom, not from the top."

On one occasion, Paule was assigned to pick up a large sum of money from a bank in the center of town:

> I was never afraid, except when I had to pick up that money. I was scared stiff. I told myself: "They will question me, and I will not be able to explain it." Whenever I could think of good explanations, I felt fine, but for such a large sum of money I did not have any explanation at all. At the bank nobody asked me anything, and the money was handed over without a word. The bank was clearly in connivance.

Paule reflected that her apprehension during the bank episode was unusual. She was not at all a fearful person, and she was good at masking her feelings:

> I don't know why I was the one to be sent. I was often sent on errands, perhaps because I had an easy time establishing contact with people. I was young, and when one is young one does not see the danger, and one always believes nothing will happen.

She remembered one day when she had an appointment with the head of a children's home. Jeanne had told her to meet him in a coffeehouse, where he was going to provide her with addresses of hiding places. She waited for two hours, but he failed to show up. The next day, she learned that he had been arrested on his way to their meeting. Another time, she was asked to bring a false identity card to a Jewish man in hiding. The streetcar she was traveling in was stopped, and passengers were searched. She calmly presented her own identity card and nothing else happened to her. She left the streetcar and the neighborhood and delivered the false identity card some hours later.

According to Paule, the CDJ saved 2,571 children. This was the number of names found in secret notebooks Andrée kept. Paule knew nothing about these notebooks. She simply received addresses and followed through. She had the impression that the children she had escorted had been routinely baptized. She touched briefly on the children's adaptation to their new surroundings. "For those who were not from a very religious background, it could be all right, but when they came with their *crolekes* [Flemish slang for "locks of hair," in reference to the sidelocks of ultra-Orthodox Jews] it was so much harder."

Catholics were not the sole rescuers of the children; people from all walks of life took part, with some making extraordinary efforts to ensure the children's well-being. As Paule recalled:

> A miner was hiding a Jewish child. He asked to work deeper in the mines. This harder work entitled him to additional rationing stamps he could use for feeding the child. I find that fantastic!

How did she travel around the country? She hitchhiked, obtained rides on trucks, sometimes traveled by train, and at other times walked. When escorting children, she mostly used the train. She worked until the Liberation and even a short time afterward, when the CDJ transformed itself into the social welfare organization Aide aux Israélites Victimes de Guerre (AIVG; Aid to Jewish War Victims).

The aftermath of the war brought many new tensions. Paule discussed at length—and with much emotion—the matter of the children's retrieval. It was obvious that she felt deeply moved by the painful events that occurred. An office was opened where families could try to find out where their children were hidden. If children's parents came in search of them, there was rarely a problem. However, if other relatives—even an aunt or uncle—arrived, there could be difficulties when families in which children had been hidden would refuse to relinquish them. Paule remembered the case of one little girl who had wound up spending the night at her home because it was too late to escort her to her hiding place until the next morning. After the war, when the girl's relatives came to retrieve her, the family who had hidden her did not want to give her back. Just three years old, she herself preferred to stay where she was, with the person who had been like a mother to her. It was not uncommon for younger children to become very attached to their rescuers and not to recognize their own mothers. Paule believed that this case ended in court.

She commented that these attachments to rescuers were very strong, especially when the one rescued was an only child. In contrast, in a convent or with a person caring for many children, such an intense bond would not form. Though the stories she recalled did not pertain to children hidden in convents, these stories deserve to be noted in light of their importance to her and to her sense of justice. She praised some relatives of hers, a childless couple who hid a little girl whose parents had been deported. Though strictly practicing Catholics, they did not try to convert the girl and sent her to a secular school. With their blessing, she eventually went to Israel and married there. Another family, who were Freemasons, rescued two youngsters whose parents did not return. They wanted to adopt the children and "behaved very correctly," said Paule, even offering to send them to a Jewish school and raise them as Jews. But the AIVG, acting in the name of the Jewish community, insisted on placing them in an orphanage—euphemistically called a "home"—set up after the war to care for children whose parents had been exterminated. In retelling these events, Paule seemed torn once again by the heartbreaking dilemmas that had arisen.

There were other dangers for the children. One boy was placed at the seashore, which had been heavily fortified by the Germans against an Allied invasion. While out playing, he found a bomb. It exploded when he touched it, shattering his leg. Paule was assigned to pick him up by chauffeur-driven car. She still remembered where she had delivered the boy and wondered, during our interview, what had happened to him.

The end of the war also brought personal problems. Paule and Claire Murdoch were dismissed; the rationale was that there were enough Jewish social workers to help the Jewish war victims. "At the time, it hurt me because I wanted to know what would happen to the children," said Paule. Her dismissal, however, is not corroborated by other sources.[3] She looked for other employment, eventually leaving Belgium to work in camps for displaced persons in Germany. Claire Murdoch left for Africa, and they never saw each other again.

In the interview, Paule discussed at length how she lived after the war. After working for a year in Germany, she came back to Belgium and married the man who had driven her on many of her escort assignments. Essentially, she kept quiet about her war activities. After her husband died in 1958, with two small children, she needed to find a job. She could not find social work in Antwerp, where she lived, because her Flemish was too weak. In her forties, she was at an age when it is hard to take up any profession. So she went to work in an office, though she had sworn never to do so. In 1962, she met the man who became her second husband. He was Jewish, but even he did not know about her wartime activities. She had never told them to anybody, although there were opportunities. For example, she attended a dinner party in 1965, shortly after Yvonne Nèvejean had been honored as a Righteous Among the Nations. When Nèvejean's name came up in conversation, Paule was too timid to mention that she had known her.

It took thirty more years for her to break her silence. While a guest in the Antwerp home of an official from the Association of the Hidden Child, she listened to her host relate how he was hidden with his parents during the war. When he mentioned Andrée Geulen, Paule remarked that she knew her and had worked with her. He exclaimed: "What do you mean you have worked with Andrée Geulen?" Finally, the stories came pouring out.

Did Paule keep silent for so long out of modesty? Perhaps, but she argued that she thought her wartime experiences would not be of interest to anyone. Her granddaughter, however, recently asked her why she had never talked, telling her how much she would like to know the details of her activities as a child escort.

Paule then asked me: "Do you know when I understood what I had done?" She answered her own question: "It was in Israel." In May 1998, she was among fifty Righteous Among the Nations who were invited to celebrate the fiftieth anniversary of the founding of the State of Israel at a ceremony at Yad Vashem. There were Righteous Among the Nations of all European nationalities—many from Poland, even some from Germany:

> Pointing to a person in our group, one man said in his speech: "I have been hidden by this Righteous Among the Nations. I am here with my wife, my children, and my grandchildren. Thanks to her, my family has been reconstructed." At that moment, I understood. I said to myself: "I have also done so. I had never realized it. I am happy to have done so. After all, it was something useful."

Making this day especially memorable for Paule, the ceremony was also attended by the seven-day-old girl, now grown up, whom she had rescued.

Paule's longtime reticence about telling her experiences illustrates very well how the rescue of Jewish children was veiled in silence in the decades following the war. It was not a part of the social discourse. Early on, the emphasis was on the contentious fight for the souls of orphaned children: Would they return to being Jewish, or would they remain Catholic? Further, until the 1970s, the genocide of European Jews in general was not recognized in its specificity. Jews were victims similar to, and amalgamated with, all others. In other words, Jewish suffering was not perceived in its particularities.[4] Having been hidden ranked very low in the hierarchy of victimization. These children were perceived as simply having been lucky—so they remained silent.

In the later decades of the twentieth century, the hidden Jewish children gradually acquired moral status as war victims. They began to create associations, search for their rescuers, and manifest their gratitude. In the 1990s, Paule Renard could narrate a story that would find interested listeners. She was recognized as a Righteous Among the Nations in 1997, later than Andrée Geulen but earlier than Claire Murdoch (on whose behalf she and Andrée extended a major effort). Unfortunately, because of the painfully slow bureaucratic process, Claire passed away before she could be officially recognized. She was honored posthumously as a

Righteous Among the Nations, and her daughter came from London to accept the medal in her name.

By the end of our interview, Paule wanted to define more fully how others had seen her and how she saw herself. She noted that she had been interviewed by the Spielberg Foundation, remarking with amusement that her second husband's story had required more tapes than hers had. She then described how, at an exhibition on hidden children held at the University of Brussels in 1998, she was addressed as Solange and easily assumed her war persona while examining wartime photographs and encountering former hidden children and Yvonne Jospa, whom she hadn't seen since the end of the war. Then she launched into a description of her background, as if to justify to me—and perhaps even to herself—how she had acted during the war.

She did not come from a practicing Catholic home. She went to Catholic school because, at the time, it provided a better education than the municipal school. Her father, who was in the grain business, was not Catholic, but when the nuns—"the little Sisters," her father called them—organized their yearly fair, he would help to raise money for them because "they did a lot of good." Her parents were broad-minded; they brought her up without any prejudices and taught her to value all human beings equally.

And so, coming full circle, she ended:

> At meetings in Antwerp, many have asked me to try and find people who had been hidden with them in the convents. And I have managed to satisfy them. I adore doing that.

ANDRÉE GEULEN-HERSCOVICI

Among the escorts, Andrée Geulen-Herscovici has achieved the most renown. The 2002 film *Un simple maillon* (Just a link) was based on her wartime activities. In it, she and some formerly hidden children movingly describe her rescue work. She was honored as a Righteous Among the Nations in 1989. On April 19, 2005, she received the Mensch award—bestowed annually in Brussels by a secular Jewish organization—for her lifetime contribution to the Jewish community. (April 19 is doubly symbolic. On that date in 1943, the Warsaw Ghetto revolt broke out. Simultaneously, three young men stopped the twentieth convoy train, which was transporting Jews from their concentration point—the Dossin barracks in Malines—to Auschwitz. After some carriages were opened, people jumped out and fled; some succeeded in saving themselves. It was the only attempt made in occupied Europe to attack a deportation train.)

Because many aspects of Andrée's life have been thoroughly documented, I shall describe her first by examining what she has recalled in many interviews, as well as in the film. My interview with her then completes the picture.

Andrée Geulen was born in Brussels in 1921 to a liberal bourgeois family. "I had never heard talk of the Jewish problem," she remembered. She had been interested in the events of the Spanish Civil War while she was in high school and made food packages for refugee children. She trained as an elementary school teacher, and in 1942 she began substitute teaching. In the film, she says:

> One evening the initial shock happened while I was working in an institution housing children on vacation. I was giving good night kisses to the children in bed, and one latched on to me and said, "Miss, I like you, so I will tell you. René is not my real name; in reality I am called Simon. You know, I am Jewish, and I am hidden. My parents have put me here, but don't tell anybody." I was horrified that children had to hide and suppress their name.

Some children in her class wore yellow stars. Revolted, she ordered every child in her class to wear an apron, so that the Jewish students' stigma would not be displayed.[5] Eventually, all these youngsters vanished, having been arrested during the night with their parents. Andrée was revolted both by the sight of the star and the children's subsequent disappearances.

In the summer of 1942, roundups of Jews followed calls for "work." When the CDJ, which included Yvonne Jospa, Ida Sterno, and Maurice Heiber, organized a plan to save Jewish children, Andrée was living in Brussels at a private boarding school, Gatti de Gamond, where she supervised children and taught a few courses. Odile Henri-Ovart, the school's director and the mother of one of Andrée's friends, had accepted Jewish children among her pupils. She received regular visits from Ida Sterno, who eventually asked Andrée to join the branch of the CDJ that helped escort children to hiding places. Sterno spelled out the considerable danger: If she was caught by the Nazis, Andrée risked imprisonment and deportation to Germany. Nevertheless, she accepted immediately. Soon afterward she found herself in the midst of the terrifying hunt:

> In spring 1943, in the middle of the night, the SS stormed into the school with much commotion and many screams. I ran into the children's rooms. All were up and trembling. The Germans screamed. . . . The Jewish children were taken to Malines [the transit camp for deportation]. Odile Henri-Ovart, her husband Henri Ovart, and her daughter Dédée were arrested and imprisoned. Dédée was later freed, but both her parents were deported and died in the camps.

FIGURE 1. Ida Sterno and Andrée Geulen (right), Committee for the Defense of Jews members, just after Sterno was released from the Malines camp in 1944. (*Courtesy of Andrée Geulen-Herscovici*)

FIGURE 2. Committee for the Defense of Jews member Paule Renard during the war. (*Courtesy of Paule Renard-Andriesse*)

FIGURE 3. Professor Chaïm Perelman, one of the founding members of the Committee for the Defense of Jews, and his wife, Fela Liwer-Perelman, who set up Jewish elementary schools when Jewish children were expelled from the public ones. (*Courtesy of Noemi Perelman-Mattis*)

FIGURE 4. Mother Cécile Stinger, head of the Couvent de la Miséricorde, Héverlé, near Louvain, where more than sixty children were hidden. (*Courtesy of Annette Apelbaum*)

FIGURE 5. Sister Marie Beirens (second from right) and Sister Augusta Loret (second from left), originally from the Héverlé convent, with two former hidden children who had lived there during the war. Photo taken in 2005. (*Suzanne Vromen*)

FIGURE 6. Sister Hilde Casaer, Institut Paridaens, Louvain. Photo taken in 2000. (*Suzanne Vromen*)

FIGURE 7. Sister Marthe Sibille, Institut des Soeurs de Notre Dame, Chimay, sitting between her siblings. (*Courtesy of Sister Marthe Sibille*)

FIGURE 8. Father Julien Richard. (*Courtesy of Father Julien Richard*)

FIGURE 9. First Communion of hidden child with guardian angel. (*Courtesy of Marie Charendorf-Robers*)

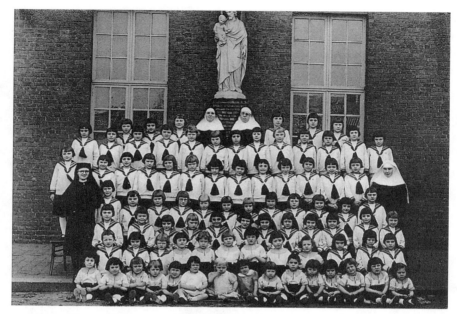

FIGURE 10. Group of very young children in Héverlé convent with Sister Augusta (right), Sisters Eugénie and Marguerite-Marie (middle top row), and a postulant (left). 1943 jubilee photo. (*Courtesy of Annette Apelbaum*)

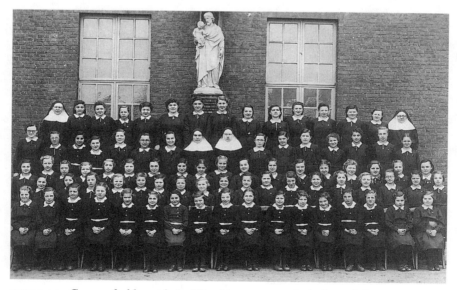

FIGURE 11. Group of older girls in Héverlé convent with (right to left) Sisters Clémentine, Ida, Lucie, and Julienne. In the front row (fifth and sixth from right) sit two interviewed Jewish children. 1943 jubilee photo. (*Courtesy of Annette Apelbaum*)

FIGURE 12. Sister Helene Baggen's boys with priest. (*Courtesy of Sister Baggen*)

FIGURE 13. Sister Helene Baggen's boys. (*Courtesy of Sister Baggen*)

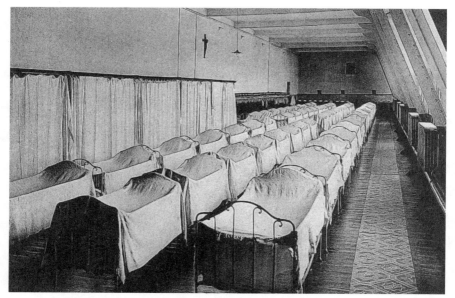

FIGURE 14. A dormitory. (*Archives des Soeurs Provinciales de Dom Bosco, Grand-Bigard [Groot-Bijgarden], Belgium; Courtesy of Sister Albertine Colson*)

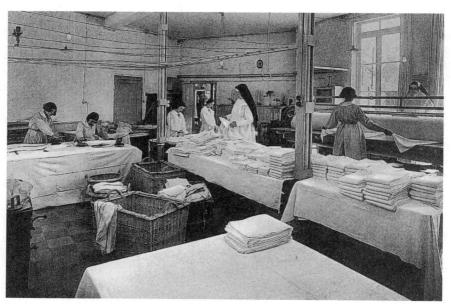

FIGURE 15. Ironing room. (*Archives des Soeurs Provinciales de Dom Bosco, Grand-Bigard [Groot-Bijgarden], Belgium; Courtesy of Sister Albertine Colson*)

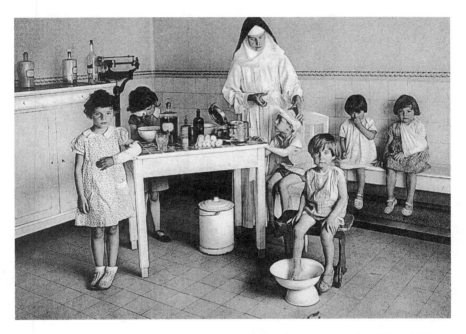

FIGURE 16. Dispensary. (*Archives des Soeurs Provinciales de Dom Bosco, Grand-Bigard [Groot-Bijgarden], Belgium; Courtesy of Sister Albertine Colson*)

FIGURE 17. Home economics. (*Archives des Soeurs Provinciales de Dom Bosco, Grand-Bigard [Groot-Bijgarden], Belgium; Courtesy of Sister Albertine Colson*)

FIGURE 18. Nursery classroom. (*Archives des Soeurs Provinciales de Dom Bosco, Grand-Bigard [Groot-Bijgarden], Belgium; Courtesy of Sister Albertine Colson*)

FIGURE 19. Small boys' refectory. (*Archives des Soeurs Provinciales de Dom Bosco, Grand-Bigard [Groot-Bijgarden], Belgium; Courtesy of Sister Albertine Colson*)

FIGURE 20. Sewing workshop. (*Archives des Soeurs Provinciales de Dom Bosco, Grand-Bigard [Groot-Bijgarden], Belgium; Courtesy of Sister Albertine Colson*)

FIGURE 21. Girls' courtyard. (*Archives des Soeurs Provinciales de Dom Bosco, Grand-Bigard [Groot-Bijgarden], Belgium; Courtesy of Sister Albertine Colson*)

FIGURE 22. Convent buildings. The part on the right was occupied by Nazis; Jewish families and children were hidden in the other buildings. (*Courtesy of Helene Baumerder*)

FIGURE 23. Parlor. (*Courtesy of Helene Baumerder*)

FIGURE 24. Sewing classroom. (*Courtesy of Helene Baumerder*)

FIGURE 25. Exercise class. (*Courtesy of Helene Baumerder*)

FIGURE 26. Gymnastics. (*Courtesy of Helene Baumerder*)

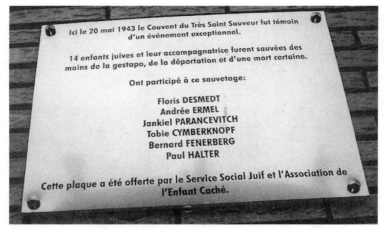

Ici le 20 mai 1943 le Couvent du Très Saint Sauveur fut témoin
d'un événement exceptionnel.

14 enfants juives et leur accompagnatrice furent sauvées des
mains de la gestapo, de la déportation et d'une mort certaine.

Ont participé à ce sauvetage:

Floris DESMEDT
Andrée ERMEL
Jankiel PARANCEVITCH
Tobie CYMBERKNOPF
Bernard FENERBERG
Paul HALTER

Cette plaque a été offerte par le Service Social Juif et l'Association de
l'Enfant Caché.

FIGURE 27. Plaque commemorating the rescue by the Armée Belge des Partisans of fourteen Jewish girls and the person accompanying them who were denounced and discovered after being hidden in the Couvent du Très Saint Sauveur, Anderlecht. (*Courtesy of Annette Apelbaum*)

FIGURE 28. Plaque on the former parish home of Father Joseph André, Namur, who, risking his life, saved many Jews during the war and helped immigrants and the needy after the war. A translation of the plaque is on page 140. (*Courtesy of Daniel Dratwa, Jewish Museum of Belgium*)

The occupiers ordered Andrée to leave the school. She knew that there were Jewish boarders who had been away and were expected back. The Germans were lying in wait for them. She left the building and stood guard in the neighborhood. When she saw the children approaching, she signaled them from afar to turn back, so they would avoid falling into the trap.[6] She then rented an apartment with Ida Sterno.

As historian Maxime Steinberg has noted, Andrée joined the children's section of the CDJ at a decisive moment for the rescue of Jewish children. This underground organization, in existence since August 1942, was finally extending its reach, having received clandestine funds in the spring of 1943. In her opening remarks in *Un simple maillon*, Andrée says:

> We were a dozen women, Jewish and non-Jewish, who fought against the Gestapo. The non-Jewish ones were most often in streetcars, trains, and dangerous places. I think one has to tell the story of the quiet courage of these women who risked everything to save children. I was a simple link in a vast network.

Contrary to her modest disclaimer, Andrée became in reality a central figure in the CDJ. She knew its leaders, was well informed about its procedures, and carefully preserved its archives after the war. To this day, she represents the living memory of the CDJ.

In the film, she continued:

> To hide three thousand children demanded a lot of work! After the extensive roundups we had to act fast. Yvonne Jospa and Brigitte Moons searched for hiding places and informed Ida Sterno. Solange, Catherine, and I—who were not Jewish—made contact with the families, for it was easier for us to circulate in the Jewish neighborhoods. When places were found, we had to fetch the children to bring them there. The one among us three who had visited the family previously escorted the child to the hiding place. This was for me the most difficult moment. To tear the child from home. The separation! The children did not cry. The older ones reasoned with their mothers. The little ones trusted me immediately when I told them that we were going to the countryside to see cows and chickens. I think that if I had had children at that time, I would not have had the courage to take them away from their families, while refusing to tell their mothers where we were hiding their children. I did not cry with them. I was always afraid of arriving too late, telling myself, "Maybe this night the child will be rounded up."

In another interview, she reiterated the same major point:

When I remember the firmness with which I refused to tell mothers where I was taking their children, I realize that my harsh behavior was only possible because at the time I had no children of my own and I knew nothing about maternal love. . . . But this sternness allowed the saving of many lives.[7]

Some recalled Andrée as young, energetic, and beautiful. One man remembered how, when he was ten years old, he was instructed to bring his one-year-old brother to her. He had to cross Brussels by streetcar to reach the meeting point. There, a lady casually passed by and said to him, "What a pretty baby." They chatted, and he handed over his brother, his heart beating with fear. A few days later, Andrée appeared at his parents' hiding place to pick him up. He had to convince his mother to let him leave. He was her last child, and she did not want him to go.

Another formerly hidden child recalled:

The doorbell rings. A good-looking blonde woman in a shiny black raincoat stands at the door. Everything happens very fast. She gives us her instructions: "As of now, you are called Henri Ledent, and your brother's name is Maurice." She takes us firmly by the hand and leads us away with our small suitcases. Mother cries.

Andrée acted fast and spoke little. Only much later did she reveal how she suffered from these heartrending tasks. One child she had taken to a convent cried silent tears when she left him. After stepping out of the convent, she sobbed shamelessly, because she already loved the little one she had to abandon. For her, he symbolized all the innocents so relentlessly hunted.

In an interview with Joost Loncin, Andrée provided further details:

The parents did not hide the children by themselves. Sometimes we picked them up; other times, a neighbor, a friend, or a teacher brought them to an agreed-on meeting point—for example, at a railroad station from which a group of children were scheduled to leave for some youth hostel. In such a group, we would succeed in including three or four Jewish children. I could not fetch them all at the same time. When I was leaving with just one child, I would first pick up her suitcase, deposit it at the railroad station, and then return to fetch her. The Jewish neighborhoods were constantly patrolled; a woman with a child and a suitcase would have been especially conspicuous and suspect. As women, we confronted the Gestapo. All alone. The Gestapo knew that an organization existed. They realized it repeatedly during the roundups. When Jews were rounded up, the Germans didn't find any children. They did not succeed in seizing us into their clutches. Parents were interrogated, but they knew nothing because we had not revealed where we were placing their children. They could not be coerced into betraying us.[8]

Andrée recalled other episodes that illustrated the Nazis' cruel "hunt after the Jews." Once she arrived to pick up a twenty-month-old baby. As she stepped out into the street, pushing the infant in a stroller, the Gestapo arrived and closed off all of the surrounding streets to prevent escapes. While she walked along, people were being rooted out of the houses all around her. She had arrived in the nick of time to save the baby. On other occasions, supportive doctors in maternity wards signaled the CDJ when newborns needed to be rescued; at the same time, the doctors attempted to care for the distressed mothers.[9]

Esta Heiber invented an ingenious system to keep track of the children and their hiding places. She split the list of names into five notebooks. One list included the children's real names; a code number was assigned to each one. The second list showed the same numbers next to the false names given to the children and their dates of birth. The third noted the children's code numbers in numerical order, each with the child's real address. The fourth listed the hiding places with their own assigned numbers. The fifth contained the false names alongside the codes of the hiding places. The five notebooks were hidden separately.[10] Only if all had been found and laid next to each other could everything be revealed. The false names had a Belgian ring to them, but retained some similarity to the real ones. Zimmerman became Timmermans; Steinberg mutated to Van Steenbergen; Weinberg morphed into Van Wijnsberghe. So, for instance, if Zimmerman was coded 20 in the first list, the second would say "20 Timmermans May 10 1938." The third notebook would list "20 Bruxelles, rue des Vierges 6." The fourth notebook showed the number 400 assigned to and placed next to the orphanage of the Sisters of Mercy in Héverlé. The notation in the fifth would show "400 Timmermans." Reading the notebooks simultaneously, one would conclude that Zimmerman, alias Timmermans, born in 1938 and living in Brussels, was hidden in the orphanage of the Sisters of Mercy. The Nazis never found these notebooks.

Asked in an interview whether she ever felt afraid during her rescue work, Andrée answered, "Quite often." For example, she remembered an occasion when German soldiers boarded a train on which she and several children were riding:

I felt that the soldiers knew that "my" children were Jewish and chose not to react. Fear especially of the deadly look of the Jewish traitor called Jacques, employed by the Gestapo, who combed the streets of Brussels to ferret out Jews. Fear of being followed.[11]

Andrée knew during the war that deportation led inexorably to extermination. The CDJ learned of the existence of gas chambers following a trip taken by Victor Martin, a young academic. He left for Germany in 1942 on some academic pretext. He was secretly charged by the Independence Front, an important Resistance organization, and by the CDJ with finding out the fate of deported Jews. When Martin returned, he revealed: "People are being burnt." He had contacted workers around the camps who told him about the chimneys.

After the war, Andrée helped reconstruct a devastated community through her work in the social service agency set up to care for Jewish orphans and war victims. In 1948, she married Charles Herscovici. Fleeing from Brussels, he had found refuge in Geneva. His parents, who were of Rumanian origin, had died in Auschwitz. After his return to Belgium, he became a lawyer. Both he and Andrée remained steadfastly active in democratic, pacifist, and antiracist causes, opening their home to peace activists from around the world.

Andrée maintained her contacts with the children she had hidden, and they—as well as those parents who survived—never forgot what she had done for them. "It was a great privilege to continue to help them, in guiding them in their studies, for example," she said in an interview. Andrée's own two daughters remarked that their parents at first spoke little about the war, but much about contemporary political events. One said:

> When we were young, we were often intrigued by these strangers, who, when they saw our mother, fell into her arms and hugged her with much emotion. Eventually, we came to understand what she had done. Today, she and our father speak freely of the past with our children. Our children have always considered her as a kind of celebrity, as they have watched her being interviewed on TV and featured in the press.[12]

In 1979, Myriam Abramowicz and Esther Hoffenberg produced a documentary on the rescue of Jewish children entitled *Comme si c'était hier* (As if it were yesterday). Abramowicz was born in Belgium to parents who were hidden during the war and later immigrated to the United States. Shot on a shoestring budget, this was the first—and is still the most extensive—attempt to tell the Belgian rescue story on film. Maurice Heiber, one of the founders of the CDJ, sent the producers to interview Andrée Geulen. As Myriam Abramowicz reported:

> She and her husband received us warmly. It was the first time that she had told the story in front of any camera. She had kept these famous notebooks, allowing the identification of the hidden children through

an ingenious coding system invented by Heiber's wife, Esta, linking for each child the real identity, the fake one, and the hiding place.

The 1991 Hidden Child gathering in New York City meant a return to the past for Andrée and many of the former boys and girls who owed their lives to the escorts. Endowed with an extraordinary capacity to remember, she had become the hidden children's memory. Giving press interviews, speaking in schools, participating in meetings of hidden children in Belgium and abroad, featured in *Comme si c'était hier*—in all of these settings, Andrée ceaselessly recalled her CDJ comrades, such as Brigitte Moons and Ida Sterno, two indispensable links in the rescue network. At the same time, she gave credit to all those who contributed to the efforts to save Jewish children in particular: "The parish priests and the good sisters, without whom we could not have hidden so many children, most of whom were placed in convents."

My own conversation with Andrée focused mostly on points that were not developed during her previous interviews. Her first remark was that the government in Belgium, in contrast to that of France, did not extend help in the roundups of Jews. In Antwerp, there were two particularly violent roundups in which local police were involved, but when the police in Brussels were asked to collaborate, the officials in charge refused all cooperation. The dirty work had to be done by the Nazis themselves.

She then mentioned that she did not understand why Jews voluntarily registered when the Germans made it mandatory. Prewar identity cards in Belgium did not specify a religion, and no official census of Jews existed. Then in October 1940, a German decree required Jews to register in the municipalities where they lived, under threat of dire punishment for the whole family in case of noncompliance. Andrée stressed how unwise it had been to register. She noted that Yvonne and Ghert Jospa, founding members of the CDJ, never did; therefore, they were never found out and hunted as Jews. The Jospas' refusal to register was the exception, however. I found myself arguing with Andrée and trying to explain that the compliant behavior was motivated by the desire to remain in good legal standing, in the belief that legality would ensure protection and illegality would heighten vulnerability.

In fact, I was trying to justify my own father's actions. I remembered vividly how hesitant he had been, and how finally he had decided to register in order to protect us all. He had no way of knowing that registration, paradoxically, could lead to death. I felt that Andrée did not understand how vulnerable foreign Jews were feeling at the time, confronted as they were with an unpredictable enemy and a lack of protection by the host government. In retrospect, of course, noncompliance was much wiser, but how could we have known? I was surprised by how deeply I felt the need to argue heatedly and to justify my father's action. After all, I was the interviewer, but my expected professional objectivity deserted me completely.

In 1942, the foreign Jews without Belgian citizenship, who made up about 94 percent of the country's Jewish population at that point, were the first targets of German roundups for deportation. Andrée noted that the occupiers had assured Queen Elizabeth of Belgium, the Queen Mother, that Jews with Belgian citizenship (the remaining approximately 5 to 6 percent of the nation's total Jewish population) would not be deported. The Germans answered any protests Belgian officials voiced against the roundups with the xenophobic argument "These are not your citizens." Therefore, the roundups were not stopped, though Andrée thought some unsuccessful interventions were attempted.

A year later, the occupiers reneged on their promise. In a single night in 1943, those Jewish Belgian citizens who had relied on the Nazi assurances were mercilessly rounded up and forcibly taken from their homes to fulfill deportation quotas. The Belgian authorities did not publicly protest the seizure of their own citizens, even though this operation demonstrated the total failure of their "policy of the lesser evil"—their acceptance of the deportation of foreign Jews in exchange for immunity for the small minority of Belgian Jewish citizens.[13]

Later in our interview, Andrée came back to this subject in more detail. When the first deportations occurred, the occupiers, as noted, retorted to the protests of the Belgian authorities, "They are foreigners, and we are sending them back where they come from. They are leaving to work; there are Belgians who are also leaving for work. Why not the Jews?" However, when old people and six-month-old children were seized, it became clear that they were not going to be part of the labor pool.

At that point, the occupiers declared: "We do not want to separate families." They always had an argument. So when a child was rounded up when alone—caught in a park, for example—an intervention was made: "You said you were deporting families; this child is alone." Then the Germans would hand the child over to the Association des Juifs en Belgique (AJB; Association of Jews in Belgium), which the Germans had set up (with Jewish notables nominally running it) to facilitate the enactment of their policies. The association operated a temporary legal ghetto of orphanages for children whose parents had been deported and an old-age home. In order to keep up the pretense that deportation was intended for labor, the occupiers said that those sent to these facilities were not considered fit to be part of the labor force transported east. In reality, they were holding pens, maintained as a reserve and at the mercy of Nazi intentions. The children and old people in them could be deported at any time.

Andrée referred to Belgium as a country that had been welcoming to refugees. As an example, she mentioned having worked in 1939, before the outbreak of the war in western Europe, with a *Kindertransport* (a children's transport).[14] The children were housed in the only secular orphanage in Belgium at the time. With the German invasion of Belgium on May 10, 1940, they were evacuated to France and later were thought to have reached Switzerland. One little girl missed the evacuation and spent the war in the orphanage. Andrée noted that she was in frequent contact with her. Since our interview, this person has published her account of these events, in which she revealed that five other children from that *Kindertransport* also lived in the orphanage throughout the war.[15]

Andrée then reflected on the larger impact of the CDJ's activity. After the first roundups, the general advice was: "Go and hide." But how could a family with four children disappear? By finding hiding places for the children, the CDJ gave the parents a chance to try to rescue themselves. As soon as the Resistance had spirited the children away to safety, the parents could leave for the countryside or the Ardennes, the hilly, less densely populated part of the country. Andrée summarized: "So we accomplished a double task. We hid the children, and we made it possible for the parents to go underground."

Andrée pointed out that during the war a whole series of support institutions for children was created. As examples, she cited the Aide paysanne aux enfants des villes (Rural Help to City Children), and the Homes Léopold III (named after the reigning king). Members of the Belgian nobility set up two large homes for children whose parents were imprisoned in Germany. The CDJ established connections with all of them, won over the people in charge, and also received help from some government officials. As a result, these institutions accepted many Jewish children. The children of prisoners only came for shifts of two to three months; the Jewish children remained permanently until the war's end. Andrée was in touch with all of these institutions. She recalled in particular the many children hidden in the three or four Homes of Léopold III, which were located in the region of Tournai, near the French border.

Andrée gave much credit to the help given by the Jeunesse Ouvrière Chrétienne (JOC), the Catholic-sponsored Christian Workers' Youth movement. At the beginning of the war, its chaplain, Father Pierre Capart, founded four youth centers for young people between the ages of fifteen and eighteen. The JOC helped immensely, hiding fifty-eight Jewish boys in its centers. Father Capart accepted appeals for help that were delivered to a private mailbox he kept, an uncommon way of seeking aid. Andrée used to meet him once a week; he gave her a dozen letters each time. All of this was done clandestinely, and not widely known.

How was secrecy enforced? Although she was quite central to the Resistance committee, Andrée says,

> I did not know the office where the children were registered. When
> information needed to be transmitted—the parents' address, the

children's names, the places where they were hidden—we didn't go to the office. We fixed a rendezvous in the waiting room of a doctor or in the back room of a store. We met with the office employee and we handed over all bits of paper. The information was then inscribed into those famous notebooks.

Protective walls between the people involved in the children's rescue were rigidly maintained. For example, Andrée never knew Yvonne Jospa's real name or where she lived. Such precautions lessened the fear of betrayal. They worked well until the last months of the war, when Ida Sterno was picked up. Fortunately, with the help of bribes and the end of the Occupation, she was not deported (see fig. 1 of the photo gallery). Unfortunately, she died soon after the war.

Andrée then related a well-known feat of the Resistance (to which we will return in another chapter). Due to a denunciation, the Gestapo had come to round up fifteen Jewish girls hidden in a convent in Anderlecht, a suburb of Brussels. Sister Marie Aurélie, the head of the convent, asked for a delay of a day in order to prepare the girls for their departure and pack the few belongings they were allowed to take with them. She was so convincing that the Gestapo agreed to her request. There are different versions about what happened next. According to Andrée, Sister Marie Aurélie alerted her parish priest about the Gestapo's visit and its intention to seize the girls; the priest, in turn, contacted the Resistance. Two men arrived, told Sister Marie Aurélie not to worry, and whisked the girls out through a back door. The nun insisted that they shoot her, to demonstrate to the Nazis that she had tried to prevent the girls' flight. They did not comply. Instead, the rescuers came back later, cut the telephone lines, tied up and gagged all the nuns, and staged a disorderly scene—to prove to the Germans that the convent had put up a brave fight. When the Gestapo returned the next day, there was anger but no dire consequences for the nuns.[16]

"The Germans were more cautious toward the nuns," Andrée commented. She did not know any nun who was arrested during the war, though a large number of the children hidden through the CDJ were placed in religious institutions. With the one exception mentioned earlier, there were no secular orphanages before the war. There were only two Protestant institutions in Brussels, since Belgium was predominantly a Catholic country, and "the base of the hiding places were the convents," Andrée said.

Brigitte, whose real name was Suzanne Moons, was a non-Jewish member of the CDJ and the organization's primary contact with the nuns. While Andrée claimed that she was usually well received in Catholic institutions and found a number of hiding places, she noted that Brigitte had easier access into the convents, in part because she carried an official letter of introduction from a high Church authority asking that all possible help be extended to its bearer. This letter has not been found since the war, and some historians believe it may be mythical. But Andrée did not doubt that it existed. Without such a missive, Andrée surmised that Brigitte would have had a more difficult time locating receptive convents. As for the letter's date, Andrée thought it was sometime in 1942, but she was not sure.

After the Liberation, the wartime attitude of the Church was hotly debated. Doubts were cast on whether it had fulfilled its moral responsibilities, and it was criticized because it had made no public appeals to the nation to come to the aid of Jewish citizens, as occurred in France.[17] Andrée did not share these doubts. She recalled to historian Lieven Saerens how she traveled once a month to the headquarters of the cardinal of Belgium in Malines to pick up a list of hiding places. She described the layout of the place, indicating the location of the office and detailing her reception by the cardinal's personal secretary, René Ceuppens, who would hand her the list. "It is not true that the Church did nothing, really not true," Andrée forcefully declared.

Saerens eventually found in the cardinal's archives a letter of thanks written after the war. Ida Sterno had signed it. Andrée quoted by heart what she remembered of the text: "Homage and gratitude by our population to the members of the Church, thanks to whom a large number of our children have been saved from the worst sufferings."[18] She then reiterated that the majority of the children were hidden in Catholic families and in institutions directed by priests and nuns. She added that she wasn't aware of a single convent that refused to accept children. An enormous number participated in the rescue, she said, although she was unable to be more precise. "I never counted them," she admitted. Then Andrée sounded a note of caution:

> Some convents were poor; they were often begging orders. There were children in Mons [a town southwest of Brussels] who were in bad shape. We took them out because the children complained. We placed them somewhere else. Some children were very happy in convents, others very unhappy. One should not idealize.

Our conversation then led to the convent in Héverlé, near Louvain, where I had interviewed Sister Marie Beirens. Sixty to seventy children were hidden there through the efforts of the CDJ. Some sources claim that the figure was higher. Andrée suspects that others may have been hidden there by Father Bruno Reynders, who placed children through his own network. She remarked that some of the former children hidden there still visit the surviving nuns. Though the children formed emotional bonds with some of the nuns, on the whole these bonds were not as strong as those that emerged in surrogate families.

How did the hidden children fare in the aftermath of the war? According to Andrée, they did well on the whole. She mentioned the children featured in her film as examples of high achievers. But then she reflected that the girls who ended up in the orphanages established after the war were channeled only into programs that trained them in typing and nursing:

> The boys were told: "You are alone, you do not have parents, but we, the social services, are here for you. If you work hard, if you are courageous, we will pay for your university studies." The women today are extremely resentful about the gendered way they were treated at the time.

In Andrée's opinion, the hidden children had not been traumatized and needed very little psychiatric help.[19] Relying both on her experience and her closeness to so many children, she thought that they had succeeded very well in all fields. Those who did not pursue higher education went into business, and she hardly knew of any who did not "feel well in their skin."

On the subject of gratitude, she emphasized her uninterrupted contact with the former hidden children and noted that each New Year she receives a thousand cards, which she can only acknowledge collectively with a published announcement. She recalled attending their graduation ceremonies, weddings, and celebrations of their children's births. "I have always remained in touch with them, always," she said. "This is to tell you how I love them." In our interview, Andrée did not mention how many children she rescued, but she had previously estimated that she escorted at least three hundred boys and girls to their hiding places.[20] The hidden children have remained a crucial part of her life and are frequent visitors in her home:

> On one occasion, when we were having a wedding for five former hidden children, my oldest daughter, who was then three or four years old, asked to speak, and said to them: "Before being born, I already had brothers and sisters." Nice, don't you think? She adores them; they behave like siblings with each other. And my grandchildren know them also. Two years ago, the hidden children celebrated my eightieth birthday.

In concluding the interview, Andrée responded to my question about how the rescue has been commemorated by pointing to the initiative of the former children themselves. A plaque was placed in Jamoigne—where eighty-three children were hidden—and in Cul de Sarts as well, through the initiative of a former hidden child, Marcel Frydman. A plaque was also affixed to the house of Father André in Namur. As for the convents themselves, they simply considered that they had done their duty. Andrée acknowledged that there has been little commemoration by the Church, and she reiterated that its critics reproached it for not having taken a public stand against the deportations. She concluded: "Probably it was because the cardinal was cautious."

Andrée was asked to give the inaugural address when the Belgian Hidden Child Association was formed soon after the 1991 gathering in New York City. She gave me a copy of this address. The text reveals much about her feelings and summarizes her life. There is no better ending for this account.[21]

"Miss Andrée, why may I not say that my name is Esther?" This question, asked by a six-year-old, summarized the dark years of the hidden child. What does one answer to such a deceptively simple question? I answered her: "Esther is a marvelous name, but where you are going, it is better that you should be called Jeanine." What else could I say? Fifty years later, I still have not found the real answer. How can one explain today that there was a barbaric period in which to be called Esther, Rachel, or Jacob was dangerous? How can one tell that children were hunted, and that they were forced to begin wandering when they were so very young? To survive, one needed to be hidden. Some were placed in five or six hiding places successively. They also had to hide their name, their religion, their maternal language. They had to be silent about their address, their family.

In May 1991, 1,600 hidden children gathered in New York City, and we experienced hours of intense emotion. All spoke, some for the first time, about the drama of their childhood, a childhood stolen from them. Every narrated life was a long and sad story. The wounds recalled were not those of bombardments or earthquakes, but injuries to the soul, which do not scar easily. These ex—hidden children talked about the separation from their parents, the entrance into another milieu in which the religion, the customs, and even the language were often different. They talked about nocturnal fears, hidden tears, forbidden prayers, also about a conversion not always forced, and the guilt of having called "Mom" somebody who was not their mother. And then, when peace returned, it was the separation from a surrogate family, often painful, or, much worse, the sorrow of not ever finding again either father or mother, or grandfather or grandmother. The feeling of floating, of being manipulated like an object, once again placed in an orphanage, in a location not freely chosen nor appropriate but only because there was room. And there were those who were listed for possible adoptions abroad, where, once more, they had to begin: another family, another language, another school.

With so many hardships piled on a child's head, one could have feared the worst. But it really did not happen. Most of the hidden children, as soon as peace returned, bounced back on their feet, and with extraordinary tenacity and combativeness, studied or learned a trade. And when in New York, we heard about their social and familial successes, we felt, Yvonne Jospa and I, great joy and pride. Inevitably there were some failures, but the hidden children have survived. Where in the aftermath of the war we had found three orphans, we met in New York a family of twenty-two persons.

That alone justified the fight carried out by the Committee for the Defense of Jews. In this army of shadows, led essentially by women, my place was that of a simple little soldier. Alas, many have disappeared. Maurice Heiber, Ida Sterno, Brigitte Moons, all played much more important roles. If you have asked me to speak today, it is probably because I was the youngest in our resistance movement. But that place of little soldier was, I think, the best one, because it brought me into contact with you, and you were such wonderful children, so courageous! At the moment of separation, it was you who consoled your parents, those parents whose strength of character I so admired, the strength needed to separate oneself from children often so very young. All this has been an unforgettable experience, and fifty years later I am receiving marks of such affection that they make my life so marvelous.

After those two war years in which I shared your fears and your pains, nothing has ever been the same. I touched very closely the stupidity and the horrible cruelty of racism, and all my life ever since, through education and by example, I have fought that monster. It has not been vanquished, and one hears today again shouts and slogans that had been expected to disappear. Recently neo-Nazis from Germany have invaded the streets of Brussels, shattering storefronts and looting, reminding us of horrible events. So I have a last message for you: I have read that your organization intends to send to schools speakers against racism. Racism and anti-Semitism are rearing their ugly head in the world and even in our country, they occur daily, and daily they have to be fought.

It remains for me to wish you luck, to offer you my memory and my archives to help you reconstruct your history and your past, to assure you of my affection, to express my gratitude once more for all you have given me. Thank you for having made me what I am.

REFLECTIONS ABOUT PAULE RENARD AND ANDRÉE GEULEN

The two escorts I interviewed provide a living history of the children's section of the CDJ. Although these two women have very different personalities, their attitudes toward their wartime tasks were similar. Both vividly remembered the heartbreak of separating children from their families. This task was made even worse because they could not openly acknowledge the harshness of their actions or express empathy. They had to act fast, feigning impassivity while facing distraught parents. Their feelings were irrelevant; what mattered was gaining the parents' cooperation and the children's immediate trust and obedience. It was certainly appropriate and in keeping with traditional gender roles that women would be used as escorts; parents trusted them to care for their children, even if only temporarily. Yet what these women had been asked to do was by necessity a violation of the essential meaning of family.

Paule and Andrée each had her own style in relating to the children she escorted, using various strategies to entice them. At the time, these young and childless women were at the outset of their careers; they had relatively little experience with children, but they made up for it by being imaginative, inventive, quick-witted, and practical. Above all, they were dedicated. Both expected maturity from children who had reached the age of seven or eight. In almost all cases, they received it. Paule remembered her ability to relate to people even though she didn't know Yiddish. Andrée recalled her concern that she would arrive at a home too late, after a roundup had taken place. Both excelled at masking their feelings. When they cried, no one witnessed their tears.

The need for secrecy was characteristic of all Resistance work. Paule and Andrée differed in how they abided by the CDJ's strict procedures. Paule noted that she was instructed to tear up any paper trail and remember all information by heart. Andrée spoke of transmitting paper messages in bits so that, if confiscated by the Nazis, they could not be understood. Whatever the process, the fewer CDJ employees the women were involved with, the safer they were. They recognized that fear was both inevitable and surmountable. Extremely cautious, Paule kept even her mother in the dark about her risky work. If she was arrested, her mother could not be implicated in any way.

They both lauded Ghert and Yvonne Jospa for their wisdom in not registering as Jews when the Nazis mandated it early in the Occupation. As noted, I was sensitive to this issue. Who could have imagined how monstrous the Nazis would prove to be, since their behavior was outside the bounds of what human beings were known to do? Perhaps Paule and Andrée also underestimated the Nazis' implacable resolve for racial extermination. In the absence of registrations, the Nazis would have resorted to other ways of casting their murderous net, perhaps catching Jews listed as members of synagogues and organizations, searching neighborhoods regarded as primarily Jewish, and scrutinizing the existing register of foreign nationals.

Paule and Andrée were both motivated by humanitarian concerns, though neither mentioned patriotism specifically. This is understandable, given the work they chose to do and the subjects covered during my interviews with them. They felt an obligation to help others, an obligation Nehama Tec has labeled a "universalistic perception."[22] Social psychologist Eva Fogelman would have categorized them as "moral and network rescuers."[23] By the time Paule and Andrée joined the civilian resistance in 1943, Belgium had been under occupation for nearly three years. During that period, numerous anti-Jewish ordinances were promulgated. Besides the racial registration, hotels, restaurants, coffeehouses—eventually all businesses—had to display notices if they were owned by Jews. Jewish civil servants, teachers, lawyers, judges, and journalists were forced to give up their jobs.[24] Yet Paule and Andrée seem not to have been aware of these measures; at least they did not mention them in the interviews. This reflected in part how well the German occupiers succeeded in obscuring the Jewish problem from the public. In stark contrast, the ordinance published on June 1, 1942, that mandated the wearing of a yellow star by any Jew older than six who appeared in public caused widespread reaction among the Belgian population. Most were angered or saddened by this blatant act of discrimination, although some Fascist collaborators seized upon the opportunity and molested Jews in the streets.[25]

Even more eye-opening for Andrée than the yellow stars was the sudden disappearance of the Jews. By the time the CDJ recruited her in the spring of 1943, she was very much aware of the Nazi solution to the "Jewish problem." She had been exposed to it face to face. When Paule ended her studies in the spring of 1943, she was liable to be drafted for compulsory labor service in Germany. The draft had been instituted in October 1942 to overcome severe labor shortages and as a means of economically exploiting the occupied countries.[26] Paule had been exempt from the draft while she was a student. To be officially employed as a social worker—while in reality clandestinely escorting children for the CDJ—solved for her the draft threat. At about the same time, as a result of an extensive resistance to the draft and intense negotiations with the Belgian secretaries-general (heads of ministries), the occupiers renounced drafting women for labor in Germany, except for domestic service.[27] Still, Paule chose not to abandon her escort work. Like Andrée, she was wholeheartedly committed to her humanitarian values. In our interview, she talked about the variety of tasks she had undertaken in the CDJ, as did Andrée, who also described the controversies that occurred after the war.

Both escorts remembered how difficult it had been to retrieve the children after the Liberation. In this chaotic situation, and after the extermination of so

many parents, the fate of the new orphans was hotly debated. The escorts suffered
in sympathy for the children and the adults—both those who were suddenly
deprived of the young ones they had cared for and the relatives who wanted to
reconstruct families. Their main tasks were to alleviate economic and social
hardships and to facilitate the reintegration of orphaned children. Paule detached
herself rapidly from the new organization that emerged from the CDJ.[28] The
abrupt severing of her ties with the organization may have contributed to her long
silence about her war activities, and to her sense that what she had done had been
of little importance. As she remarked in our interview, she would have liked to
know the fates of the children she had escorted.

After the war, the paths of the two escorts diverged markedly. Andrée had
been more central to the organization and was a great friend of Ida Sterno, who
remained in the AIVG, the social welfare service that succeeded the CDJ. So
Andrée continued her work, now with the AIVG. She stayed in touch with many
of the children she escorted. However, her daughter remarked that as a girl she
never heard about her mother's activities—in contrast to her own children's
awareness of their grandmother's celebrity. Andrée's reputation grew as time
passed and as she helped many rescued children reintegrate into normal life. Her
concern for the children allowed her to maintain continuity in her life. Yet it was
not until 1979 that she spoke for the first time in front of cameras, revealing to a
wider audience the Resistance activities of the CDJ. With her husband, she
continued to fight against racism and anti-Semitism, and adopted pacifist causes.
Eva Fogelman has remarked about the rescuers she studied: "Most network rescuers continued to be politically active. The same political instincts that made
them oppose Hitler compelled them to fight other politically oppressive parties."[29]
Andrée was radicalized by the war and has remained a political activist.

In contrast, Paule abandoned her wartime activism, returning entirely to
private life. She retained few contacts with her CDJ colleagues, never seeing Catherine Murdoch again and running into Yvonne Jospa fifty years after the war's
end. Though she married a man who had shared in her wartime activities, she was
soon widowed. She struggled to earn a living as a single mother until she remarried.
After long years of silence and anonymity, her recognition as a Righteous Among the
Nations became very important to her.

Andrée was sanguine in asserting that most of the hidden children were
not traumatized by their war experiences and had become successful adults. To
discuss this opinion in depth was not possible within the constraints of our
interview. The subject has been widely studied, yielding a continuum of con-
clusions, with emphases ranging from devastating trauma to complete resilience
and readaptation. The former hidden children who have remained in touch with
Andrée may well be a self-selected, resilient group whose members are *bien dans
leurs peaux*—they feel at ease in their skins. Her view of them was colored by their

visible professional achievements, yet these may not necessarily account for contented inner lives. Furthermore, less well-adjusted adults may have opted not to stay in touch with her. Given the historical circumstances, her opinion is understandable; an optimistic viewpoint, however, may require nuances.

Andrée is focused on her historical role, and on the roles of her colleagues. For this task, she is endowed with extraordinary powers of recall. By offering the ex—hidden children her memory and her archives, by helping them to reconstruct their history, by showering them with her deep and unwavering affection, she has acquired an iconic stature for them and an important place in the history of the Belgian resistance as a whole.

THE BELGIAN RESISTANCE

While these interviews provide some texture to the escorts' lives, as well as arresting details about their activities and personalities, by themselves they tell just part of the story. To complete it, the rescue of Jewish children in Belgium needs to be put in context. How was the CDJ established and what were its overall activities? How were the deportations carried out? How were they resisted? What other resistance activities were carried out in Belgium? These are some of the questions that need to be addressed in order to reach a full understanding of the rescue of Jewish children and an appreciation of its importance.

The CDJ was established by the communist Front de l'Indépendance (FI; Independence Front), one of the major movements of the Belgian Resistance. In June 1941—a year after the Nazis occupied Belgium—Germany invaded its former ally, the Soviet Union. At that point, the Belgian Communist Party, which until then had remained neutral toward the occupiers, was outlawed and its militants relentlessly persecuted. The Party's goal became the liberation of the homeland. By that fall, the Resistance movement was launched in the name of patriotism, and the FI organized as a broad national Resistance coalition. The strategy of the FI was twofold: armed actions by partisans and civil resistance through alliances with different social and political groups. The FI mobilized support for resistance among workers, farmers, police officers, judges, teachers, doctors, and youth organizations. The FI eventually developed into "an energetic and diversified movement,"[30] though it did not succeed in uniting all political factions.

One of the most successful achievements of the FI was the establishment of the CDJ, whose name has double meaning: a committee to defend Jews and a Jewish defense committee. In other words, it implies a need both to protect Jews and to empower them to defend themselves. To a large extent, the CDJ succeeded on both fronts. Ghert Jospa, a Jewish engineer of Rumanian origin and a founding FI member, and his wife, Yvonne, persuaded the leadership to establish this committee after the wearing of the yellow star of David was mandated, the situation of the Jews deteriorated, and the roundups began. Among the eight individuals who founded the CDJ were seven Jews and one non-Jew—Emile Hambresin, a left-wing Catholic who had long fought against racism and later perished in one of the camps. An important founding member of the CDJ was the philosopher Chaïm Perelman, a Jewish faculty member at the Free University of Brussels and a Zionist militant, who enjoyed a high intellectual standing both in Jewish and non-Jewish circles. He met for the first time with Jospa and Hambresin in his home in Uccle, a southern suburb of Brussels, and agreed to join them. His cooperation was vital and made it possible to progress in setting up the Resistance committee.[31] His wife, Fela Liwer Perelman, soon joined him. Their home became a haven for many secret meetings throughout the war. Nearly all of Belgium's Jewish organizations were represented on the CDJ. This was an important achievement, because it united people from opposite ends of the political spectrum: Communists, Zionists of all persuasions, and Belgian and foreign Jews. Most significantly, a large number of non-Jews were soon included in the upper echelons of the organization as well as in its rank and file. All who joined the CDJ were allowed to preserve their own political identities. Members of the FI considered the rescue of Jews an integral part of their work.

The CDJ clandestinely installed an extensive administration, including a service for forging identity papers, rationing cards, and rationing stamps; a network of hiding places for children systematically separated from their parents; a service offering assistance to impoverished Jewish adults without resources; and departments for press, propaganda, and finances. There was interdepartmental cooperation. The department for forged documents was so efficient that it generated a supply beyond the CDJ's own needs. It wound up selling quality forgeries to members of other Resistance movements as well as various individuals. The proceeds were used to finance the CDJ's activities.

When deportations began on a large scale, parents tried to save their children at least. Some found hiding places by themselves, but this was not sufficient for the large number of children needing help. The CDJ was an efficient response to racist deportation. It addressed first the problem of children who were abandoned due to their parents' deportation, then those threatened by deportation themselves. The recently created group understood that its primary task was the placement of children in a systematic, consistent, and responsible way. The committee began to function officially in September 1942, but the rescue of children was so pressing that it started even before the CDJ was completely formed. Soon afterward, adults who escaped the first roundups were also helped to enter the underground so they, too, could evade "the final solution."

The CDJ discovered greater rescue possibilities than it had expected. The grassroots clergy played an important role, while the higher echelons of the Church hierarchy maintained a cautious silence. Maxime Steinberg has argued that the hidden Jews could not have survived clandestinely without the organized Jewish defense.[32] At the height of the CDJ's activities, the names of about twenty-four hundred children were contained in the famous notebooks described in the Andrée Geulen interview. These represented about half of the children that the Nazis were not able to deport. As successful as this seems, many more were victims of Nazi barbarism: 5,093 children under the age of sixteen were deported, 145 of them younger than two years with the youngest just thirty-nine days old.[33]

During the three months after the Germans initiated their roundups—from the end of July through October 1942—the Jewish population of Belgium was reduced by about one-third. As Maxime Steinberg has noted, seventeen thousand Jewish men, women, and children were deported in one hundred days.[34] The Jews who were rounded up were incarcerated in the barracks of the Caserne Dossin in Malines, a town conveniently situated between Antwerp and Brussels, the two major centers of Jewish population. The convoys that left the Caserne Dossin for the east were labeled "evacuations for labor," but the brutality of the roundups, the stuffing of victims into cattle cars, and the inclusion of children and old people fed fears that this human cargo was destined for a much worse fate. Over the next two years, until the end of the Occupation in the fall of 1944, another eight thousand Jews were caught and deported; among them were over one thousand Jews who were Belgian citizens. It became difficult to fill the convoys to capacity; once the element of surprise had been removed, Jews went underground and were hard to catch. The Nazis were thwarted in their efforts to meet deportation quotas, and the convoys left irregularly. In the end, about half of Belgium's Jews managed to escape deportation and extermination. While some survived using their own initiative and resources, many others received help from the Resistance and the local population.

The speed and the viciousness of the first roundups had been a painful surprise. The Nazis had been facilitated in this despicable work by the AJB, created by German ordinance at the end of 1941. Made up of Jewish notables appointed by the occupiers, the AJB was meant to control the Jewish population, to engage in welfare activities, and to serve the occupiers' aims. Its officials and employees were not directly threatened by deportation; they were expected to facilitate the centralization and emigration of others.[35] Under direct German orders, the AJB distributed so-called employment cards to all of those summoned to Malines. This helped to maintain the deception that the purpose of the convoys was to furnish forced labor in the east. A member of the AJB conscientiously prepared lists of deportees. As Andrée Geulen mentioned in her interview, the deportation orders were accompanied by threats of collective punishment—retaliation against family members and the entire Jewish community if those summoned did not show up. In spite of these threats, many of those summoned did not appear voluntarily, so they were barbarically rounded up. On July 25, 1942, a team of partisans called Armée Belge des Partisans, which included many Polish Jews, set fire to the AJB's index file containing the names of the country's Jewish population; unfortunately, it was only a duplicate.[36] On August 29, while the roundups were being carried out, the same team murdered the AJB's "employment" agent.[37] After he was killed, the Nazis no longer requested lists of Jews; they carried out the roundups on their own. These violent Resistance actions served as potent alarm signals and convincing proof of the need for disappearing into clandestinity.

As already mentioned, at the onset of deportations in 1942, the Nazis had granted Jews holding Belgian citizenship immunity from deportation—in order to carry out their operations against foreign Jews without arousing opposition from the general population. It was a shrewd xenophobic tradeoff, but it did not last. A year later, in 1943, the sudden roundup of all the Jewish Belgian citizens who had relied on their supposed immunity was the only large roundup the occupiers had the opportunity to carry out after the fall of 1942.

Some members of the CDJ also held official positions in the AJB. Acting as double agents, they engaged in secret Resistance activities while enjoying relative protection within the AJB. For example, Maurice Heiber, an AJB member, had the main responsibility for the children's section of the CDJ. The AJB assigned Heiber the task of setting up an orphanage for children of deported parents in We-zembeek-Ophem. Officially, these children were labeled as abandoned. Because this orphanage was an official venture, it also came under the purview of the ONE. This was a government agency created in 1919 to promote children's health and to reduce child mortality, and it was headed by Yvonne Nèvejean. The ONE, in turn, was dependent on Belgium's Ministry of the Interior and the Family. Heiber confided to Nèvejean that he was worried about German intentions toward these children; she promised to protect them if need be. Heiber's fears were soon confirmed. In October 1942, the children and their caretakers were suddenly rounded up and brought to the Caserne Dossin to fulfill a deportation quota. A non-Jewish housekeeper in the orphanage alerted Nèvejean, who immediately appealed to Queen Elizabeth, the Queen Mother, to intercede with German authorities. Other interventions took place as well. Those arrested were eventually freed and returned to the orphanage. From then on, Nèvejean devoted herself to the CDJ's rescue mission. She used all of her resources to find placements and provide subsidies. She intervened at a time when the CDJ was running out of money. While some placements were free, many were not. Nèvejean also provided safe helpers whom she chose from her intimate circle. A while later, she formally joined the CDJ as a member of the children's section. She also sat on its finance committee.[38]

In August 1944, as Allied forces were advancing across Europe, the Nazis were preparing one last roundup—the deportation of the children and the elderly in the institutions run by the AJB. The plan was to arrest them all at once and dispatch them on the twenty-seventh convoy, the last deportation convoy scheduled to leave from Malines to Auschwitz, before withdrawing the occupying forces from the country. The fact that the Germans planned this final roundup even as they themselves were retreating before the Allied forces defies understanding. It certainly underscores the fanaticism with which they clung to their racist ideology. Aware of the menacing situation, the AJB—at its last meeting before disbanding and going underground—decided to transfer the elderly to the Brussels social welfare services and to seek the help of the CDJ in hastily dispersing the six hundred children from its orphanages. Thanks to Yvonne Nèvejean's persuasive calls throughout the country and to her helpers, this mammoth operation was hurriedly accomplished. The Allied forces advanced rapidly. The twenty-seventh convoy never left; Brussels was liberated on September 4, 1944.

The rescue of Jewish children owes much to Yvonne Nèvejean-Feyerick (as she was known after her marriage). As head of the ONE, she held a key official position that gave her oversight over a large number of children's institutions. She was thoroughly aware of what hiding places were available across the country, and she used her wide network of connections to seek placements. Through her own organization, she provided financial assistance; she also raised considerable funds from banks and clandestinely from the Belgian government-in-exile in London. She was undoubtedly a major figure who made the rescue possible. And while it is true that she joined an existing rescue organization that counted many devoted members, her boundless support was crucial to the expansion and overall success of the CDJ. When she died in 1987, Yvonne Jospa eulogized her: "Nèvejean was driven by her love for children, her antipathy towards any form of discrimination, and her . . . defiance against the Nazi occupation. Her paramount concern was to provide the same opportunities for Jewish children as for non-Jewish ones."[39] Nèvejean provided Jewish children with more than equality of opportunity: she gave them the gift of life. In February 1965, she became the first Belgian woman to be honored as a Righteous Among the Nations.[40] In 1996, the Belgian Postal Authority issued a stamp in her memory.

The FI and the CDJ were only two of a large number of Resistance organizations in Belgium, and while the CDJ rescued a large number of Jewish children, others also undertook that mission. Families acting individually called on non-Jewish friends and acquaintances to hide their children. Others were brought to priests who had their own Resistance networks and connections. Father Joseph André in Namur, as mentioned in the interview with Paule Renard, placed many children and adults, as did Father Bruno Reynders, a Benedictine priest. Both cooperated with the CDJ but maintained their independence from it. Father Jan Bruylandts arranged many hiding places. Father Louis Jamin hid a large number of girls in Banneux, east of Liège. They were brought to him through the Resistance network of the lawyer Albert Van den Berg, who worked closely with Monseigneur Louis-Joseph Kerkhofs, the bishop of Liège and Limbourg. Van den Berg paid with his life for his rescue efforts.

The rescue of Jewish children is a clear example of a successful civilian resistance, in the way Jacques Semelin has conceptualized it.[41] In contrast to those using armed resistance, civilian resisters had no intention of attacking the enemy directly. They sought to foster survival by thwarting the occupiers' murderous intentions and to preserve the values threatened by the Nazi regime. As Paule Renard remarked, she joined the CDJ because "it was not normal that people be arrested because they were Jews." Likewise, Andrée Geulen was revolted by the sight of the stigmatizing yellow star. The civilian resistance in Belgium developed ideological dimensions through the underground press, and its appeals for help increasingly sensitized the wider population. As mentioned earlier, the CDJ unified different political factions under one umbrella and ensured that organizations opposing the occupiers saw saving Jews as an integral aspect of resistance. It successfully avoided divisive ideological issues and, in this way, provided the social cohesion that Semelin deems essential for the emergence and efficient functioning of a civilian resistance movement.

Belgian government authorities were both a help and an obstacle to this civilian resistance. The registration of Jews by municipalities throughout the country in October 1940 was undoubtedly a racist census, an act against all the tenets of the country's constitution. As noted in the introduction, prewar Antwerp was a hotbed of anti-Semitic organizations. During the war, the freely raging anti-Semitism prevalent in Antwerp—called by Lieven Saerens a "culture of hate"—and specifically the collaboration of its municipal police in brutal roundups are inexcusable facts. On the other hand, authorities in Brussels refused to handle the distribution of yellow stars and would not allow policemen to participate in roundups. Some of the city's municipalities even extended precious help in forging documents.[42]

A public outcry by religious authorities against the deportations might have enhanced the legitimacy of the civilian resistance, but this did not occur. Instead, caution prevailed. This lack of action was counterbalanced by limited confidential assistance from the head of the Catholic Church and, more important, by the extensive practical support of many clergy who recognized their moral responsibilities and took action on their own. In her interview, Andrée Geulen mentioned how she received lists of possible hiding places from René Ceuppens, secretary of Belgium's Cardinal van Roey, and she described the unconditional help extended to her by the Catholic-sponsored youth organization JOC. It must be noted, however, that Andrée joined the CDJ in the spring of 1943. By that time, the tide of the war was turning against the Germans, and the Belgian Catholic hierarchy was becoming bolder in its opposition to the Occupation. In March 1943, Cardinal van Roey publicly and forcefully denounced the draft for forced labor in Germany.[43] The Belgian "resisting conscience" was thus reinforced and civilian resistance greatly legitimized. But the survival of Jews and thousands of others who evaded the Nazi labor draft remained a major challenge for the civilian resistance until the Liberation.

In assessing the different Belgian resistances, armed and civilian, Fabrice Maerten points out that resisters were a minority phenomenon, even by the end of the war.[44] They included between 2 to 3 percent of the population who were old enough to resist—roughly those between the ages of sixteen and sixty-five. About 20 percent of them were women. More than thirty thousand resisters fell into enemy hands, and about half of them lost their lives. The last eight months of the Occupation in 1944 were the most dangerous, as both the violence of the Resistance and the repression against resisters grew. Many foreigners were among the resisters. Civil servants were more likely to be involved than people in other occupations, who felt less threatened by the new regime, according to Maerten. Farmers began to participate significantly only after those who were avoiding forced labor sought hiding places en masse in the countryside, joining other fugitives.

An overview of Resistance activities shows great diversity: providing escape routes for hundreds of downed English pilots; developing intelligence networks and drafting the multitude of reports that were relayed to the government-in-exile in London; maintaining a vast underground press for dissemination of information and the continuation of a democratic public debate; sabotage; killing of collaborationists as a deterrent to others; preventing destruction of bridges at the time of Liberation. This is but a partial list. In addition, there was what Maerten calls "humanitarian" resistance—helping families of political prisoners and prisoners themselves, as well as labor draft evaders and Jews.

The interviews with the escorts have shown that many women were actively engaged in the CDJ's efforts to rescue children. It is not surprising that women were essential to this mission: the rationale for their tasks was rooted in their traditional gender roles. Protecting children, feeding them, clothing them, checking up on their well-being, paying for their keep—all of these were "feminine" occupations. Some skills, however, such as assessing hiding possibilities and breaking up families, had to be learned, and the risks of leading secret lives accepted. Women were essential in separating children from their families; they were trusted as surrogate mothers, even if only temporary ones. Organizing the rescue in all of its facets went far beyond traditional gender roles. In contrast to many other Resistance organizations, women in the CDJ's children section occupied decision-making positions from its inception.

Maerten has described women's activities throughout the Belgian Resistance in some detail.[45] In the Communist Party, a number of women became couriers and providers of support services. They found housing and food for men who were being hunted; distributed clandestine newspapers; arranged mail drops and meeting places; supplied services to the armed partisans of the FI; transported arms; and helped families of political prisoners. Some participated in public protests demanding a better food supply. The women collected money for those living underground, as well as for their families. Especially noteworthy was how some of these women helped Russian prisoners escape from work in the Belgian coal mines. One resister estimated having helped seventy-six such prisoners. When the male heads of Resistance groups were arrested, women occasionally replaced them. In summary, dozens of women made vital contributions to communist Resistance activities, especially in the southern region of Charleroi. They facilitated the armed resistance but were not visible within it. Many were arrested and sent to Ravensbrück, the concentration camp for women established in eastern Germany.

Women were active in other Resistance groups as well. Wherever there was a clandestine press, women had large production and distribution responsibilities. In the network called Zéro, they helped to collect intelligence. The network Comète was the most important conduit for the evacuation of downed Allied pilots. The group was responsible for the return to England of about 770 airmen—almost a quarter of all the pilots rescued in occupied Europe.[46] For two years, this network was headed by Andrée De Jongh, a former nurse. In 1941 she established an evacuation route for hidden airmen through France and across the Pyrenees into Spain, a neutral country. From there, the pilots could reach England. At the height of the network's activities in 1942, up to fifty men a month were spirited to safety. After having passed back and forth to Spain thirty-seven times, De Jongh was arrested and deported. The network continued its activities, though on a lesser scale, until just before the Liberation. Fifty-five women lost their lives; many more, De Jongh among them, endured life in concentration camps.

Some women joined the Resistance at the urging of family members— brother, father, husband. At first they helped; eventually they became accomplices. Some were moved by concern for the suffering of those being persecuted. After the war, some of them neglected to seek recognition for their heroic endeavors. They acted as if with the end of the conflict, public affairs were no longer of concern to them. Those who had aided their husbands in Resistance work considered that help as natural and not worthy of tribute. This is perhaps an indication of how they felt about their place in the Resistance.

Maerten notes that these women were not so different from those who had fought in World War I. On the whole, they were subordinate to men and given little initiative. De Jongh was a striking exception, yet her group's success was so spectacular that the English at first doubted her existence, believing she was a symbolic figure. No other woman headed a Resistance network. Military leaders had little confidence in women; war was considered the business of men. Only three women out of three hundred Belgian agents were sent on special missions to London.[47] In sum, while women participated in all forms of resistance except violent action, there was a great reticence to give them decision-making posts. Though they were the essential infrastructure—"the ground floor of the underground," as Schwartz has described their wartime work in France—they were perceived as nothing more than auxiliaries.[48]

Verhoeyen and Maerten both ask whether, after the war, women's participation in the Resistance had an emancipatory effect on gender relations and on the social position of women in general. Verhoeyen leaves the question unanswered, while Maerten deals with it in a nuanced way. In his interviews with female resisters, Maerten found that they did not see themselves as fighting for social change in general, even less for a change in their place in society. They wanted a return to prewar society. They felt motivated by patriotism, a value transmitted by family and implying attachment to the existing social order, not to emancipation. However, their increasing participation in the public sphere through Resistance activities indicated progress, for the prewar depression had negated what small steps forward women had made. In addition, more egalitarian gender relations developed while women were participating in Resistance activities. Simultaneously, women acquired a greater self-confidence. These experiences made it harder to readapt to the postwar society's traditional gender expectations.

Those who participated in the Resistance—men and women alike—endured common experiences and upheavals that were impossible to communicate to others. Some forged strong bonds and in returning to normal life, they let any idea of feminine emancipation disappear.

Through their engagement in public life, some female resisters tried to foster new values after the war. They soon realized that they were incapable of changing their society. Doubly marginalized by their status as resisters and as women, they adapted to their world, participated in the baby boom, and went on to acquire—like many women since the 1960s—a certain degree of material comfort and greater personal autonomy.

Verhoeyen and Maerten question the emancipatory potential of women's Resistance activities in the postwar world and maintain that these had no effect. This is not surprising for many reasons. First, the new roles women undertook in the Resistance were expected to be short-term, appropriate only for the duration of the war. More important, the culture they drew on to make sense of their experiences was characterized by a nationalist and militarist discourse that reinforced traditional notions of gender relations. When national solidarity, heroism, and sacrifice are extolled, expressions of women's rights and needs are unlikely to emerge. If they do, they are easily discouraged and interpreted as selfish and divisive. When such a cultural discourse is prevalent, it is difficult for women to develop a consciousness of themselves as a socially defined group and to challenge taken-for-granted assumptions.

Further, the postwar world stressed the need to restore family life and encouraged pronatalist policies, while playing down women's demands for employment opportunities and equal pay. At the same time, postwar notions of femininity in the popular media revived conventional gender relations; the war years were perceived, individually and collectively, through the same lens. Memory was also gender-specific. In France's postwar commemoration of the Resistance, women who had displayed great courage but were less visible than men received less recognition. "French women in the Resistance, because German soldiers read them as women, often escaped detection when men could not. Indeed, the contribution of these women was, in the postwar period, when awards were being made, unreadable for French politicians as well."[49] It is likely that this statement could also apply to the women in the Belgian Resistance. The trajectories of commemorations of priests and nuns involved in the rescue of Jewish children show the same gendered pattern.

Clearly, the Resistance did not create a potential for change in women's social position. Embedded in a culture sustaining traditional gender relations, women were not politically influential or well enough organized in the immediate postwar world to foster such a change. Furthermore, women resisters were too few in number to alter the situation. It is fair to expand the question and ask whether the Resistance in Belgium triggered any social change in general. As Lagrou has concluded, "The resistance was almost by definition an ephemeral phenomenon, destined to disappear as soon as the occupation . . . it resisted was over."[50] It never embodied claims for transforming society, either its gender relations or social classes. The everlasting legacy of the Resistance lies in its humanitarian achievement—the preservation of so many lives.

4

Memory and Commemoration

To complete the stories of the hidden children and their rescuers, it is necessary to consider who was commemorated, when, and by whom. The ways in which the life-saving actions have been remembered in testimonies and commemorated ultimately do justice to the exceptionality of the events and ensure their continued relevance.

The word "testimony" derives from the Latin word for witness, in the sense of seeing and awareness. As James Young has argued, to testify is to create knowledge about both oneself and one's world.[1] Testimony is a means through which individuals come to know themselves. Interviewer and interviewee generate a shared project. The Holocaust violently overthrew conventional social relations and cultural practices, producing a profound sense of disorientation for individuals, a disjunction between worlds. In testifying about their experiences, the hidden children recreate themselves and establish threads of continuity between who they were before the war and who they have become subsequently. The narratives also commemorate parents, both those who died and those who survived. At the same time, the witnesses perceive themselves as waging a fight against Holocaust denial. For example, by publicly presenting their narratives to schools and by selecting what they wish to transmit, they attribute to their lives a significance that reaches far beyond their personal experience.

The Hidden Child: The Emergence of a Concept

Until the late 1980s, the formerly hidden children were not seen as a well-defined category of victims, nor did they perceive themselves as such. Immediately after the war, they had been rapidly silenced, both within their families and the larger society. As the historian Saul Friedländer, himself a hidden child, described it, they had lived on "the edges of the catastrophe; a distance—impassable, perhaps."[2] When they wanted to narrate their war experiences, they were told categorically: "You were lucky, you did not suffer."[3] There was no place for them on the hierarchy of the war's victims. What mattered was the torment of deportees, prisoners of war, those condemned to forced labor. The children had escaped the range of tortures the Nazis inflicted. Their wartime lives lacked drama and aroused no interest; they did not become a part of the social discourse on martyrdom. To their parents, relatives, and the institutions that were caring for them, it was most important that they catch up in their studies and acquire economic independence. The children were swept up in these concerns as well, so they smothered their war experiences, buried them in their inner selves, and turned their gaze to the future.

In retrospect, this silencing is not surprising. As Pieter Lagrou has noted, postwar memories were shaped by a desire to reestablish the nation's self-esteem— a search for patriotism and epic heroism.[4] Consequently, writing about Jews, he argued:

> When heroism, choice and ideology are the criteria, the victims of genocide do not stand out. Persecuted for something they did not choose, for the simple reason of being born Jewish, they are placed at the bottom of the hierarchy of martyrs.... The victims of genocide were not commemorated because they could not be integrated in a national epic, because their memory was inert in the chemistry of postwar commemoration.[5]

As the entire Jewish genocide was not commemorated in its specificity, there was no reason to call attention to the ex–hidden children. Only after two decades had passed, in the aftermath of the trial of Adolf Eichmann, was the silence finally broken. Jewish victims gradually ceased to be amalgamated with all other victims of Nazi persecution. As Annette Wievorka has remarked, the searchlight of history finally focused on the victims and opened up the era of the witness.[6]

It took longer for the children to emerge as a distinct category of victims. As mentioned previously and worth reiterating, in 1979, amateur filmmakers

Myriam Abramowicz, living in the United States but born in Belgium to a formerly hidden family, and Esther Hoffenberg made a documentary about the Committee for the Defense of Jews (CDJ) that recounted how individuals and institutions in Belgium had saved children. It remains to this day the most historically significant and comprehensive film about the rescuers.[7] Entitled *As If It Were Yesterday*, the film had profound resonance and influence. Eventually Abramowicz suggested convening an international conference of hidden children. Abraham H. Foxman, national director of the Anti-Defamation League and a former hidden child from Poland, decided to sponsor the conference.

The First International Gathering of Children Hidden during World War II took place in New York City in 1991, forty-six years after the end of the war. Until that event, which attracted sixteen hundred former hidden children from twenty-eight countries, surviving hidden children had no formal status, no institutional representation, and no public voice. On the heels of the conference, numerous associations of ex–hidden children were formed throughout the world, and in these forums their experiences were finally articulated and legitimized: "After decades of silence, hidden children finally uncovered their buried pasts, and openly shared their special histories with one another, with spouses, with children and with the outside world."[8] Still, the Belgian government did not grant hidden children the moral standing of war victims until 2001. It took two more years for them to be given the right to petition for minimal material claims.

The emergence of the concept of the hidden child and the structures of memory it has given rise to exemplify what French sociologist Maurice Halbwachs refers to as *collective memory*—a memory that encompasses individual memories and transforms them into a totality, providing a site for a rhetoric of survivorship and agency.[9] Individuals have memories, but what is remembered depends on the social context. People remember in interaction with others, as members of groups. By sharing their experiences of being hidden and constructing their collective memory, the ex–hidden children expanded their experiences from the personal to the political, with lasting consequences.

After the war, to what extent did children maintain contact with those who had hidden them? Did parents show gratitude, and if so, in what way? Parents wanted their children to forget their Catholic socialization as quickly as possible. Those parents whose children had been enveloped in an intense and satisfying spirituality had to undertake a powerful resocialization process. Although they were immensely relieved that their children had survived, there was little room for gratitude. New lives had to be forged as quickly as possible. These new beginnings were not easy; property, means of livelihood, and lives had been lost. In reconstructing their families, parents reached out to the difficult present and a hopeful future. They had no place for the past. In the process of normalizing Jewish families, there was no room for relationships with nuns, as maternal as they might have been. As we have seen in the account of the young woman who tried to sneak out to Sunday Mass, her resocialization was abrupt and painful. Other parents were more prudent and understanding, and within these families the process took longer. Gratitude was not a priority for parents: it was not considered essential to the recovery process.

Parents intensely questioned whether the convents' motivation for hiding the children had been primarily economic. Parents and the Resistance had paid monthly sums for the youngsters' upkeep. The economic well-being of the convents varied markedly. Some, such as the Sisters of Charity of Ghent, were quite wealthy. Others, like the Sisters of St. Vincent de Paul, were so poor that they had to beg food from farmers. Orphanages were particularly destitute. Clearly, hiding children was a way of increasing income. Yet there were convents that did not take them in, so there was something special about those convents that elected to do so and accepted the risk.

Concentrating on this presumed financial motive in some sense relieved parents of having to feel grateful to the convents. It was twenty years before many hidden children, as grown adults, began renewing their relationships with—and manifesting their gratitude toward—the clerics who had saved them. One of the ex–hidden children I interviewed returns periodically to the convent where she was hidden, laden with presents. Many ex–hidden children have seen to it that nuns, priests, and laypeople are recognized as Righteous Among the Nations. The rescuers who have been so honored have been immensely proud of it.

By acquiring a publicly recognized moral status, by identifying themselves and associating in groups throughout the world, and by recounting their lives, the ex–hidden children have changed from silent victims into witnesses and actors engaged in a dynamic reconfiguration of memory.

Lawrence Langer has argued that survivors inevitably live with a fractured self.[10] Multiple voices emerge from the same person in testimonies and unanswerable questions arise. Recalling an anguished past leaves surviving victims divided between pain and relief, preventing them from constructing an integrated self, and bearing both the need and the inability to recover from loss. For Langer, the process of testifying does not imply the attribution of meaning to experience. Retelling is simply a process of reliving. This argument revives the discussion between philosopher Henri Bergson and sociologist Maurice Halbwachs in the first quarter of the twentieth century, at the time when Halbwachs was developing his concept of collective memory. Bergson argued that memory is a simple repository of past experiences activated by remembering. Upholding the social aspect of memory, Halbwachs countered that remembering is a reflexive activity shaped by concerns with the present.[11]

Langer takes a Bergsonian approach: When victims talk, they are not engaged in a process of reflection. No meaning can be wrung from their experiences; no sense can be made of them. The memories are repositories for pain and suffering. However, disagreeing with Langer, one can argue that testimony is integral to the construction and maintenance of self and identity. Testimony allows for the restoration of continuity, an essential element of individual and social life. In telling stories, survivors structure and give significance to experience, fusing past and present. Langer analyzed testimonies from camp survivors, who rank highest in the hierarchy of Holocaust victimization. But not all testimonies are one-dimensional, and those testimonies that are not descriptive of the ultimate evil of the camps do not necessarily reveal a fractured self. On the contrary, they may disclose a reflexive awareness seeking continuity of identity. Furthermore, survival seems to inspire narratives that seek to provide a legacy. As survivors assume "the duty to remember" (*le devoir de mémoire*), they perceive themselves as transmitting the meaning of past events to the next generations.[12]

There were significant consequences as the children emerged from their silence, began to tell their stories, and forged a collective memory that was socially constructed and maintained.[13] In a sense, their memories became more than their private possessions. As Richard Sennett reminds us, French sociologist Emile Durkheim believed that solidarity is created by remembering together.[14] By sharing their memories, the ex–hidden children framed their social bonds. Now members of a distinct category, they felt empowered to claim collective rights and voice collective demands, for example to receive moral recognition as war victims. In reconstructing their stories, some realized that the important actions of their rescuers had never been recognized.

The emergence of the concept of the hidden child illustrates Eviatar Zerubavel's point that commemoration is regulated by social rules that define what should be remembered and what is to be forgotten. As members of mnemonic communities, we have a collective memory—a shared past jointly remembered and commemorated.[15] Who, what, why, when, and how we commemorate is affected by the groups we belong to. Collective memory should not be seen necessarily as monolithic and harmonious. It can be fragmented and a source of conflict. There are different ways and intensities of "belonging." Nevertheless, there is no doubt that after the 1991 gathering, the ex–hidden children acquired a new identity by constructing their collective memory. Robin Wagner-Pacifici has suggested that memories are never formless; they are "shared significance embodied in form."[16] This describes exactly the mission of Yad Vashem, the remembrance institution of Israel, which honors the Righteous Among the Nations, a new term in twentieth-century European history describing the non-Jews who risked their lives to save Jews.

YAD VASHEM: THE INSTITUTIONALIZATION OF MEMORY AND THE RIGHTEOUS AMONG THE NATIONS

Located in Jerusalem and formally called the Holocaust Martyrs' and Heroes' Remembrance Authority, Yad Vashem is the official Israeli institution for the commemoration of the Holocaust. The name derives from the Bible—Isaiah 56:5, in which God promises a memorial (Yad) and a name (Vashem), hence everlasting memory, to those who keep God's covenant. Discussions about the need for such an institution began as early as 1942, fueled by reports of the ongoing genocide. Yad Vashem was finally established in August 1953, when the Israeli Knesset unanimously approved the Holocaust Martyrs' and Heroes' Remembrance Law.[17]

The commemorative mission entrusted to Yad Vashem is inspired by the desire to mark both martyrdom and redemption. According to the law establishing the institution, Yad Vashem is expected to commemorate (1) "the six million members of the Jewish people who died a martyr's death at the hands of the Nazis and their collaborators; (2) "the communities, synagogues, movements . . . and cultural institutions destroyed"; (3) "the fortitude of Jews who gave their lives for their people"; (4) "the heroism of Jewish servicemen, and of underground fighters"; (5) "the heroic stand of the besieged ghetto population and the fighters who rose and kindled the flame of revolt to save the honor of their people"; (6) "the sublime, persistent struggle of the masses of the House of Israel, on the threshold of destruction, for their human dignity and Jewish culture"; (7) "the unceasing efforts of the besieged to reach Eretz Israel in spite of all obstacles, and the devotion and heroism of their brothers who went forth to rescue and liberate the survivors"; and (8) "*the Righteous Among the Nations who risked their lives to save Jews.*"[18]

In addition, Yad Vashem was charged "to collect, examine and publish testimony of the Holocaust and the heroism it called forth, and to bring home its lessons to the people"; "to promote a custom of joint remembrance of the heroes and victims"; and "to confer upon the members of the Jewish people who perished in the days of the Holocaust and the resistance the commemorative citizenship of the state of Israel, as a token of their having been gathered to their people." In other words, it has the duty to be both "custodian and creator of national memory."[19] In fulfilling this weighty mandate, the Jerusalem-based institution has become a national shrine devoted to research and education. At the same time, by memorializing people throughout the world, it reaches out globally and transcends national borders. It also has constructed and maintains a sacred commemorative landscape. Among its numerous buildings and monuments, many poignantly address Holocaust destruction. These include a Memorial Chamber, a Hall of Names, and the Valley of the Destroyed Communities. Others monuments celebrate heroism. Thus Yad Vashem's narrative oscillates between two poles: from remembrance of Jewish martyrs and heroes to redemption by the birth of the state.[20]

Within Yad Vashem's landscape is the Avenue of the Righteous Among the Nations. It is lined with carob trees, each planted in honor of an individual rescuer. When space for additional trees ran out in the last decade, a garden dedicated to the Righteous was added. It features a wall on which the names of rescuers are engraved by country.

The term Righteous Among the Nations, translated from the Hebrew Hasidei Umot Haolam, originated in the Babylonian Talmud. Down through the generations, it has become an expression of esteem for a non-Jew with a favorable attitude toward Jews.[21] After the war, it was chosen to signify non-Jews who had risked their lives to save Jews.

In the decade after its establishment, Yad Vashem pursued its building program, established a museum, and struggled to obtain the resources necessary for its research and educational goals. During that time, there was no interest in implementing the commemoration of non-Jews. The institution devoted its attention to those who had died in the hells of the concentration camps, not those who had managed to avoid them. The trial of Adolf Eichmann changed the situation.

The trial of this notorious Nazi killer took place in Jerusalem in 1961. In contrast to the Nuremberg tribunals, held soon after the war's end, Eichmann's trial laid out in full detail the horror and scope of the Jewish genocide. It also highlighted remarkable examples of heroism. Witnesses questioned about receiving help while they were persecuted and hunted recalled non-Jews who had risked their lives to save them and others. The prosecutor painted a stark dichotomy between Eichmann and the rescuers, paying collective homage to the latter. At that time, Yad Vashem started receiving many letters requesting recognition of the Righteous Among the Nations. As Gensburger points out, public opinion—both in Israel and internationally—expressed

> its wish to show that the Jewish people does not only want to punish, condemn and judge the criminals, that it is not only animated by a desire for vengeance but also by the desire to manifest gratitude towards the Righteous Among the Nations who have risked their lives to save Jews.[22]

Paradoxically, while the Eichmann trial dramatized evil, it also recognized goodness. Shakespeare wrote: "The evil that men do lives after them; the good is oft interred with their bones."[23] The Jewish people resolved not to let that happen. Responding to pressure from the World Jewish Congress and numerous individuals, Yad Vashem created a special department to fulfill its mandate toward the Righteous and adopted the planting of trees as a symbolic way to honor them.

Tree-planting symbolizes connection to the land and has patriotic overtones as a metaphor for a Jewish sense of rootedness after a two-thousand-year exile from the land of Israel.

Inaugurating the tradition, twelve honorees were chosen to plant trees along the Avenue of the Righteous Among the Nations on Holocaust Memorial Day in 1962. One of them, Oscar Schindler, was absent. A few days earlier, he had been the target of a polemic by two persons he had saved; they now accused him of financial opportunism. Others came forward to defend him. A week later, flanked by three hundred people he had rescued, Schindler planted his tree. The incident merits mention, both because of Schindler's subsequent fame—the result of Steven Spielberg's 1993 film *Schindler's List*—and its immediate and significant consequences at Yad Vashem. Learning a lesson from the controversy, the institution established an independent and permanent public commission to evaluate the merits of each proposed Righteous, in effect creating "a Tribunal of The Good."[24] Memory alone had proved insufficient to ensure an official commemoration that would be accepted as both legitimate and just.

The members of this evaluation commission are public figures—lawyers, historians, many of them Holocaust survivors. It is chaired by a Supreme Court judge; the first chair in 1962 was Justice Moshe Landau, who had presided at the Eichmann trial. The commission's task is to scrutinize all applications for recognition based on evidence provided by those who were rescued and other relevant documentation. Over the years, the commission has developed an intricate and cumbersome process of authentication that demands steadfast perseverance from the petitioners and at times taxes their patience, as my interviewees mentioned. As survivors are aging, they are concerned by the slowness of the process. Sadly, the honor now is very often bestowed posthumously.

The criteria for admission to this "unique international hall of fame" stipulate that the non-Jew has to have saved a Jewish life during the Holocaust in full awareness of risk to his or her life, freedom, and safety.[25] It must have been done without expecting a reward, monetary or otherwise, as a condition for the aid provided. In addition, the evidence must show that the rescuer's role was active, *making* the rescue happen, as opposed to passive—for example, simply refraining from turning in a Jewish fugitive.[26] Over time, diplomats who provided assistance have been honored, in effect expanding the meaning of the act of rescue. Only individuals are considered for the honor; groups and institutions are excluded from recognition.

In addition to being honored on the memorial wall, each person designated as Righteous is awarded a specially minted medal and a certificate of honor. One side of the medal contains a sentence from the Talmud—"Whoever Saves One Life Saves the Whole World"—written in relief in French. Above the sentence is sketched a view of Yad Vashem and the words, in both Hebrew and French, "From the grateful Jewish people." On the verso, the Talmudic sentence is written in Hebrew and arrayed in a circle around a globe of the world. Two hands, seemingly surging from nowhere at the bottom of the medal, reach across barbed wires and pull on a cord strung around the globe, as if disseminating the words across the world. The medal and certificate are awarded at ceremonies held either at Yad Vashem or, most often, in the country where the rescuer lives or lived. Diplomatic representatives of the State of Israel award the medal and certificate to the rescuers or their kin in the presence of local authorities, the rescued persons, families, and friends. These are ceremonial occasions marking the successful closure of a lengthy seeking to express gratitude in a public and significant way. Closure is thus offered to both the rescuer and the rescued. The public presentations also become widely reported media events.

Yad Vashem and the honoring of the Righteous exemplify the dynamic interaction between historical events and the forms of collective memory that are available for their preservation. In other words, Yad Vashem embodies a formal translation of important past events and provides a memorializing discourse, giving them a collective shape, symbolic meanings, and political dimensions.

What events are adopted for commemoration? Social drama, but also social repair.[27] In the Holocaust drama that Yad Vashem memorializes, destruction and its victims predominate. However, by creating and honoring the Righteous Among the Nations, the institution provides an opportunity to repair in some measure the devastated social fabric. It empowers the surviving Jewish victims to initiate a process in which they seize their past, reconfigure it, and redirect it toward reconciliation with non-Jews. In choosing to follow the trajectory of gratitude, the end point becomes reconciliation. As Gensburger has remarked in discussing the appropriation of the Righteous in French historical memory through the inauguration of a monument to them in Thonon-les-Bains in 1997, suffering and heroism are united through the figure of the Righteous.[28] What she fails to point out is that by bestowing the honor, the suffering is symbolically overcome. Yet Gensburger rightly indicates that the help given by the Righteous was often carried out with the cooperation of Jewish resistance networks. In a way, underscoring the role of the Righteous simultaneously provides an opportunity to recognize the work of these networks. As we have seen, this fusion between resistance and righteousness certainly applies to individuals in Belgium. For example, children hidden in convents at the initiative of the CDJ years later requested Righteous recognition for the nuns who had cared for them. Thus narratives of honor also indirectly apply to the CDJ.

The cultural forms through which the Righteous are honored, especially the medal, reflect moral, political, and aesthetic considerations. The text on the medal enlarges the moral stature of the rescuers. Their act is morally globalized. And the cord around the globe links the individual rescuer to those around the world who accomplished similar heroic acts. Or, in another possible interpretation, the rescuer is tied to all the rescued. The moral universality, however, is joined to a political particularism. The rescuer is reminded in two languages and by the sketch of Yad Vashem that the gratitude emanates from the Jewish people and from Israel in particular. The inscription of the rescuer's name and country on the memorial wall provides a permanent enshrinement. A symbolic link is thus created between the State of Israel, the individual rescuer, and the rescuer's nation. Who owns collective memories is a question Wagner-Pacifici raises, but "ownership" is not an appropriate term. The recognition of the Righteous is a process that involves individuals, the collectivity of the rescued, and the State of Israel in the incarnation of Yad Vashem. The latter grants the title, judges the behavior, and draws on the Righteous for its narrative of redemption. At the intersection of private, collective, and historical memories, the figure of the Righteous is endowed with great moral strength and at the same time presents a political statement.

The ex—hidden children have used the procedure put in place by Yad Vashem to memorialize their rescuers for a variety of reasons. It gives them the opportunity to exercise legitimate power. They can be actors in the public world for a recognition that they see as just, uncontroversial, and long overdue. At last they can compensate for their long period of silence. The process also enhances the depth and intensity of their memories, anchoring their identity to the past and affirming it in the present. In justifying the honor, the citations describing the acts of rescue by clergy often mention that they exerted no pressure for conversion. For the rescued children, the connection to Judaism is thus reaffirmed. They as well as the rescuers are at the center of the process. Their indispensability is confirmed. They gain strength as moral beings who are paying a debt and dispensing joy to their aging rescuers.[29] Finally, it is important to the rescued that the title be awarded in a public ceremony, for they expect this celebration to be didactic, exemplary, and reconciliatory.

The participation of the State of Israel in these commemorative ceremonies has several implications. The nation has positioned itself as an intermediary between the rescued and the rescuer. It claims to represent the Jewish people as a whole and Holocaust survivors in particular. Undertaking the process of recognition and petitioning the Yad Vashem commission activates this claim. Israel's participation is essential and its centrality never in doubt. The Righteous ceremony has symbolic purposes. First, it marks the reintegration and reconciliation of Jews, so fiercely marginalized during the war, with non-Jews in Belgium and elsewhere. Second, by its presence Israel implies a guarantee that surviving Jews will never again be victimized, proclaims itself their protector in the present and for the future, and ensures their allegiance. Third, having completed a rigorous authenticating process, the Yad Vashem commission and the State of Israel affirm their moral authority in commemorative matters. These aspects are not in conflict; in fact, they complement each other.

What does being honored as Righteous Gentiles mean to the recipients? Once they agree to participate in the process, they look forward to a positive outcome.

Sometimes humility may be an obstacle, especially for nuns. They contend that what they did was to be expected; it was simply the humane thing to do. There is also the question of responsibility for the rescuing acts, which is sometimes difficult to determine because participants are deceased. As the process follows its course, individual nuns are concerned about being singled out for the honor. They often insist on the inclusion of others, in particular their mothers superior. As mentioned, Yad Vashem never gives the award to an institution such as a convent. But sometimes in the public citation that summarizes the rescuing acts of an honored nun, other sisters receive an honorable mention though not the title itself. At other times, when enough proof has been supplied that two nuns in the same convent are worthy of recognition—for example, a living nun and her deceased mother superior—both have been honored in the same ceremony, although the title is bestowed individually. This is done to the great satisfaction of the living honoree, who has often played an instrumental role in documenting the actions of her deceased colleague.

What some of the nuns I interviewed seemed to appreciate about the whole process was that it reestablishes contact with the children they sheltered. After years of not knowing how the children fared after the war, they now know that their former charges have thrived and that they themselves played an essential role in making that outcome possible. They appear humble but proud that they were not mere bystanders during the war. When I interviewed Father Richard, he displayed with great pride his Righteous medal, along with photographs of his trip to Israel, where he had been invited to Yad Vashem for ceremonies marking the fiftieth anniversary of the founding of the state. At the time the title is bestowed, the honorees suddenly find themselves in the public spotlight, at the center of media events and the subjects of glowing newspaper articles. They accept the title as an extension of honor for the Church at a time when the Church in Belgium has lost many members. There is another dynamic as well. As the number of Righteous recognitions began to grow as a consequence of the 1991 Gathering of Children Hidden during World War II, expectations of recognition and entitlement also grew. For example, in my interview with Sister X, she expressed disappointment that she had lost track of Solange, a girl she had cared for during the war. The younger woman would have been an essential witness in any endeavor to achieve recognition as a Righteous. In sum, to become Righteous Among the Nations is perceived by the nuns as an affirmation of their humanity and an acceptable way to be a part of the public world, if only momentarily. The title is generally the only honor they will ever be granted. It is different for some of the priests who created or were major participants in Resistance networks.

The honoring of the Righteous in all its aspects represents an intense manifestation of collective memory, in the sense that it fuses public events and private memories. Moreover, it illustrates the way memory is a social practice: embedded in social action, it produces and *forms* social relations.[30]

COMMEMORATIVE TRAJECTORIES

The number of honorees has additional implications. The list of Righteous Among the Nations recognized by Yad Vashem through January 2007 includes 21,758 individuals worldwide.[31] There are 1,443 persons from Belgium, among them forty-seven nuns and fifty-two priests.[32] Though the clergy make up only a small percentage of the total number of Belgian Righteous, they saved a high proportion of individuals. For example, the Couvent de la Miséricorde in Héverlé sheltered at least fifty children. Two persons from that convent have been honored as Righteous: Sister Marie Beirens, whom I interviewed, and Mother Superior Cécile Stinger, who received the title posthumously.[33]

When comparing the dates of recognition of the Belgian nuns and priests, two very different trajectories of memorial recognition emerge. Before 1992, seven nuns were recognized; since then, forty have been honored. Thirty-two priests were recognized before 1992, but since then only twenty. Looking at it another way, 15 percent of the honored nuns were recognized prior to 1992; in contrast, 60 percent of the priests received the award during that period. This shows clearly that the role of the priests in the saving of Jewish children and adults was very visible; they were active in the Resistance and among the public in general. Rewarding their preeminence and importance, recognition was granted to them relatively early. The mothers superior and the sisters remained quasi-invisible until the hidden children gained status and definition. After the 1991 hidden children gathering, the women clergy slowly emerged from the shadows, as the children they had sheltered gathered evidence for their recognition.

I chose to divide the clergy into those recognized before and since 1992 because I wanted to determine how strong the impetus for recognition became after the 1991 gathering, which formally marked the end of the ex–hidden children's silence. The figures for the recognition of nuns may suggest the impact. Nine nuns were honored in 1994, the largest number of clergy in any one year. Eighty-five percent of the nuns who have been honored received the recognition since 1992. I think this indicates that until recently, and with a very few exceptions, the nuns' role in the resistance to the Nazi occupation of Belgium was not institutionally recognized.

In developing his concept of civilian resistance during World War II, political scientist Jacques Semelin has rightly argued that such unarmed opposition was first and foremost aimed at ensuring survival. Its intention was to rescue what could be saved, and the hiding of the Jewish children fits this definition perfectly. In Semelin's terms, the nuns were clearly civilian resisters.[34] He points out that for a long time only those who participated in the more dramatic armed resistance were honored with national commemorations; it is relatively recently that civilian resisters have been given a commemorative space. He mentions specifically the appropriation of the French Righteous into national memory through the afore-mentioned monument.[35] Semelin also argues for enlarging the meaning of acts of resistance to include, among others, the youngster who carried messages, the elderly person who provided mailboxes and safe spaces for secret meetings, the printer of leaflets, the policeman who informally warned of arrests, the farmer who hid those avoiding forced labor, and the employee who forged identity cards.[36] He believes that people of all generations who engaged in these and similar activities should be included in an all-embracing national remembrance. Here he seems to be searching for and advocating the recall of the texture of civilian resistance—in other words, the many acts of resistance that were embedded in everyday life during the war, unrecognized but essential. Judith Greenberg raises a similar point in regard to caregiving activities by women resisters.[37]

Within the civilian resistance itself, I think that a comparable commem-orative pattern developed. In celebrating rescue, attention focused first on the priests who were the best known, those who had established their own resistance networks and were significant and visible actors. So, for instance, the two priests who each had helped large numbers of adults and children were honored early. Father Bruno Reynders was recognized as a Righteous in 1964 and Father Joseph André in 1968. In a sense, they exemplify the fusion of resistance and right-eousness discussed previously. Undoubtedly, they deserved this early recognition.

It is in the more private sphere of civilian resistance encompassing the less visible, more intimate acts of everyday life—in effect, the quotidian aspects of rescue—that the nuns played a significant role. The mothers superior, whose wartime decisions were essential to the children's rescue, were forgotten and their cooperation and savvy unrecognized. In the history of the Resistance, they re-mained in the shadows. They had two strikes against them: they were women and they were nuns. Women's participation in the Resistance in all its forms has generally not been sufficiently acknowledged; this has been amply documented for France and applies to Belgium as well.[38] In addition, women occupy a relatively low position in the Catholic Church hierarchy, and convents are gendered insti-tutions. There was little incentive to underscore the important role the mothers superior played. The awarding of the Righteous honor is a compensation for some, but by no means a complete one.

THE CATHOLIC CHURCH, COMMEMORATION, AND THE FIGHT FOR THE SOULS OF THE CHILDREN

While many Jewish children were hidden and saved in Catholic institutions, the Catholic Church itself has neither emphasized nor significantly commemorated these deeds in an official way. When I undertook this study, I knew, of course, that the Catholic Church is a hierarchical institution. Though matters of dogma are centralized, I also was aware that bishops and cardinals make autonomous decisions. In spite of the passive attitude of Pope Pius XII during the Holocaust, I thought that I would find directives to rescue Jewish children emanating from the higher echelons of the Belgian Catholic Church. I was wrong. Publicly, the Church in Belgium remained just as silent as the Vatican, and the matter of its official position is much debated in Belgian postwar historiography.[39] I had wrongly assumed that plaques on Belgian convents would declare the number of rescued Jewish children hidden in each of them. I had expected the Church itself to have had a hand in placing these plaques, thereby asserting a moral high ground. Yet the Catholic Church has not formally commemorated the rescue of Jewish children by Belgian convents. Instead, it has followed what I call the politics of silence.

Before dealing with the reasons behind this silence, it is necessary to outline the attitude of the Church during the Occupation. Cardinal Joseph-Ernest Van Roey, archbishop of Malines and primate of Belgium during World War II, practiced during the Nazi occupation what has been labeled "the politics of the lesser evil." His main concern was to maintain the interests and autonomy of the Church. Through a pragmatic and opportunistic attitude, he sought a *modus vivendi* with the occupier. He adapted to the new situation and avoided open confrontations. The German military administration, the Miltärverwaltung, was conscious of the moral power of the Church, so to maintain peace and order it did not touch Catholic institutions. It let the Church keep control over its domain.

A second concern of the cardinal was to retain the unity of the country by attachment to the monarchy, embodied by King Leopold III, to whom the cardinal was very loyal. This unity was threatened by divisive Flemish nationalism in the north. Before the war, Leopold III had been politically neutral. After the Nazi invasion on May 10, 1940, he believed that Germany would win the war, and he remained in the country while his government fled to London. The cardinal was very devoted to the monarchy as a system and to the king as a person. In the south, in the diocese of Liège (which at the time also included the province of Limbourg), Bishop Louis-Joseph Kerkhofs exhibited the mindset of a resister, in marked contrast to the resigned attitude of the cardinal and other bishops. Catholic clergy and organizations throughout the country saved many Jews, but Liège was the only bishopric where the fight against their persecution was to a certain extent centralized. Neither the cardinal nor Bishop Kerkhofs protested the treatment of Jews openly, but in his diocese Kerkhofs instigated and organized help and rescue, and he encouraged his priests to act likewise. It wasn't until 1943 that the cardinal made a public protest—against the Nazis' conscription of Belgians for forced labor and their stealing of church bells to be melted down for war purposes. In spite of protests, a total of 4,568 bells were seized.[40] Informally, the cardinal did not oppose the help extended to Jews by many members of his church. In spite of numerous appeals for help addressed to him personally, his rare interventions through his secretaries were on behalf of Jews who were Belgian citizens.[41] The fate of the Jews, as the cardinal perceived it, entailed deportation, not extermination. This did not warrant endangering the survival of the Church as an institution, all the more so as he felt unsure of an Allied victory until late in the war. Therefore, there was no moral public stand by the Church. Other than the shining exception of Bishop Kerkhofs, the initiative for rescue came from grassroots clergy, for whom the defense of human values was by far the most vital consideration.

After the war, the concern for unity grew stronger, given the outcry against the king's wartime behavior, which culminated in a period of unrest known as "the royal crisis." The Church's interests were vested in restoring harmony and supporting the monarchy, not in defining and honoring resisters and rescuers. Because the lion's share of the resisters and rescuers had come from the south, it was felt that commemoration would only elicit comparisons and drive an even larger wedge between the Flemish north and the French-speaking south.

Another reason for the lack of commemoration was suggested by the priest I interviewed. Parish priests responded to parental pleas and found hiding places for the children in individual families and within convents and colleges. Priests created rescue networks and worked independently or in close cooperation with the CDJ. Nuns sheltered children of all ages. It was members of the lower clergy who filled the moral vacuum left by the Catholic Church hierarchy through its failure to speak out publicly against the persecution of the Jews and to organize their protection. By publicly commemorating its lower clergy, the Church's leaders could have triggered comparisons with their own behavior. They would have been compelled to confront questions about their relative passivity. Even more difficult, they would have been required to justify their attitude.

Further, soon after the end of the war, the Church became preoccupied with the burgeoning Cold War. World War II quickly became past history. Antifascism was easily and rapidly replaced by fervent anticommunism. In those pressing political circumstances, the topic of the humanitarian rescue of Jewish children did not carry any weight. It was irrelevant to the ideological discourse in vogue at the time.

This silence was in line with the general attitude about Jewish victims and the neglect of a Judeocentric memory, as Pieter Lagrou has pointed out. Furthermore, foreign Jews, who made up about 94 percent of Belgium's prewar Jewish population, were the first to be deported. Some attempts were made to protect the tiny minority of Jews who were Belgian citizens, but the Nazis reneged on their promises, and these efforts eventually failed. Commemorating specifically the Jewish victims could have highlighted this flagrantly xenophobic discrimination.

In addition, priests and nuns live in a culture of humility. As institutions that advocate a humble way of life—and as gendered institutions—convents are not well placed for commemorative recognition. As one of the nuns I interviewed reported, when it was suggested to her mother superior that she deserved recognition, she responded that she had done only what was to be expected. Yet those who have been recognized by Yad Vashem have been very proud of the honor, and in the case of nuns, they have involved their whole convent community in the acceptance. In recent decades, resistance to recognition has weakened, and public appreciation of the clergy's moral stance during the war has been welcomed.

A significant factor in the lack of commemoration was the contentious fight waged after the war over the retrieval of Jewish orphans from Catholic environments. As already mentioned, some of the rescued children had been converted to Catholicism and baptized while in hiding, and those who went back to their families underwent the process of resocialization and a return to Jewish identity. But others faced a much more complex dilemma: When it was discovered, only after the end of the war, that some of the children's parents had been exterminated, a fight took place for their souls, in the striking expression of historian Hanne Hellemans, who has thoroughly investigated this topic. Had the rescues been a purely humanitarian issue, or were they motivated by the desire to save souls and Christianize? Unfortunately, the efficient collaboration between Jewish and Catholic organizations to ensure rescue during the war was replaced in peacetime by a sharp conflict over "the children question"—the fate of converted and baptized Jewish orphans.[42]

With the end of the war, the Aide aux Israélites Victimes de Guerre (AIVG; Aid to Jewish War Victims, the reconstituted CDJ), the large social welfare organization that assisted surviving Jewish war victims, both adults and children, considered itself the representative of the Jewish orphans and acted in the name of the Jewish community. In Nazi-occupied Europe, one and a half million Jewish children had been exterminated, and barely one hundred thousand had survived. With half of Belgium's Jewish population destroyed by Nazi barbarism, every rescued child was considered precious and deemed essential to be removed from the Catholic environment. The AIVG wanted each orphan raised in the parents' tradition and at the same time hoped to ensure a long-term Jewish presence in Belgium. To retrieve the orphans placed through the CDJ during the war and give them back their Jewish identities, the AIVG adopted a variety of tactics. Whenever possible, it entrusted the child to extended family members, for example an aunt or a grandparent. The AIVG also established institutions where the children were cared for until they reached the age of eighteen. These facilities, financed by the American Joint Distribution Committee, were known as homes rather than orphanages, signaling the organization's intention to provide a quasi-familial environment.[43] The AIVG also set out to retrieve Jewish children who were not on the CDJ lists—youngsters who had been placed directly by parents or through other Resistance networks.

Some Catholic authorities, but not all, claimed that orphans who had been converted and baptized in individual homes and convents should remain Catholic. After all, baptism is an irreversible sacrament that requires an obligation to lead a Catholic life. The Catholics, among them Father Reynders and Bishop Kerkhofs, were determined to thwart the efforts of the Jewish organizations to return these orphans' former identities to them and reintegrate them into the Jewish community.

In January 1945, a few months after the end of the Nazi occupation of Belgium, Father Reynders wrote a document that was meant to offer guidelines about the "legal situation of Israelite children." He began by describing the wartime collaboration between the CDJ and the major Catholic networks and priests involved in hiding children. He noted that, except for a few instances resulting from "ignorance, excessive zeal, misguided fervor and narrow-mindedness," there had been no pressure to convert the children to Catholicism.[44] Understandably, the children had been required to behave according to Catholic traditions for security reasons. But, the priest argued, "many of these children, endowed with an uncommon intellectual curiosity and a sensitive religious attitude, became passionate for Catholic life and doctrine."[45] Nearly always, he added, they were baptized with the parents' consent. If the parents had been deported, baptism was deferred until their eventual return. Father Reynders marveled at the remarkable religious fervor of the converted children. He therefore objected to the AIVG's desire to erase all traces of contact with Catholics and subject the children to "a bath of Judaism or neutrality." "An experience is an experience, whatever the circumstances that provoked it, and it would be unacceptable that the children be forbidden to freely draw the consequences from it," he wrote.[46]

In seeking to outline a legal statute that would allow these youngsters to remain in a Catholic environment, Father Reynders questioned the very existence of "the Jewish child" by asking what criteria should be used to define them.[47] Nationality? A Jewish nation, he wrote, is only a hope for part of the Jewish population (in 1945 the state of Israel did not yet exist). Most just want to become citizens of the country that has received them. Religion? There are so many Jews who do not practice Judaism. Race? That was a notion inherited from the Nazis and unacceptable under Belgian law. Following this reasoning, the Catholic protagonists dismissed as worthless the AIVG's argument that the orphans belonged to the Jewish community. From the Catholic perspective, it was crucial to ensure through legal channels that the converted and baptized rescued children would continue to lead Catholic lives. Therefore, it is not surprising that some Catholics were oblivious to or chose to ignore the concept of a Jewish people and a Jewish culture. By defining the distinction between being Jewish and non-Jewish as intrinsically and solely racist, they used to their advantage an anti-Nazi rhetoric that often succeeded in eliciting the sympathy of the courts.

In developing their cases, some Catholics argued that when parents did not return, three issues had to be considered: the affective bonds between the rescued and their rescuers, the presumed will of the parents, and the religious situation of the child. According to them, affective bonds forged during the war had priority over blood ties, so the rescuers who cared for the children should have precedence over any relatives who claimed them. The parents' choice of hiding place for their children was seen as the best indication of parental will. Those who had been entrusted with the care of the children should acquire custody. And according to canon law, the baptized were to remain Catholic for the remainder of their lives. Even nonbaptized believers should remain Catholic if they wished to, because Belgian law assured them the right to freedom of religion.

Both parties appealed to the Ministry of Justice for general rulings on the matter; both requests were rejected. Meetings between the two parties were fruitless. The Catholics refused to concede that the Jewish community deserved to bring up the children. They objected to the concept of "giving them back": in their eyes, one could only give back to those from whom one has received—in this case the parents, not any Jewish community as such.[48] The real issue, however, was not the meaning of being Jewish, but the fact that in Catholic theology, "anyone who has been baptized is a subject of the Church."[49]

Belgian historian Hanne Hellemans has studied this issue in depth. She emphasizes the differences that arose at the time within the Jewish community, for example between Zionists and non-Zionists, the Right and the Left, the religious and the nonreligious. Accusing the AIVG of being too lax and secular in its retrieval efforts, three different Jewish Orthodox organizations joined forces in 1947 to pursue the matter more actively and set up religious orphanages. Dissensions notwithstanding, I believe that the retrieval of the children by the Jewish community was of the utmost importance to all of the Jewish organizations acting on the youngsters' behalf—far more important than issues such as whether they would be raised as Orthodox or secular Jews and whether they would immigrate to Palestine, and later Israel, or remain in Belgium. Jewish communities have never been monolithic, and the chaotic conditions after a horrendous war were far from conducive to overcoming political and religious differences. Though the dissensions between the AIVG and the religious organizations were regrettable, in contrast to Hellemans, I do not think that these were a major issue.

From my perspective, the Catholic organizations' refusal to release the Jewish orphans from their Catholic milieu amounted to an effort to achieve a new kind of annihilation. Retaining the children was unfair to the parents who had died because they were Jews; it misjudged entirely their real intentions and blithely erased the children's past. In handing over their children, parents wanted them to stay alive. The circumstances created by the Nazis forced them to undertake these actions, and they used any means of survival at their disposal. Hiding their children in a Catholic environment was one of the few means available. They knew that they were in danger of being deported, but they did not necessarily expect to be exterminated. For the parents who stayed alive by hiding and for the few parents who came back from the camps, the Catholic position and Belgian law recognized their rights; they had no problem in reclaiming their children. But it was specifically because the other parents were exterminated that some Catholic organizations wished to obliterate the converted and baptized orphans from the Jewish people and "save" them from being Jewish. In my view, this amounted to a double annihilation.

To be fair, however, I must recognize that my argument may be criticized for two reasons. First, it neglects to take into account the feelings of surrogate families who had strong affective bonds with the children they had raised. They understandably wanted to adopt the orphaned children and give them a family home, which they considered an environment far superior to an AIVG institution. Second, my argument does not consider the children's own wishes. Both objections have merit. Nevertheless, because Holocaust cruelty created a new category of Jewish children—baptized orphans—the refusal to give them the opportunity to return to their heritage amounted to handing the Nazis a double victory. Furthermore, these children would eventually gain the freedom to choose; once they grew up, they could embrace whatever identity they wished. Clearly, I have struggled with the issues. But let me point out that courts and other organizations at the war's end made no systematic provisions to recognize the complexity of the situations and resorted to ad hoc, variable resolutions.

Courts sometimes rendered strange verdicts. For example, one court ruled that two girls were to stay in a convent because that would have been their parents' desire. These girls, however, were the daughters of a synagogue sexton. It is hard to imagine that their father would have freely chosen life in a convent for them.[50]

After the Jewish organizations realized that the argument of belonging to the Jewish community would not hold up in court, they shifted their strategy to assert the primacy of blood ties. They searched for relatives far and wide, sometimes going so far as to produce bogus family members. Sometimes the children were returned. Brachfeld cites a case where a child was finally entrusted to the custody of an uncle when the convent's mother superior was paid the substantial sum of money she had demanded.[51] The decision whether blood or affective ties had priority varied from judge to judge. Sometimes court orders were not followed. Children were secretly hidden to prevent their retrieval, in spite of rulings demanding their return.[52] The famous case of Henri Elias, who was claimed by an uncle but vanished behind convent walls where he was brainwashed into being an anti-Semite, took twelve years to be resolved.[53] Hidden in a convent in 1943, he was turned over after the war to the fanatic Fernande Henrard, who had made it her mission to prevent orphaned Jewish children from being returned to their relatives. She had Henri Elias baptized and then hidden in various Catholic institutions, while his uncle, his only surviving relative, was searching for him. She instilled in the child fear of the Jews, while he suffered abusive treatment and was tossed from institution to institution. The slow judicial process ended in 1957, when his uncle finally won his guardianship. Henri Elias has detailed his long ordeal in dispassionate terms, under which his pain is palpable.[54]

Cardinal Van Roey was the epitome of ambivalence in these matters. Sometimes he advised the return of the children to their original milieu and avoided being entrapped in an official position in favor of Catholic caretakers. At other times he sent contrary signals. In one documented case, he agreed with both sides. This controversy began in 1947; in 1955, the two children in question were still living with the fanatic Fernande Henrard. She had had them baptized and was adamantly opposed to their leaving her influence and faith.[55]

The rescuing families stressed their emotional ties to children they had cherished and argued that the youngsters should not be deprived of their love. Religious motives predominated for the institutions. They had saved souls; they did not want to lose the results of their life's work. Lest they be damned, these saved souls had to be guaranteed a Catholic education. In some cases, anti-Semitism prevailed. In a desire to prevent the children's return and "save" them from a Jewish education, some Church authorities instilled in the youngsters a hatred of Jews. As for the Belgian authorities, the existing custody laws did not give preference to family. The interest of the child was the determining factor, and the judge was the final arbiter.

The Belgian cases arose against the background of large commotions in France and the Netherlands over the issue of the children's retrieval. But in Belgium, which was not lacking for divisive issues, all parties wanted to avoid a broad conflict between religious and secular forces over the children. By eschewing an official attitude, Cardinal Van Roey could at most be accused of passivity, but not of explicit cooperation. The Belgian rabbinate adopted a moderate position. It felt a deep gratitude for the predominant role the Catholics had played in the children's rescue. After wide consultations in 1956, the rabbinate decided not to publish the names of eighty-five Jewish children known to be in Catholic hands, thus avoiding the possibility of "eighty-five Finaly-like affairs," a reference to a retrieval controversy that had aroused much anger in France.[56] Henri Elias refers to the same incident in the title of his autobiographical article.[57] The Belgian state considered the issues private.

For a time, personal relationships between the Jewish organizations and a few Catholics were strained. They perceived each other as fanatics and dogmatists, but the controversies did not turn into long-lasting conflagrations.[58] The Jewish community never forgot the Catholic role in the children's rescue. In 1964, Father Reynders was honored as one of the first Belgian Righteous Among the Nations. The children who lauded him insisted that he had always given instructions to convents in which they were hidden not to pressure for conversion.[59] Still, the psychic cost of this controversy to the children—pawns torn between identities and places—was high. The exact number of youngsters who were not reintegrated into the Jewish community will never be known. Both Hellemans and Dequecker indicate in general a relatively considerable Christianization. Dequecker, who has examined in depth the problem of baptism and conversion of Jews in Belgium during the war, concludes his study poignantly by asking, "Is it unthinkable that one day the Roman Catholic Church will officially admit that many Jews, adults and children, were baptized during World War II under dubious circumstances?"[60]

Since the fight for the souls of the orphaned children was contentious, it is understandable why the Church took no steps to commemorate their rescue. It did send delegates to commemorative events, but it was generally the hidden children who took it upon themselves to honor those who saved them. As we have seen, through Yad Vashem, Israel has become a partner in the commemorative process.

SOME NOTABLE COMMEMORATIONS

Others have also memorialized the rescuers, sometimes in cooperation with state authorities, and especially in cases where priests gave extraordinary help to the Belgian Resistance and organized the rescue of not only children but also adults. For example, in Namur there is a plaque on the Home de l'Ange, the parish house of Father Joseph André, where numerous people found refuge and were later directed to safety. The house is located on the appropriately named Place de l'Ange (Place of the Angel). Ironically, during the war it was in close proximity to German headquarters.

Born in 1908, Father André served as a parish priest in Namur from 1941 to 1957. When the first deportations occurred in 1942, he was asked for help by an acquaintance, a German Jewish lawyer. The priest arranged for a hiding place and brought the two children to his own parents. This was the beginning of the extended help network, known as l'Aide Chrétienne aux Israélites (Christian Aid to Israelites), that Father André organized to aid both adults and children. Later in the war, he worked in collaboration with the CDJ, but he never joined the organization officially or accepted its financial help. Several hundred children passed through the Home de l'Ange, most on their way to permanent locations. Some stayed with him for longer periods. Adults were placed as farmhands and domestics. Father André was charismatic and persuasive, and thanks to him the region of Namur became a zone of refuge.[61] The municipal government provided him with false identity and rationing cards. He received assistance, financial and otherwise, from numerous Catholic individuals and clerics, among them his bishop. Hunted by the Gestapo toward the end of the war, Father André had to disperse the children and go underground, until American forces liberated Namur in September 1944.[62]

A few weeks after the Liberation, Father André turned his home over to survivors and American Jewish soldiers so they had a place to observe the High Holidays; half a year later, they returned to celebrate the Passover Seder.[63] He spent a year retrieving the children he had placed all over the country and helping Jewish families cope with the difficulties of returning to a normal life. He then devoted himself to assisting the poor, the unemployed, Muslim immigrants, foreign workers, and recently released prisoners. From 1957 until his death in 1973 he served as chaplain of the prison in Namur.[64]

In 1968, Father André was honored as a Righteous and traveled to Israel to plant his tree at Yad Vashem. A year later, he was invited to the United States. Thanks to collaboration among local authorities, hidden children, and a foundation the priest had created, a plaque was affixed on his former parish home in 1979 (see fig. 28 of the photo gallery). It reads:

> To the memory of Father Joseph André 1908–1973
>
> In this place which was the Home of the Angel he lodged and saved from deportation at the peril of his life from 1941 to 1944 many Jewish children. Then he continued to welcome here refugees and immigrants of all countries.

Father André has been honored in two additional ways. The square near the prison where he served as chaplain now bears his name. More important, in December 2005 the bishop of Namur dedicated the House of Father Joseph André, a center containing all of the region's Catholic social service organizations. In his speech at the center's opening, the bishop remarked that the plaque honoring Father André had not adequately fulfilled a wish, expressed at the priest's funeral, for a monument to be erected in his memory. He then declared his hope that naming the new facility after Father André would prove a more fitting memorial to this remarkable man.

For Brachfeld, Father André represents a potent symbol of the help Catholics provided to persecuted Jews in Belgium.[65] Yet through the ways the cleric has been honored, his actions have taken on global significance. His commemorators have insisted in giving equal weight to the work he did during and after the war. It is the assistance he extended to a multitude of disadvantaged groups that is memorialized. In effect, he has become a symbol of the modern Belgian Catholic Church's extension of its traditional charity and its concerns with the downtrodden in all of their diversity.

In the town of Ottignies, near Louvain, a stele erected in 1991 recalls Father Reynders. Born in 1903 as Henri Reynders, this Benedictine priest collaborated actively during the war with lawyer Albert Van den Berg, who established his own Resistance network to rescue Jewish adults and children. For this work Father Reynders received support from the bishop of Liège. Traveling primarily by bicycle to locate placements, Father Reynders succeeded in hiding more than three hundred children and adults. He kept detailed notes that were never found by the Germans. Hunted by the Gestapo, who raided his abbey in 1944, he went into hiding. Almost immediately, he changed into civilian clothes, wearing a beret to hide his tonsure, and continued his rescue mission.

The initiative to erect the stele in memory of Father Reynders came about because of the will and tenacity of a teacher, Johannes Blum, who also published a book about the priest. In addition to a biography, it contains numerous documents and testimonies related to his rescue activities. Blum is of German origin. When he learned of the crimes the Nazis committed during World War II, he decided to immigrate to Belgium, where he adopted citizenship. He was determined to devote his life to keeping alive the memory of those who had risked their lives to work against the Occupation and its crimes, especially Father Reynders. To achieve his goal, he created an association, Les Compagnons de la Mémoire (The Companions of Memory). The organization solicited funding for the commemorative monument to the priest. Since 1991, Blum has organized annual commemorative events at the stele for schools. The association has also branched out to videotape war testimonies and organize debates about contemporary issues and the dangers of extreme rightist ideologies. It is Blum's passionate involvement that has fueled the commemoration of Father Reynders. "We learn to cultivate memory in order to live a better today," a member of the association remarked in a speech at one of the commemorations.

A recent commemoration highlighted the way the process of recognition is not always a complete one. A gripping episode in the rescue of Jewish children that occurred on May 20, 1943, has received much attention. Andrée Geulen described it in her interview, and here are additional details. Due to a denunciation, the Gestapo suddenly arrived at the convent of the Holy Savior in Anderlecht, a Brussels suburb, where fourteen Jewish girls were hidden with the young woman who was taking care of them. The girls ranged in age from twenty months to twelve years. Sister Marie Aurélie, the head of the convent, talked the Nazis into postponing the arrests for a day so she could prepare the children for their departure and pack their belongings. When the Gestapo left, she alerted a parish priest, Father Jan Bruylandts, who was sheltering several Jewish boys. Hearing the dreadful news, Bernard Fenerberg, one of the boys, in turn informed Paul Halter, a member of the

Resistance. That evening, members of the Armée Belge des Partisans came to whisk the children away, staging the flight to appear as though it had been accomplished by force. As mentioned earlier, Sister Marie Aurélie insisted that they shoot her so as to create the appearance that the nuns had resisted. Instead, they bound and gagged the nuns, cut the telephone lines, and overturned the furniture. By the time the Gestapo arrived the next day, the girls had been safely dispersed in hiding places throughout Brussels, with the help of Andrée Geulen. Because Fenerberg had acted so decisively and rapidly, Halter allowed him to become a member of his group, though he was only seventeen years old. After the war, many people claimed that they had taken part in this audacious rescue, and Andrée Geulen felt she had to set the record straight. In 2003, the Jewish Welfare Service, the Association for the Hidden Child, and former members of the Armée Belge des Partisans ceremoniously installed a plaque on the building where the convent was once housed (see fig. 27 of the photo gallery).

The plaque's text is revelatory. It recounts the rescue of the girls from deportation and certain death. It names the members of the Resistance who took part, among them Andrée Ermel, the sole woman in the group, who served primarily as a courier. But Sister Marie-Aurélie, who made the rescue possible by arguing and bravely negotiating with the Nazis, is not mentioned at all.

Clearly, the intent was to set the historical record straight. To those responsible for the plaque, and to those who might read the plaque, the people whose names are inscribed on it were the actors who accomplished this dramatic mission. Yet, incredibly, so many years after the war, that record continues to be gendered. Though a photograph of Sister Marie-Aurélie is displayed in the Museum of Deportation in Malines, in Anderlecht the nun's brave stand appears to be forgotten entirely. It is the dramatic armed resistance feat that is commemorated here, not the quieter enabling act that made that feat possible.

By examining how the rescue of Jewish children has been commemorated, it has been possible to extend the topic beyond the Belgian case and to highlight general aspects of memorializing discourses. We have seen how memory can be institutionalized, how the legitimacy of commemoration may be contested or assured, how not only social drama but also social repair may be celebrated, how gendered memorial trajectories are constructed. Sociologist Marie-Claire Lavabre aptly characterizes memory as "the past in the present" and collective memory as the interaction between lived or transmitted experiences and their official elaboration.[66] We have seen how the hidden children's experiences were for decades in contradiction with official institutional elaborations, until finally the politics of memory and shared reminiscences led to a common interpretation of the past. Finally, the commemoration of Father André illustrates a case in which the memorial discourse is shaped beyond the confines of the events themselves in order to attribute to it a larger universal significance and a didactic intention.

Epilogue

The rescue of Jewish children in Belgium is first and foremost the story of Jews saving Jews. The first rescuers were those courageous parents who willingly tore their families apart so their children could be safely hidden. In the demonic world created by the Nazis, survival was more likely when this desperate act occurred. The Committee for the Defense of Jews, the major but not sole Resistance network saving children and adults, lived up to its double meaning: It was created *by* Jews *for* Jews. Soon after it was organized, non-Jews joined it at all levels of responsibility. In the history of the Holocaust, it serves as a template of humanitarian cooperation and civil resistance transcending religion, class, and political ideologies. Remarkably, it also managed to overcome marginality and xenophobia: It was formed in a country where 94 percent of the Jewish population was foreign-born.

While this book records intense human experiences, it was not my intention to write minibiographies. As a sociologist, I am interested in the hidden children as a group; in the social context in which connections between identity, memory, and personal narratives were made during and after the war; and in the structure of the institutions—specifically Roman Catholic ones—that were involved in rescue. I was intrigued by how these institutions affected the identities of Jewish children and how those involved have interpreted this impact over the intervening years. It was crucial to examine this relationship to reach a better understanding of the children's experiences in Belgium. As described, reactions among the youngsters varied, ranging from strong resistance to Catholic socialization to complete acceptance. In the future, it would be enriching to compare these memories to those of children who were hidden with families.

Likewise, a comparison with recollections of ex–hidden children in France and the Netherlands would be illuminating. It would draw attention to the different ways national policies shaped and politicized collective memories of war experiences.

I relied on interviews, but placed them carefully in a wider context. As many scholars have argued, people's remembering of the past is crucial to understanding events.[1] It provides significant information. The interviews offer intimate and vivid slices of life; they recount and validate experiences, often dramatic, etched in memory. Complementary to historical research, they have the power to recreate the atmosphere of daily existence and emotional suffering. And if they are presented as testimonies and stories, they can forge bonds between generations. I am particularly gratified to have interviewed so many surviving nuns and the one priest who were closely involved in the rescues. Their stories deserve to be heard.

What kind of people were the nuns? As we have seen, they had diverse personalities. But they were part of a structure and organization that enabled them to extend help much more readily than families or individuals. Living in closed institutions, the nuns were removed from direct neighborly curiosity, allowing them to better veil their activities and maintain secrecy. Since convents are hierarchal organizations in which lines of authority are clearly defined, fully respected, and imbued with a spiritual imperative, the nuns followed instructions without questioning them. The sets of rules by which convents were run—designed to fulfill spiritual goals, manage the institutions efficiently, and regulate every aspect of individual behavior—created a predictable daily routine. Separation from the outside world and predictability were particularly important features; they offered a protective contrast to the sudden brutal roundups and chaotic life that reigned outside convent walls. Though Jewish children were foreign to the nuns, the teaching orders were used to dealing with youngsters who had been removed from their parents. If necessary, they could stretch their material resources by seeking help from more prosperous orders or by begging from the community at large. As clergy, they ran fewer risks than families and individuals when sheltering children. In sum, the conditions in which they lived provided good rescue possibilities. Within the convents and orphanages, the nuns had the potential to combine fundamental goodness with Christian duty. The war offered them an extraordinary opportunity to do this; fortunately, they seized it. Of course, not all nuns displayed courage, but refusals by convents to hide children are not well documented. Father Bruno Reynders reported several instances, as did one of my interviewees.

In a more general way, this research has shown that highlighting gender and childhood offers a nuanced image of the Catholic Church. Placing nuns and hidden children at the center of my concerns has brought out the decisive role played by mothers superior in agreeing to hide Jewish children in their convents and in running their institutions in wartime under the constraints of an occupied country drained of resources. Their participation in the Resistance was not only noteworthy but also essential. In a sense, they were the end point of Resistance rescuing activity: their convents were the solution to the search for a relatively stable and secure hiding place. Without the agreement of the mothers superior, rescue would have been much harder.

The relationships between the nuns and the hidden children have been revealed in all their complexity. Given the diversity of Catholic institutions and the difficult circumstances, it is not really surprising that the treatment of the hidden children ranged from tenderness to cruelty. What is noteworthy, however, is that the situation offered some nuns the opportunity to express maternal feelings that to this day have not been forgotten.

From a wider perspective, as mentioned in chapter 4, accounts of rescue raise the general question of motive. Humanitarian values survived obliteration during the dark period of Nazi savagery. Why did rescuers act when so many remained bystanders, averting their eyes and minds from the cruel events around them? Numerous explanations for the existence of goodness in the face of evil have been suggested, in an attempt to predict when and where individuals will act heroically. Dr. Mordecai Paldiel, former director of the Righteous Among the Nations Department at Yad Vashem, has been immersed in tales of heroic rescuers. He feelingly described them as "the sparks of light which cracked the darkness of the Nazi world."[2] Drawing on philosopher Emanuel Levinas's concept of "personal ethics rooted in one's relations to others," Paldiel believes that the rescuer possesses a commitment to care and a recognition of responsibility for the other person, both of which are triggered by face-to-face encounters.[3] In fact, it was the shock of encounters with hunted and starred children that compelled Andrée Geulen and Paule Renard, the two escorts I interviewed, to join the rescue network, at the risk of torture, deportation, and death if they were caught.

Social psychologists Eva Fogelman and Samuel and Pearl Oliner attribute the rescuers' exploits to a core of solid humanitarian values and compassion acquired in childhood.[4] In her latest empirical study, Pearl Oliner also examines whether religion is a factor. Fogelman maintains that a moral imperative is important.[5] In pathbreaking works, sociologist Nechama Tec identified six characteristics of altruism shared by rescuers of the Jews.[6] These include individuality (meaning a marginal position in one's social environment), independence, a general commitment to the needy, self-appraisal as neither heroic nor extraordinary, an unplanned initial rescue act, and a universalistic perception of Jews as essentially helpless beings depending on protection from others.

All of these characteristics but one apply to Andrée Geulen and Paule Renard. They held universalistic views: to them, Jewish children had become helpless, hunted human beings; the young women considered this unacceptable, and they wanted to help. But they were *not* in marginal positions in their social milieux. In fact, of the six characteristics proposed by Tec, this one seems the most dubious in the Belgian situation. Fathers André and Bruno Reynders, for example, were solidly rooted in their environment and relied on their expansive network of connections.

Sociologist Mary Gallant places more emphasis on situational variables.[7] She maintains that where Resistance networks were strong, rescue was more likely and had a better chance of succeeding. While this was certainly true in Belgium, it still leaves unanswered the question why so few chose to join these networks.

The altruistic actions of their rescuers gave the hidden children the gift of life but could not grant them a normal childhood. Their sufferings affected their adult lives profoundly and in many ways. For example, in raising their own children, the former hidden children often lacked a parental role model. Obviously, they would have preferred parenting without bearing the weight of a painful history. They tried to shield their children from the negative impact of the past, but psychologists note repeatedly that they nevertheless transmitted their anxieties. There has been great interest in the extent to which surviving children were permanently traumatized by their experiences. Investigations range from studies examining damaged lives to those emphasizing great resilience and resistance to adversity.[8] Studies also have pointed out that disproportionate numbers of child survivors are engaged in careers in the helping professions.

Here is not the place to evaluate these diverse findings. As mentioned previously, my interviewees often referred to experiencing underlying anxieties, but these did not prevent them from developing constructive responses to their shattering experiences and leading fulfilling lives. Psychiatrist and child survivor Robert Krell recently pointed out that large-scale studies of Holocaust survivors and their children have shown that they function within the normal range when compared to Jews born and raised outside Nazi-occupied Europe.[9] However, the term "Holocaust survivor" includes so many different categories of people and such diversity of painful experiences that generalizations are difficult to establish. Much remains to be studied on this difficult topic.

In speeches honoring rescuers as Righteous Among the Nations and at other commemorative ceremonies, the former hidden children often make a link between their past and the current necessity of fighting contemporary racism, xenophobia, and the resurgence of anti-Semitism. They are simultaneously engaged in a process of empowerment and of universalization. For former escort Andrée Geulen, the connection with contemporary events is more alive than ever. The survivors realize that their very presence brings the Holocaust into the realm of the visible and puts their memories on the stage of life. As they are aging and becoming fewer in numbers, the linkage to contemporary events opens up a new space for their feelings. At the same time, it provides some reassurance that their experiences will not fade into oblivion.

In addition to showing the historical and institutional context that framed the experiences of the former hidden children, the nuns who sheltered them, and surviving Resistance escorts, this book has examined how collective memories emerge, how they are institutionalized, how gendered memorial trajectories are constructed, and how the politics of commemoration have been played out in Belgium. What remains to be seen is whether the figure of the Righteous Among the Nations will be appropriated by the Belgian state. In neighboring France, a plaque honoring the Righteous (in French, the Just) was recently very ceremoniously unveiled in the Panthéon, the building in Paris housing the remains of the country's "great men."[10] It was a widely reported media event. At the intersection of collective and individual memories, the figure of the Righteous has emerged to symbolize all those who refused to participate in the persecution of Jews by French authorities and resisted by engaging in rescue. In that discourse, the fact that the State of Israel has been the first to define and honor these heroes has been deemphasized. The Righteous have been embraced by France; by extension, they represent and unify all its resisters. These ceremonies have had an echo in Belgium. However, because of the country's deep internal divisions, the politics of commemoration play out differently and may fail to have a similar unifying effect.

Recently, researchers at the Center for Historical Research and Documentation on War and Contemporary Society in Brussels (www.cegesoma.be) have published a 1,114-page report documenting the Belgian collaboration with Nazi Germany during the war. Entitled *Docile Belgium*, it documents that "Belgium adopted a docile attitude providing collaboration unworthy of a democracy in diverse and crucial areas for a disastrous policy toward Belgian and foreign Jews."[11]

It is hard to judge so soon the overall effects of this belated acknowledgment. My book devotes much attention to the Resistance and to the Righteous Among the Nations. It provides a timely balance, in a sense even a very modest counterweight to the accusatory report and its painful revelations, for it illustrates behavior that seems now more than ever exceptional.

Throughout the book I have tried to avoid a redemptive triumphalism. This is a story of cooperation and rescue; it attests that humanitarian values survived and were not completely obliterated in the face of the Nazi horror. It is easy to be lured into a happy ending: Children were rescued and rebuilt their lives! Yet there is no triumph here. If nothing else, I hope my work illuminates and provides a deeper understanding for how so-called lucky children were cheated out of their childhoods, suffering losses and sacrifices impossible to evaluate. The haunting truth is that more than five thousand Jewish children under the age of sixteen were deported from Belgium and exterminated. Every single one should have lived.

| APPENDIX |

Nuns Honored as Righteous Among the Nations

Names are taken from the *Encyclopedia of the Righteous Among the Nations: Rescuers of Jews during the Holocaust. Belgium*, edited by Dan Michman and published by Yad Vashem (though published in 2005, this encyclopedia only records honorees until the end of 1999). Asterisks denote nuns interviewed in the book. Dates indicate when the nuns were honored by Yad Vashem. Text is taken from the encyclopedia. Page numbers refer to the specific encyclopedia entry.

1965 Sister Mathilde (Marie Leruth), Soeurs de Charité Saint Vincent de Paul, Orphelinat La Providence, Hodimont, Verviers (p. 170).

1979 Sister Ghilaine De Vogel, Paroisse Moorsel, Flanders (p. 182).

1980 Mother Marie Xavier, Mother Superior, Couvent du Sacré-Coeur, Nivelles (Nijvel), south of Brussels (p. 275).

1982 Sister Marguerite (Henrica Beyls), originally from Héverlé near Louvain, fled to Couvent des Ursulines, Auvillar (Tarn-et-Garonne), France (p. 47).

1982 Sister Céline (Germaine Robaeys), originally from Héverlé near Louvain, fled to Couvent des Ursulines, Auvillar (Tarn-et-Garonne), France (p. 221).

1982 Sister Théophilus (Marguerite Waffelaert), originally from Héverlé near Louvain fled to Couvent des Ursulines, Auvillar (Tarn-et-Garonne), France (p. 268).

1983 Sister Maria Désirée Van Gerwen (became a nun after the war; she is not included within my statistics) (p. 256).

1990 Mother Liguori (Martha Putzeys), Mother Superior, Institut Mater Dei, Couvent des Sœurs de la Charité, Louvain (p. 213).

1992 Sister Berthile, Mother Superior, Institut Imelda, Brussels (p. 45).

1992 Sister Mechtilde, Institut Imelda, Brussels (p. 45).

1992 Sister Judith Eulalie, Mother Superior, Institut Dames de Marie, Brussels (p. 115).

1992 Mother Superior Hillegonda, Couvent des Franciscaines Missionaires de Marie, Malines (p. 140).

1993 Sister Marie de St. Augustin (Nicolas), Mother Superior, Couvent Bon Pasteur, Bury-lez-Raucourt, near Bon Secours, Hainaut province (p. 196).

1994 Mother Marie Chrysostome, Mother Superior, Couvent des Carmélites, Ruiselede, northeast of Tielt, West Flanders (p. 67).

1994 Sister Madeleine Hospel, Mother Superior, Soeurs de Notre Dame, Chimay, Hainaut (p. 142).

1994 *Sister Marthe Sibille, Soeurs de Notre-Dame, Chimay, Hainaut (p. 142).

1994 Mother Superior Marie-Agnès, Notre Dame des Sept Douleurs, Brussels (p. 180).

1994 Sister Marie Eustelle, Notre Dame des Sept Douleurs, Brussels (p. 180).

1994 Sister Marie Cécile, Notre Dame des Sept Douleurs, Brussels (p. 180).

1994 Sister Odonia, Franciscan Couvent des Franciscaines, Doel, north of Antwerp (p. 200).

1994 Sister Roberta, Couvent des Franciscaines, Doel, north of Antwerp (p. 200).

1994 Sister Marie Thérèse Thierry, in charge of clinic, Bertrix, near Neufchateau, Luxembourg province (p. 242).

1995 Sister Madeleine Herbecq, Mother Superior, Clinique St. Elisabeth Ecole d'Infirmières, Bois de Breux, Chênée near Liège (p. 138).

1995 Sister Germaine Bribosia, Clinique St. Elisabeth Ecole d'Infirmières, Bois de Breux, Chênée near Liège (p. 138).

1995 Sister Madeleine Moguet, Clinique St. Elisabeth Clinic Ecole d'Infirmières, Bois de Breux, Chênée near Liège (p. 138).

1995 Sister Urbaine (Marie Josephine Schoofs), Mother Superior, Soeurs de la Charité, Notre Dame du Bon Conseil, Auderghem (Brussels) (p. 229).

*Sister Marie-Reine (Hubertina Verstappen), Sister Rodriguez (Franziska Catharina Weber), and *Sister Bridget (Bridget Fitzgerald) lived in this convent and are given an honorary mention in the Encyclopedia (p. 229).

1996 Sister Eugénie Bertrand, Mother Superior, orphanage, Wasmes, near Mons (p. 46).

1996 Sister Louise-Marie (Claire Delepaut), Mother Superior, Ecole Sainte Lutgarde, Lasne, near Waterloo (p. 88).

1996 Sister Ferraille, Institut Médical des Dames Hospitalières du Sacré Cœur, Brussels (p. 117).

1997 Sister Marie Gérard (Agnès Coussemaeker), Mother Superior, Institut de la Providence, Templeneuve, west of Tournai (p. 74).

1997 Sister Aline de la Purification (Germaine Delcuigne), Mother Superior, Filles de la Sagesse, Durbuy (p. 87).

1997 Sister Véronique Overkamp, Couvent des Soeurs de Misericordia, St. Georges-sur-Meuse, southwest of Liège (p. 202).

1998 Sister Euthalie, Mother Superior, Institut Saint Joseph des Sœurs de la Miséricorde, Rosseignies, Hainaut (p. 115).

1998 Sister Germaine (Maria De Pauw), Institut Saint Joseph des Sœurs de la Miséricorde, Rosseignies, Hainaut (p. 115).

1998 Sister Berthe Naveau De Marteau, Mother Superior, Couvent du Sacré Cœur, Jette (Brussels) (p. 194).

1998 Sister Dora (Anna Otto), Mother Superior, Couvent de Notre Dame de Sion, Antwerp (p. 201).

1999 Mother Cécile Stinger, Couvent de la Miséricorde, Héverlé, near Louvain (p. 239).

1999 *Sister Marie Beirens, Couvent de la Miséricorde, Héverlé, near Louvain (p. 239).

1999 Sister Marie Alphonse Vandermolen, Mother Superior, Weeshuis Onze Lieve Vrouw, Herenthals, east of Antwerp (p. 262).

Names of honorees after 1999, obtained by correspondence with Dr. Mordecai Paldiel, former director of the Righteous Among the Nations Department at Yad Vashem; Irena Steinfeldt, current director of the Righteous Among the Nations Department at Yad Vashem; and Helene Potezman of the Israel Embassy in Brussels.

2000 Sister Marie-Ignace (Jeanne Richard), Institut Michotte, Liège.

2001 Sister Marie Louise, Soeurs Franciscaines, Soignies.

2001 Sister Marie-Aurélie (Eugénie Leloup), Les Sœurs du Très Saint Sauveur, Anderlecht (Brussels).

2001 Sister Andrée Frère, Pauvres Sœurs de Mons, Ciney.

2001 Sister Véronique Van Acker, Pauvres Sœurs de Mons, Ciney.

2002 Sister Emilie (Catherine Yvens), Filles de la Croix, Ecole Ste. Julienne, Bois de Breux, Chênée, near Liège.

2003 *Sister Hélène Baggen, Couvent St. Vincent de Paul, Louvain.

2003 Sister Léontine Van Schoonbeeck, Couvent St. Vincent de Paul, Louvain.

2006 Mother Raphaël (Thérèse Falise). Abbaye Bénédictine Paix Notre-Dame, Liège.

| NOTES |

Introduction

1. The concept of the "hidden children" has been used only since the last decade of the twentieth century to describe children concealed in many ways from the Nazis in order to escape annihilation.

2. Maerten, Selleslagh, and Van den Wijngaert (1999, 9, 91).

3. M. Steinberg (1983, 1998).

4. Dwork (1991, 32); Fogelman (1993, 293).

5. Frydman (1999, especially 202–207).

6. Silberman (1995, 4).

7. Dwork (1991, 270).

8. Fogelman (1993, 307).

9. Michman (2000, 20–38).

10. Friedländer (1991, 182).

Chapter 1

1. Schram (2004, 272).

2. Interview with the author in Brussels, April 7, 2000.

3. Dequecker (2000, 237).

4. Hellemans (2005).

5. The American Jewish Joint Distribution Committee, commonly referred to as the Joint or JDC, is an organization that has aided millions of Jews throughout the world since its founding in 1914. During World War II, it secretly provided funds to the Resistance in Belgium through Switzerland. After the war, it funded for many years the institutions that cared for the Jewish orphans.

6. The Nazis set up the Association des Juifs en Belgique (AJB; Association of Jews in Belgium), through which they sought to control the Jewish population. This organization was responsible for social welfare and was ordered to set up orphanages for children of deported parents and old-age homes. These were in reality holding pens. Their occupants, children and the elderly, could be deported at any time by Nazi decision. At the end of the war, as the Germans were preparing to deport the children from the orphanages in their last convoy to Auschwitz, the AJB disbanded and appealed to the Resistance to disperse the children and hide them in safe places. In a couple of days, six hundred children were hidden in a marathon operation. Andrée refers to the children from one of the AJB orphanages located in Wezembeek who arrived suddenly to be sheltered temporarily in her convent.

7. De Vos (2004, 210).

8. The most illustrious example of a Judeo-Christian is the recently deceased Cardinal Jean Marie Lustiger, the head of the Catholic Church of France and the archbishop of Paris. Born a Jew in 1926, he converted to Catholicism when he was thirteen years old. When he was reproached for his conversion, he would insist that he was as Jewish as all the members of his family who were exterminated in Auschwitz and other camps. In August 2007, his funeral in Notre Dame Cathedral in Paris began with the chanting of Kaddish, the Jewish prayer for the dead.

CHAPTER 2

1. Hellemans (2005).

2. Liebman (2005).

3. For more details on Jacques the Jewish traitor, see M. Steinberg (1987, 2: 191–217).

4. This was the fate of the principal of the boarding school Gatti de Gamond in Brussels and of her husband. The Resistance escort Andrée Geulen was living and teaching in that school.

5. This last point is appropriately illustrated in my interview with Sister Casaer.

6. De Vos (2004, 210).

7. Eddy Louchez argues that in order to survive, one had to use the black market (see Louchez 1999, 119).

8. The Secours d' Hiver was a social welfare organization created in October 1940 under German auspices to distribute additional food, soup, and cod liver oil to school children.

9. A coalition of local Resistance groups.

10. McNamara (1996, 613).

11. De Vos (2004, 210); Struye and Jacquemyns (2002).

12. Quoted by Sister Casaer in the alumnae newsletter she kindly sent me, *Paridaens Driemaandelijkse Kroniek*, 1988, in her article "Wat Niemand Weten Mocht," p. 8.

13. De Meyer (2005, 45).

14. The Oeuvre Nationale de l'Enfance (ONE; National Children's Bureau) was a Belgian government—subsidized agency supervising children's homes and childcare services. It was created in 1919 to promote children's health and reduce child mortality.

15. M.-E. Hanoteau, quoted in Wynants (2000, 244, my translation).

16. Wynants (2000, 249).

17. Ibid., 256.

18. Ibid., 253.

19. M.-J. Aubert, quoted in Wynants (1992, 84).

20. Ibid.

21. Wynants (1992, 84).

22. Ibid., 85.

23. Ibid., 88.

Chapter 3

1. Paule Andriesse-Renard died in October 2006.

2. The expression "White Russian" was used to designate the forces who fought against the Bolshevik Red Russians and communism in the aftermath of the 1917 revolution. By extension, the term refers to Russian traditionalist exiles who emigrated after the Red revolution.

3. In our interview, Paule said that she had been fired. However, in a subsequent conversation Andrée Geulen stated that Paule had left voluntarily. I attempted to check the two different versions. In telephone conversations Catherine Massange, the most expert historian of the Aide aux Israélites Victimes de Guerre (AIVG), and Irène Zmigrod-

Rosenstein, an AIVG social worker in the immediate postwar period, both thought that Paule's version was unlikely. Both stated that the AIVG had no systematic policy for preferential Jewish employment and had continuously employed both Jewish and non-Jewish social workers. It is plausible that Paule left the AIVG for financial reasons.

4. Lagrou (2000a).

5. Paldiel (2000, 298).

6. Michman (2005, 128).

7. Baumann (2005, 11).

8. Loncin (2006, 2–3).

9. La boite à images (2006, 1).

10. Andrée Geulen kindly provided this description in a letter to me, May 24, 2006.

11. For more details about the notorious Jewish traitor, Jacques, who was employed by the Gestapo to detect Jews by examining their physiognomy, their accents, and their gestures, see M. Steinberg (1987, vol. 2, chap. 6).

12. Baumann (2005, 13).

13. Schreiber (2004, 173).

14. In 1938–1939, nearly ten thousand Jewish children from Germany, Austria, Poland, and Czechoslovakia were allowed to emigrate without their parents to England, Belgium, and the Netherlands in groups called Kindertransports. Most of them never saw their parents again.

15. Scheraga (2006).

16. Maurice Heiber, the head of the Committee for the Defense of Jews, was arrested. See M. Steinberg (1987, 1: 159). He was later released. A photo of Sister Marie Aurélie is displayed in the Museum of Deportation and Resistance in Malines.

17. The archbishop of Toulouse, Monseigneur Saliège, openly protested the treatment of Jews in his pastoral letter of August 1942, writing: "The Jews are human beings, they are our brethren. A Christian may never forget it" (Gensburger 2004, 25). See also M. Steinberg (1998, 64). Monseigneur Théas of Montauban and Cardinal Gerlier of Lyon also expressed protests.

18. Saerens (1999).

19. Andrée Geulen disagreed with the psychologist Marcel Frydman (1999), who emphasized the traumatization of the hidden children.

20. Michman (2005, 128); Paldiel (2000, 300).

21. Andrée Geulen kindly gave me the full text of her speech.

22. Tec (1998).

23. Fogelman (1998).

24. M. Steinberg (2004, 307–308).

25. Schram (2004, 272–273).

26. Selleslagh (1993); Warmbrunn (1993).

27. Warmbrunn (1993, 232).

28. See note 3 for another version.

29. Fogelman (1998, 673).

30. Lagrou (2000b, 40).

31. L. Steinberg (1978, 137).

32. M. Steinberg (1987, 20).

33. Brachfeld (2001, 192); M. Steinberg (1998, 98).

34. M. Steinberg (1984).

35. Michman (2004, 319–340) argues that the Germans developed two models of headship: a local one—usually called the Judenrat or Jewish Council—and a countrywide one. The AJB was the latter. Michman thinks this model was less "useful" to the Nazis.

36. Lagrou (2000b, 48).

37. L. Steinberg (1978, 141).

38. Brachfeld (2001, 93); M. Steinberg (1998, 130–136).

39. Michman (2005, 194–195).

40. Nèvejean was the first woman honored for her own actions and not as part of a couple. In 1964, the Lozdyck and Van Haesendonck couples were honored; Queen Elizabeth was honored in May 1965, and Sister Mathilde Marie Leruth in September 1965.

41. Semelin (1993, 2001).

42. A recent and extensive report by Belgian historians entitled *Docile Belgium*, presented to the Belgian Senate in 2007, documents the widespread collaboration of governmental authorities at all levels with the Nazi persecution of Jews.

43. Semelin (1993, 96), mentioning also that no similar denouncing ever occurred about deportations of Jews.

44. Maerten (2006).

45. Maerten (1989).

46. Ibid., 170.

47. Verhoeyen (1992).

48. Schwartz (1987, 147).

49. Higonnet and Higonnet (1987, 38).

50. Quoted in Moore (2000, 55).

CHAPTER 4

1. Young (1988).

2. Friedländer (1991, 155).

3. Interview with Sophie Rechtman, president of the Belgian Association of the Hidden Child, in Brussels, March 22, 2000. She also said, "I did not see myself as a hidden child, but as a child of a deportee."

4. Lagrou (2000a, 290).

5. Ibid., 290–291.

6. Wievorka (1999).

7. The film is focused on the rescue of Jewish children by the Committee for the Defense of Jews. It does not include earlier rescue initiatives. For example, Fela Liwer Perelman, with the help of Jeanne Daman, dispersed and rescued children from the Jewish schools she had created by hiding them with private Belgian families (Michman 2005, 77–78; personal communication from Noémi Perelman-Mattis).

8. http://www.adl.org/hidden/history.asp.

9. Halbwachs (1925, 1941, 1980).

10. Langer (1995).

11. Vromen (1986, 2007b).

12. Ricoeur (1999).

13. Halbwachs (1980); Yerushalmi (1982).

14. Sennett (1998).

15. Zerubavel (1996).

16. Wagner-Pacifici (1996, 301).

17. Gensburger (2004); Laqueur (2001, 697–700).

18. Young (1988, 246; my emphasis).

19. Ibid.

20. Yad Vashem has recently greatly expanded its museum and all its facilities.

21. Michman (2005, xiv).

22. Gensburger (2004, 29; my translation).

23. *Julius Caesar*, act 3, scene 2. I thank my friend Yaffa Schlesinger for reminding me of this quotation.

24. Gensburger (2004, 33).

25. Paldiel (1993, 3).

26. Ibid.

27. Wagner-Pacifici (1996, 303).

28. Gensburger (2002, 315).

29. The historian Sylvain Brachfeld secured the title of Righteous Among the Nations for his rescuer, Sister Leruth, in 1965, one of the earliest nominations for Belgium.

30. Olick and Robbins (1998).

31. Yad Vashem Web site, www.yadvashem.org.

32. These numbers were obtained from Michman (2005), Brachfeld (1989, 2001), and correspondence with Helene Potezman of the Israeli Embassy in Brussels; Dr. Mordecai Paldiel, former director of the Righteous Among the Nations Department at Yad Vashem in Jerusalem; and Irena Steinfeldt, the department's current director.

33. The obituary for the mother superior provided by Sister Beirens calls her Cécile Stinger. However, Michman (2005) gives her name as Cécile Stingers.

34. Semelin (2001, 5).

35. See also Gensburger (2002).

36. Semelin (2001).

37. Greenberg (2003).

38. Greenberg (2003); Higonnet et al. (1987); Weitz (1995).

39. See especially the essays on this subject in Michman (2000) and in Maerten et al. (1999).

40. Louchez (1999, 107).

41. The time I spent in the archives of the archbishop of Malines was one of the most poignant parts of my research. When I held in my hands the letters soliciting the cardinal's help, many handwritten, some struggling with the language, they reflected despair so vividly that they left me sobbing.

42. Hellemans (2004, 187).

43. Massange (1999, 2001).

44. Papeleux (1981, 189).

45. Ibid.

46. Ibid., 190.

47. Ibid., 191–192.

48. Hellemans (2004, 193).

49. Dequecker (2000, 264).

50. Hellemans (2004, 188).

51. Brachfeld (2001, 163); Hellemans (2004, 200).

52. Hellemans (2004, 215).

53. Brachfeld (2001, 165); Hellemans (2004, 211).

54. Elias (2001).

55. Brachfeld (2001, 165); Hellemans (2004, 207).

56. Hellemans (2004, 218).

57. Hellemans (2004, 218) cites Dequeker (2000, 253) as her source for eighty-five as the number of children in Catholic hands, but Dequeker only mentions eighty-three.

58. Hellemans (2004, 215).

59. Blum (1993, 252); Brachfeld (2001, 106); Michman (2005, 219).

60. Dequecker (2000, 261).

61. M. Steinberg (1987, 163).

62. Brachfeld (2001, 100–102); Michman (2005, 36).

63. Brachfeld (2001, 100).

64. www.diocesdenamur.be/Eveque.

65. Brachfeld (2001, 104).

66. Lavabre (2001).

EPILOGUE

1. Among such scholars are Bauer (2001) and Thompson (2000, 172).

2. Paldiel (2000, 268).

3. Paldiel (2001, 343).

4. Fogelman (1994, 1998); S. Oliner (1998); P. Oliner (2004); Oliner and Oliner (1988).

5. Fogelman's book *Conscience and Courage* is to this day the most nuanced and compelling analysis of rescuers written in English.

6. Tec (1986, 1998).

7. Gallant (2001).

8. See Hogman (1988), Helmreich (1992), Fogelman (1993), Frydman (1999), Kraft (2002), Suedfeld (2001), Moskovitz (1983), Gallant (2002), Bluglass (2003), and Unglick (2004).

9. Glassner and Krell (2006).

10. For details about the Panthéon—the building and its shifting functions—see Vromen (1995).

11. The report was presented to the Belgian Senate on February 13, 2007. The quotation is from the Jewish Telegraphic Agency news, quoted in *The Voice of the Dutchess Jewish Community* 18 (2007) 3: 20.

| REFERENCES |

Aubert, Roger. 1980. 150 ans de vie des eglises. Brussels: Paul Legrain éditeur.

Baer, Elizabeth, and Myrna Goldenberg, eds. 2003. *Experience and Expression: Women, the Nazis and the Holocaust*. Detroit: Wayne State University Press.

Bankier, David, and Israel Gutman, eds. 2003. *Nazi Europe and the Final Solution*. Jerusalem: Yad Vashem.

Bartov, Omer. 1997. "Chambers of Horror: Holocaust Museums in Israel and the United States." *Israel Studies* 2, 2: 66–87.

Bauer, Yehuda. 2001. *Rethinking the Holocaust*. New Haven, Conn.: Yale University Press.

Baumann, Roland. 2005. "Andrée Geulen-Herscovici: Une vie de lutte pour l'humanité en danger." *Regards* 587: 10–13.

Berenbaum, Michael, and Abraham J. Peck, eds. 1998. *The Holocaust and History: The Known, the Unknown, the Disputed, and the Reexamined*. Bloomington: Indiana University Press.

Bigsby, Christopher. 2006. *Remembering and Imagining the Holocaust: The Chain of Memory*. New York: Cambridge University Press.

Bluglass, Kerry. 2003. *Hidden from the Holocaust: Stories of Resilient Children Who Survived and Thrived*. Westport, Conn.: Praeger.

Blum, Johannes, ed. 1993. *Résistance: Père Bruno Reynders juste des nations*. Brussels: Les Carrefours de La Cité.

Brachfeld, Sylvain. 1989. *Ils n'ont pas eu les gosses*. Herzlia, Israel: Institut de recherche sur le judaïsme belge (2nd ed. 1993).

———. 2001. *Ils ont survécu: Le sauvetage des juifs en belgique occupée.* Brussels: Editions Racine.

Buchignani, Walter. 1994. *Tell No One Who You Are: The Hidden Childhood of Régine Miller.* Plattsburgh, N.Y.: Tundra Books.

Le Cardinal Van Roey et l'occupation allemande en belgique: Actes et documents publiés par le chanoine Leclef. 1945. Brussels: M. Goemare.

Courtois, Luc, Jean Pirotte, and Françoise Rosart, eds. 1989. *Femmes des années 80: Un siècle de condition féminine en belgique (1889–1989).* Louvain-la Neuve: Academia.

———. 1992. *Femmes et pouvoirs: Flux et reflux de l'émancipation féminine depuis un siècle.* Brussels: Editions Nauwelaerts.

Dantoing, Alain. 1991. *La "collaboration" du Cardinal: L'eglise de belgique dans la guerre 40.* Brussels: De Boeck-Wesmael.

De Meyer, Marc. 2005. *De kleine memoires Paridaens 1805–2005.* Wetteren, Belgium: Erasmus.

Dequeker, Luc. [1998] 2000. "Baptism and Conversion of Jews in Belgium, 1939–1945." In Michman 2000, 235–271.

Dermience, Alice. 1992. "Femmes et pouvoir dans l'eglise catholique, 1889–1989." In Courtois et al. 1992, 115–129.

———. 2000. "L'émergence des femmes dans les eglises chrétiennes depuis les années ciquante." *Revue d'histoire ecclésiastique* 95, 3: 327–342.

De Vos, Luc. 2004. *La belgique et la seconde guerre mondiale.* Brussels: Editions Racine.

Dratwa, Daniel. [1998] 2000. "Genocide and Its Memories: A Preliminary Study of How Belgian Jewry Coped with the Results of the Holocaust." In Michman 2000, 523–555.

Dwork, Deborah. 1991. *Children with a Star: Jewish Youth in Nazi Europe.* New Haven, Conn.: Yale University Press.

Elias, Henri. 2001. "The Long Way Home: A Belgian Finaly Affair." *Hidden Child* 10, 1: 3, 11, 15.

Fara, Patricia, and Karalyn Patterson, eds. 1998. *Memory.* Cambridge: Cambridge University Press.

Fein, Helen. 1979. *Accounting for Genocide: National Responses and Jewish Victimization during the Holocaust.* New York: Free Press.

Fogelman, Eva. 1993. "The Psychology behind Being a Hidden Child." In Marks 1993, 292–307.

———. 1994. *Conscience and Courage: Rescuers of Jews during the Holocaust.* New York: Anchor Doubleday.

———. 1998. "The Rescuer Self." In Berenbaum and Peck 1998, 663–677.

———. 2002. "A Tenth-Year Follow-Up to the First International Gathering of the Hidden Child." *Hidden Child* 11, 1: 3, 6.

Friedländer, Saul. [1979] 1991. *When Memory Comes*. New York: Farrar Straus and Giroux.

———. 1993. *Memory, History and the Extermination of the Jews of Europe*. Bloomington: Indiana University Press.

Frydman, Marcel. 1999. *Le traumatisme de l'enfant caché: Répercussions psychologiques à court et à long termes*. Gerpinnes, Belgium: Editions Quorum.

Gallant, Mary J. 2001. "Social Dimensions of Rescue in the Holocaust." In Roth and Maxwell 2001, 2: 254–270.

———. 2002. *Coming of Age in the Holocaust: The Last Survivors Remember*. Lanham, Md.: University Press of America.

Gensburger, Sarah. 2002. "Les figures du juste et du résistant et l'évolution de la mémoire historique française de l'occupation." *Revue française de science politique* 2: 291–322.

———. 2004. "La création du titre de juste parmi les nations: 1953–1963." *Bulletin du centre de recherche français de Jérusalem*, November, 15–35.

Gérard-Libois, J., and José Gotovitch. 1971. *L'an 40 la belgique occupée*. Brussels: CRISP.

Gerson, Judith M., and Diane L. Wolf, eds. 2007. *Sociology Confronts the Holocaust: Memories and Identities in Jewish Diasporas*. Durham, N.C.: Duke University Press.

Gilbert, Martin. 2003. *The Righteous: The Unsung Heroes of the Holocaust*. New York: Holt.

Glassner, Martin Ira, and Robert Krell, eds. 2006. *And Life Is Changed Forever: Holocaust Childhoods Remembered*. Detroit: Wayne State University Press.

Goris, Jan-Albert. 1943. *Belgium in Bondage*. New York: L. B. Fischer.

Greenberg, Judith. 2003. "Paths of Resistance: French Women Working from the Inside." In Baer and Goldenberg 2003, 131–160.

Gross, Alan G., and Ray D. Dearin. 2003. *Chaïm Perelman*. Albany: State University of New York Press.

Guéno, Jean-Pierre, ed. 2002. *Paroles d'étoiles mémoire d'enfants cachés (1939–1945)*. Paris: Librio.

Halbwachs, Maurice. 1925. *Les cadres sociaux de la mémoire*. Paris: Alcan.

———. 1941. *La topographie légendaire des evangiles en Terre Sainte: Etude de mémoire collective*. Paris: Alcan.

———. 1980. *The Collective Memory*. New York: Harper.

Hartman, Geoffrey H., ed. 1994. *Holocaust Remembrance: The Shapes of Memory*. Oxford: Blackwell.

Hayes, Peter, ed. 1991. *The Meaning of the Holocaust in a Changing World*. Evanston, Ill.: Northwestern University Press.

Hellemans, Hanne. 2004. "Tot wie behoordt de ziel van het kind? De herintegratie van kinderen in de joodse gemeeschap na de Tweede Wereldoorlog." *Cahiers d'Histoire du Temps Présent* 13–14: 187–223.

———. 2005. Online untitled manuscript in Dutch about the Jewish children hidden during the war and the problems of their reintegration into the Jewish community after the war.

Helmreich, William B. 1992. *Against All Odds: Holocaust Survivors and the Successful Lives They Made in America*. New York: Simon & Schuster.

Herskovic, Patricia. 2002. *Escape to Life: A Journey through the Holocaust*. Jerusalem: Yad Vashem.

Higonnet, Margaret R., and Patrice L.-R. Higonnet. 1987. "The Double Helix." In Higonnet et al. 1987, 31–47.

Higonnet, Margaret R., Jane Jenson, Sonya Michel, and Margaret Collins Weitz, eds. 1987. *Behind the Lines: Gender and the Two World Wars*. New Haven, Conn.: Yale University Press.

Hirsch, Marianne. 1997. *Family Frames*. Cambridge, Mass.: Harvard University Press.

Hoffman, Eva. 2004. *After Such Knowledge: Memory, History and the Legacy of the Holocaust*. New York: Public Affairs.

Hogman, Flora. 1988. "The Experience of Catholicism for Jewish Children during World War II." *Psychoanalytic Review* 75, 2: 511–532.

Huyse, Luc. 2002. "Waarom Belgie ziek is van zijn jaren veertig." *Cahiers d'histoire du temps présent* 10: 185–193.

Iglinski-Goodman, Leah. 2003. *For Love of Life*. London: Valentine Mitchell.

Kearny, Richard, and Mark Dooley, eds. 1999. *Questioning Ethics: Contemporary Debates in Philosophy*. London: Routledge.

Kattan, Emmanuel. 2002. *Le devoir de mémoire*. Paris: Presses universitaires de France.

Klempner, Mark. 2006. *The Heart Has Reasons: Holocaust Rescuers and Their Stories of Courage*. Cleveland: Pilgrim Press.

Kless, Shlomo. 1988. "The Rescue of Jewish Children in Belgium." *Holocaust and Genocide Studies* 3, 3: 275–287.

Kraft, Robert N. 2002. *Memory Perceived: Recalling the Holocaust*. Westport, Conn.: Praeger.

Kurek, Ewa. 1997. *Your Life Is Worth Mine: How Polish Nuns Saved Hundreds of Jewish Lives in German-Occupied Poland, 1939–1945*. New York: Hippocrene Books.

La boite à images. 2006. "1940–45: Un combat pour la liberté." www.laboiteaimages .be/images/galeries/christophe_smets/un_combat/temoignage2htm.

Lagrou, Pieter. 1997. "Victims of Genocide and National Memory: Belgium, France and the Netherlands 1945–1965." *Past and Present* 154: 181–222.

———. 2000a. *The Legacy of Nazi Occupation: Patriotic Memory and National Recovery in Western Europe, 1945–1965*. Cambridge: Cambridge University Press.

———. 2000b. "Belgium." In Moore 2000, 27–63.

Langer, Lawrence. 1991. *Holocaust Testimonies: The Ruins of Memory*. New Haven, Conn.: Yale University Press.

———. 1995. *Admitting the Holocaust*. New York: Oxford University Press.

Laqueur, Walter, ed. 2001. *The Holocaust Encyclopedia*. New Haven, Conn.: Yale University Press.

Lavabre, Marie-Claire. 1994. "Usages du passé, usages de la mémoire." *Revue française de science politique* 44, 3: 480–483.

———. 1998. "Maurice Halbwachs et la sociologie de la mémoire." *Raison présente* 128: 47–56.

———. 2001. "Peut-on agir sur la mémoire?" *Les cahiers français* 303: 8–13.

Levy, Daniel, and Natan Sznaider. 2002. "Memory Unbound: The Holocaust and the Formation of Cosmopolitan Memory." *European Journal of Social Theory* 53.1: 87–106.

Liebman, Marcel. 2005. *Born Jewish: A Childhood in Occupied Europe*. London: Verso.

Loebl, Suzanne. 1997. *At the Mercy of Strangers: Growing Up on the Edge of the Holocaust*. Pacifica, Calif.: Pacifica Press.

Loncin, Joost. 2006. "Redt onze kinderen." In *Verzet.org Het Joods Verdedigingscomiteit* (JVC/CDJ), pp. 2–4. www.verzet.org/content/view/351/37/1/3/.

Louchez, Eddy. 1999. "Les congrégations religieuses sous l'occupation." In Maerten et al. 1999, 91–126.

Maerten, Fabrice. 1989. "Les femmes dans la résistance pendant la seconde guerre mondiale: Vers une plus grande part de responsabilités." In Courtois et al. 1989, 165–175.

———. 1998. "La résistance, facteur d'émancipation des femmes? Le cas du Hainaut." *Cahiers d'histoire du temps présent* 4: 173–206.

———. 2005. "The Resistance Movement: A Mirror of Belgian Society?" Paper presented at symposium entitled "Resistance and Memory in Belgium, 1940–1945," Cooper Union, New York City, October 28, 2005.

———. 2006. "La résistance en belgique, 1940–1944." In *Le Fort de Breendonk: Le camp de la terreur nazie en belgique pendant la seconde guerre mondiale, dossier pédagogique*. 3rd ed. Brussels: Editions Racine, 33–59.

Maerten, Fabrice, Franz Selleslagh, and Mark Van den Wijngaert, eds. 1999. *Entre la peste et le choléra: Vie et attitude des catholiques belges sous l'occupation*. Gerpinnes, Belgium: Editions Quorum/Ceges/Arca.

Marks, Jane. 1993. *The Hidden Children: The Secret Survivors of the Holocaust*. New York: Fawcett Columbine.

Massange, Catherine. 1999. "De l'aide aux Israélites victimes de la guerre au service social juif." *Les cahiers de la mémoire contemporaine* 1: 157–167.

———. 2001. "Hirondelles et Aiglons: Les adolescents de l'AIVG." *Les cahiers de la mémoire contemporaine* 3: 175–212.

McNamara, Jo Ann Kay. 1996. *Sisters in Arms: Catholic Nuns through Two Millennia.* Cambridge, Mass.: Harvard University Press.

Michman, Don, ed. [1998] 2000. *Belgium and the Holocaust: Jews Belgians Germans.* 2nd ed. Jerusalem: Yad Vashem.

———. 2003. "Problematic National Identity, Outsiders and Persecution: Impact of the Gentile Population's Attitude in Belgium on the Fate of the Jews in 1940–1944." In Bankier and Gutman 2003, 455–468.

———. 2004. "Jewish Leadership in *Extremis*." In Stone 2004, 319–340.

———, ed. 2005. *The Encyclopedia of the Righteous Among the Nations: Rescuers of Jews during the Holocaust. Belgium.* Jerusalem: Yad Vashem.

Moore, Bob, ed. 2000. *Resistance in Western Europe.* New York: Berg.

Moskovitz, Sarah. 1983. *Love Despite Hate: Child Survivors of the Holocaust and Their Adult Lives.* New York: Schocken Books.

Muchman, Béatrice. 1997. *Never to Be Forgotten: A Young Girl's Holocaust Memoir.* Hoboken, N.J.: Ktav.

Nysenholc, Adolphe. 2004. *Le livre des homes: Enfants de la Shoah AIVG, 1945–1959.* Brussels: Didier Devillez Editeur.

Olick, Jeffrey K., and Joyce Robbins. 1998. "Social Memory Studies: From 'Collective Memory' to the Historical Sociology of Mnemonic Practices." *Annual Review of Sociology* 24: 105–140.

Oliner, Pearl M. 2004. *Saving the Forsaken: Religious Culture and the Rescue of Jews in Nazi Europe.* New Haven, Conn.: Yale University Press.

Oliner, Samuel P., and Pearl Oliner. 1988. *The Altruistic Personality: Rescuers of Jews in Nazi Europe.* Toronto: Maxwell Macmillan Canada.

Oliner, Samuel P. 1998. "Rescuers of Jews during the Holocaust: A Portrait of Moral Courage." In Berenbaum and Peck 1998, 678–697.

Paldiel, Mordecai. 1993. *The Path of the Righteous: Gentile Rescuers of Jews during the Holocaust.* Hoboken, N.J.: Ktav.

———. 2000. *Saving the Jews: Amazing Stories of Men and Women Who Defied the "Final Solution."* Rockville, Md.: Schreiber.

———. 2001. "The Face of the Other: Reflections on the Motivations of Gentile Rescuers of Jews." In Roth and Maxwell 2001, 2: 334–346.

Papeleux, Léon. 1981. "Le réseau Van den Berg qui sauva des centaines de juifs." *La vie wallonne* 55: 129–208.

Perks, Robert, and Alistair Thomson, eds. 1998. *The Oral History Reader.* London: Routledge.

Rajsfus, Maurice. 1994. *N'oublie pas le petit Jésus: L'eglise catholique et les enfants juifs (1940–1945).* Levallois-Perret, France: Editions Manya.

Ricoeur, Paul. 1999. "Memory and Forgetting." In Kearny and Dooley 1999, 5–17.

Ringelheim, Foulek. 1987. "Les juifs entre la mémoire et l'oubli: Avant-propos." *Revue de l'Université de Bruxelles*, 1–2: 5–10.

Rings, Werner. 1982. *Life with the Enemy: Collaboration and Resistance in Hitler's Europe 1939–1945*. Garden City, N.Y.: Doubleday.

Rosenfeld, Alvin, ed. 1997. *Thinking about the Holocaust after Half a Century*. Bloomington: Indiana University Press.

Rossiter, Margaret L. 1986. *Women in the Resistance*. New York: Praeger.

Roth, John K., and Elisabeth Maxwell, eds. 2001. *Remembering for the Future: The Holocaust in an Age of Genocide*. 3 vols. New York: Palgrave.

Saerens, Lieven. 1999. "L'aide des catholiques aux juifs dans l'Archevêché de Malines." In Maerten et al. 1999, 208–237.

———. 2003. "Inleiding: Dossier Brussel en de joodse kwestie." *Cahiers d'histoire du temps présent* 12: 125–139.

Scheraga, Hilde. 2006. "My Red Chesterfield Coat." In Glassner and Krell 2006, 127–138.

Schram, Laurence. 2004. "La distribution de l'étoile." In Schreiber and Van Doorslaer 2004, 263–276.

Schreiber, Jean-Philippe. 2002. "La belgique et les juifs sous l'occupation nazie: L'histoire au-delà des mythes." *Les cahiers de la mémoire contemporaine* 4: 59–97.

Schreiber, Jean-Philippe, and Rudi Van Doorslaer, eds. 2004. *Les curateurs du ghetto: L'association des juifs en belgique sous l'occupation nazie*. Brussels: Editions Labor.

Schwartz, Paula. 1987. "Redefining Resistance: Women's Activism in Wartime France." In Higonnet et al. 1987, 141–153.

Selleslagh, Franz, ed. 1993. *Le travail obligatoire en allemagne*. Actes du symposium tenu à Bruxelles le 6 et 7 octobre 1992. Brussels: CREHSGM.

Semelin, Jacques. 1993. *Unarmed against Hitler: Civilian Resistance in Europe 1939–1943*. Westport, Conn.: Praeger.

———. 2001/2002. "Résister sans armes face à Hitler. Quelques clés pour comprendre..." *Alternatives non violentes* 121: 6–15. Institut de recherche sur la Résolution non Violente des Conflits, www.irnc.org/ANV/index.htm; also found in Centre de Ressources sur la Non-Violence de Midi-Pyréneés, http://www.non-violence-mp.org/la%20non violence_fichiers/histresista.

Sennett, Richard. 1998. "Disturbing Memories." In Fara and Patterson 1998, 10–27.

Servais, Emile, and Francis Hambye. 1971. "Structure et signification: Problème de méthode en sociologie des organizations claustrales." *Social Compass* 18, 1: 27–44.

Shapiro, Robert Moses, ed. 1999. *Holocaust Chronicles: Individualizing the Holocaust through Diaries and Other Contemporaneous Personal Accounts*. Hoboken, N.J.: Ktav.

Silberman, Lili. 1995. "Beyond Secret Tears." *Hidden Child* 5, 2: 4.

Steinberg, Lucien. [1974] 1978. *Jews against Hitler (Not as a Lamb)*. London: Gordon and Cremonesi.

Steinberg, Maxime. 1983. *La question juive (1940–1942)*. Book 1 of *L'etoile et le fusil*. Brussels: Editions Vie Ouvrière.

———. 1984. *1942: Les cent jours de la déportation des juifs de belgique*. Book 2 of *L'etoile et le fusil*. Brussels: Editions Vie Ouvrière.

———. 1987. *La traque des juifs, 1942–1944*. 2 vols. Book 3 of *L'etoile et le fusil*. Brussels: Editions Vie Ouvrière.

———. 1998. *Un pays occupé et ses juifs: Belgique entre France et Pays-Bas*. Gerpinnes, Belgium: Editions Quorum.

———. 2004. *La persécution des juifs en belgique (1940–1945)*. Brussels: Editions Complexe.

Stone, Dan, ed. 2004. *The Historiography of the Holocaust*. New York: Palgrave Macmillan.

Struye, Paul, and Guillaume Jacquemyns. 2002. *La belgique sous l'occupation allemande (1940–1944)*. Brussels: Editions Complexe.

Suedfeld, Peter, ed. 2001. *Light from the Ashes: Social Science Careers of Young Holocaust Refugees and Survivors*. Ann Arbor: University of Michigan Press.

Tec, Nechama. 1986. *When Light Pierced the Darkness: Christians' Rescue of Jews in Nazi-Occupied Poland*. New York: Oxford University Press.

———. 1998. "Reflections on Rescuers." In Berenbaum and Peck 1998, 651–662.

———. 2003. *Resilience and Courage: Women, Men, and the Holocaust*. New Haven, Conn.: Yale University Press.

Teitelbaum-Hirsch, Viviane. [1994] 2006. *Enfants cachés les larmes sous le masque*. 2nd ed. Brussels: Editions Luc Pire.

Thompson, Paul. [1978] 2000. *The Voice of the Past: Oral History*. 3rd ed. Oxford: Oxford University Press.

Unglik, Sylvia. 2004. "De l'ombre à la lumière: La vie retrouvée la question de la résilience dans une population d'enfants cachés durant la seconde guerre mondiale." *Bulletin trimestriel de la Fondation Auschwitz* 85: 55–76.

Van Doorslaer, Rudi. 2003. "De politieke nalatenschap van de Tweede Wereldoorlog in België, 1945–2000." Unpublished manuscript.

Verhoeyen, Etienne. 1992. "Resistances et résistants en belgique occupée, 1940–1944." *Revue belge de philologie et d'histoire* 70, 2: 381–398.

———. 1994. *La belgique occupée de l'an 40 à la libération*. Brussels: De Boeck-Wesmael.

Vromen, Suzanne. 1986. "Maurice Halbwachs and the Concept of Nostalgia." *Knowledge and Society* 6: 57–69.

———. 1995. "The French Panthéon: A Study in Divisiveness." *Journal of Arts Management, Law and Society* 25, 1: 27–37.

———. 2007a. "Collective Memory and Cultural Politics: Narrating and Commemorating the Rescue of Jewish children by Belgian Convents." In Gerson and Wolf 2007, 134–153.

———. 2007b. "Maurice Halbwachs." In G. Ritzer (ed.), *The Blackwell Encyclopedia of Sociology.* Oxford: Blackwell, 4: 2047–2048.

Wagner-Pacifici, Robin. 1996. "Memories in the Making: The Shapes of Things That Went." *Qualitative Sociology* 19, 3: 301–321.

Warmbrunn, Werner. 1993. *The German Occupation of Belgium, 1940–1944.* New York: Peter Lang.

Weitz, Margaret Collins. 1995. *Sisters in the Resistance: How Women Fought to Free France 1940–1945.* New York: Wiley.

———. 1998. "French Women in the Resistance: Rescuing Jews." In Ruby Rohrlich (ed.), *Resisting the Holocaust.* Oxford: Berg, 179–193.

Wievorka, Annette. 1987. "Un lieu de mémoire et d'histoire: Le mémorial du martyr juif inconnu." *Revue de l'Université de Bruxelles* 1–2: 107–132.

———. 1999. " From Survivor to Witness: Voices from the Shoah." In Winter and Sivan 1999, 125–141.

Winter, Jay, and Emmanuel Sivan, eds. 1999. *War and Remembrance in the Twentieth Century.* Cambridge: Cambridge University Press.

Wolf, Diane L. 2007. *Beyond Anne Frank: Hidden Children and Postwar Families in Holland.* Berkeley: University of California Press.

Wynants, Paul. 1992. "Le gouvernement des instituts féminins de vie active au 19e siècle en belgique." In Courtois et al. 1992, 80–100.

———. 2000. "Les religieuses de vie active en belgique et aux Pays-Bas, 19ième–20ième siècles." *Revue d'Histoire Ecclésiastique* 95, 3: 238–256.

Wynants, Paul, and Marie-Emilie Hanoteau. 1989. " La condition féminine des religieuses de vie active en belgique francophone (19e-20e siècles)." In Courtois et al. 1989, 145–150.

Yerushalmi, Yosef Hayim. 1982. *Zakhor: Jewish History and Jewish Memory.* Seattle: University of Washington Press.

Young, James E. 1988. *Writing and Rewriting the Holocaust: Narratives and the Consequences of Interpretation.* Bloomington: Indiana University Press.

———. 1993. *The Texture of Memory: Holocaust Memorials and Meaning.* New Haven, Conn.: Yale University Press.

———. 1997. "Between History and Memory: The Uncanny Voices of Historian and Survivor." *History and Memory* 9: 47–58.

———. 2000. *At Memory's Edge.* New Haven, Conn.: Yale University Press.

Zachary, Dominique. [1994, 2000] 2005. *La patrouille des enfants juifs: Jamoigne, 1943–1945.* Brussels: Editions Racine.

Zerubavel, Eviatar. 1996. "Social Memories: Steps to a Sociology of the Past." *Qualitative Sociology* 19, 3: 283–299.

———. 2006. *The Elephant in the Room: Silence and Denial in Everyday Life*. New York: Oxford University Press.

Zuroff, Effraim. 1979. "Yad Vashem: More Than a Memorial, More Than a Name." *Shoah* 1, 3: 4–9.

Zweig, Ronald W. 1987. "Politics of Commemoration." *Jewish Social Studies* 49, 2: 155–166.

| INDEX |